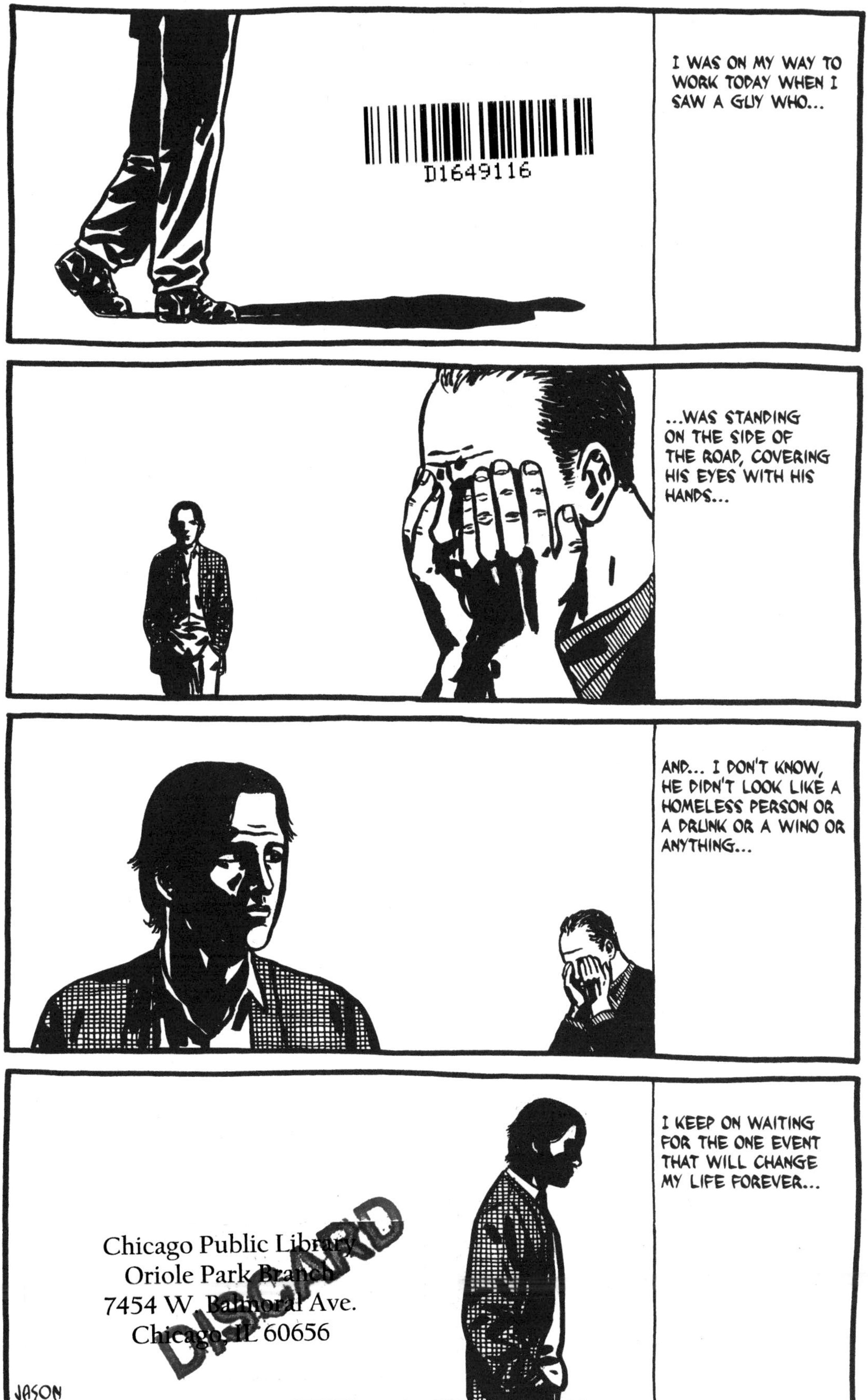
I WAS ON MY WAY TO WORK TODAY WHEN I SAW A GUY WHO...
...WAS STANDING ON THE SIDE OF THE ROAD, COVERING HIS EYES WITH HIS HANDS...
AND... I DON'T KNOW, HE DIDN'T LOOK LIKE A HOMELESS PERSON OR A DRUNK OR A WINO OR ANYTHING...
I KEEP ON WAITING FOR THE ONE EVENT THAT WILL CHANGE MY LIFE FOREVER...
JASON

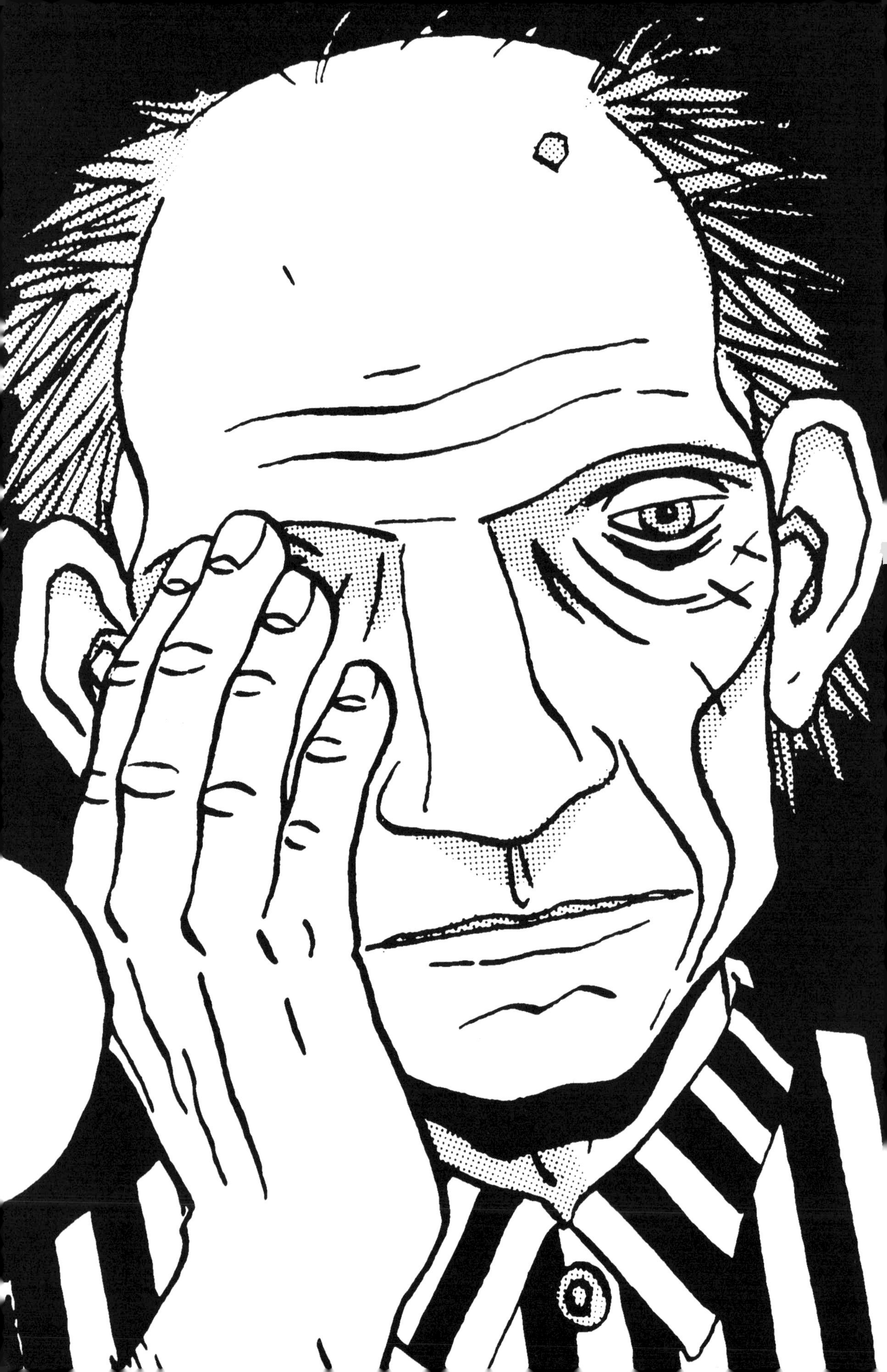

POCKET FULL OF RAIN

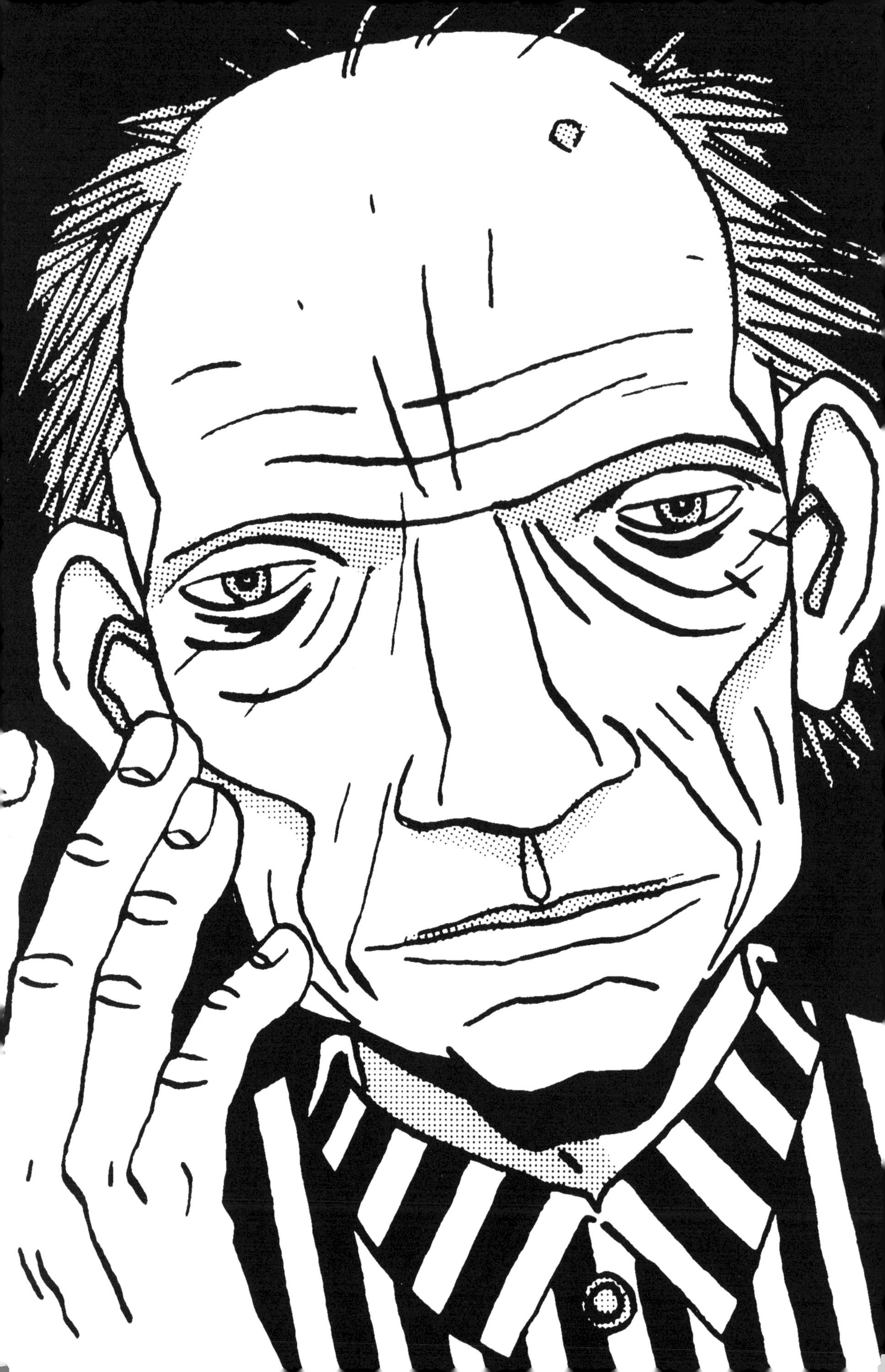

POCKET FULL OF RAIN

AND OTHER STORIES

by Jason

FANTAGRAPHICS BOOKS

FANTAGRAPHICS BOOKS • 7563 Lake City Way NE • Seattle WA 98115

EDITED & TRANSLATED by Kim Thompson
DESIGNED by Jason and Jacob Covey • PRODUCTION & LETTERING by Paul Baresh
PROMOTION by Eric Reynolds • PUBLISHED by Gary Groth and Kim Thompson

To receive a free catalog of comics, call 1-800-657-1100 or write us at the above address.

Distributed in the U.S. by W.W. Norton and Company, Inc. (212-354-5500) • Distributed in Canada by Raincoast
Books (800-663-5714) • Distributed in the United Kingdom by Turnaround Distribution (208-829-3009)

Visit the website for Jippi, who originally published Jason's work, at www.jippicomics.com
Visit the website for The Beguiling, where Jason's original artwork can be purchased: www.beguiling.com
Visit the Fantagraphics website, just because: www.fantagraphics.com

FIRST PRINTING: May, 2008 • ISBN: 978-1-56097-934-0 • PRINTED in China

WHITE RIVER JUNCTION, VT 2004

THE CENTER FOR CARTOON STUDIES AND RELATED EPHEMERA

OPEN

WHEN I FIRST BECAME A FATHER I THOUGHT ABOUT DEATH CONSTANTLY. THIS IS ALSO WHEN I FIRST STARTED READING JASON'S COMICS. SINCE THEN I OFTEN FEEL AS IF I AM A CHARACTER TRAVELING THROUGH ONE OF HIS STORIES.
- JAMES STURM

MY FIRST INTRODUCTION to the work of the Norwegian cartoonist known only as Jason was a four-page story he drew for *Comix 2000*, an international collection of pantomime comics. Out of all of the works in this massive anthology (the title was also its page count and year of publication) it was Jason's four pages that proved most memorable.

The story begins with a bird/human hobo coming upon a bed in the woods. Though a bit surprised, the hobo nevertheless stops to sleep. As he slumbers, two death-faced humanoid birds construct a proper bedroom around the slumbering hobo then exit. The hobo is awoken by an alarm clock and begins what appears to be the normal routine of getting ready for work. Before leaving his apartment he pauses in the doorway. He stands there, one hand on his briefcase, the other holding the handle of the door, turned toward the reader. This is my favorite panel of the story.

His expression is blank. Yet somehow, inexplicably so, I read a feeling of recognition and resignation on his face. He is aware that his wandering days are over. He is no longer a hobo but rather a working stiff bound by schedules and responsibilities. By merely waking up he has had some cruel joke played on him.

In almost every "how-to cartoon" book I've ever come across, there is a page demonstrating facial expressions and how cartoon characters can telegraph their emotional state with the angle of their eyebrows. Jason's faces register an incredibly limited number of expressions yet they magically convey a range of nuanced and subtle feelings. How the hell does he do it?

When you consider Jason's work, his distinct-looking characters are the first thing that comes to mind. But Jason's work is not about style or character design because beneath the steady droll expressions of his unmistakable figures (whether they be human, canine, feline, or fowl) lies intense passions. These characters are so driven that they will kill, time travel, journey to other planets, and even return from the dead to attain their heart's desires. They are all locked into relationships that are made all the more poignant by being played out against a somber world where death is right around the corner (or perhaps walking right alongside them).

THE STORIES IN THIS VOLUME were created throughout the 1990s, before Jason's anthropomorphic cast completely took over. For those who have been following his work it will be a bit strange to see him draw real people (in the same way it is to come across adults drawn by Charles Schulz).

Comic loving folks like myself are always suckers for "origin stories" and this collection is about as close as readers will get to see whence Jason derives his powers. *Pocket Full of Rain and Other Stories* reveals an incredibly bright and curious cartoonist in the early stages of a prolific career diving enthusiastically into various themes, formats, and styles. Jason covers a lot of ground in these pages: dada comic strips, homages to fellow cartoonists, absurdist noir, and cinema vérité colliding with science fiction.

Early efforts by most artists are a mixed bag at best, as they fumble about for their voice. But with the truly great ones, and there is little doubt Jason is one of the best of his generation, these stylistic discursions and experiments are poetry in and of themselves. It is easy to imagine the young Jason coming home from a lecture on Kierkegaard or having just finished a Hemingway novel or Hugo Pratt comic and dipping his pen in a jar of ink and exploring the possibilities.

Perhaps this metaphor is a bit of a stretch, but the way Jason steals from so many sources reminds me of a great singer who can cover anyone's song but makes it completely his or her own. In *Pocket Full of Rain and Other Stories* readers can hear Jason run through his "play list" for the first time. Some songs he never returns to, others he continues to hone.

I HAVE LITTLE DOUBT that in the near future, at dinner parties, classrooms, hair salons, and on-line forums, citizens of every civilized nation will engage in passionate debates over which Jason story is their favorite.

Some will argue in favor of *Hey, Wait...* for its heartbreaking depiction of childhood loss. Others will defend *You Can't Get There From Here* for generating genuine emotional depth with monster-movie clichés. Strong cases will made for *SSHHHH!*, *I Killed Adolf Hitler*, *The Last Musketeer*, and *The Left Bank Gang*.

Whoever wins these arguments will have read this book. Their choice will be informed by being able to trace it back to Jason's earliest work. And for some, this book may actually be their favorite. And who would I be to argue? In what other book does Jason venture so far and wide with such an imaginative and casual swagger? I'd buy this collection for the *Kill the Cat* story alone!

Inspired silliness, absurdist slapstick, formal excursions, black humor, the mundane, the fantastic, existential comic strips, crime fiction— it's all here. This collection is all over the place but it's all Jason, and like all his work it's funny and deep and smart and I cannot get enough of it.

James Sturm
White River Junction, VT
January 2008

James Sturm is the author of James Sturm's America: God, Gold and Golems, and the director of The Center for Cartoon Studies.

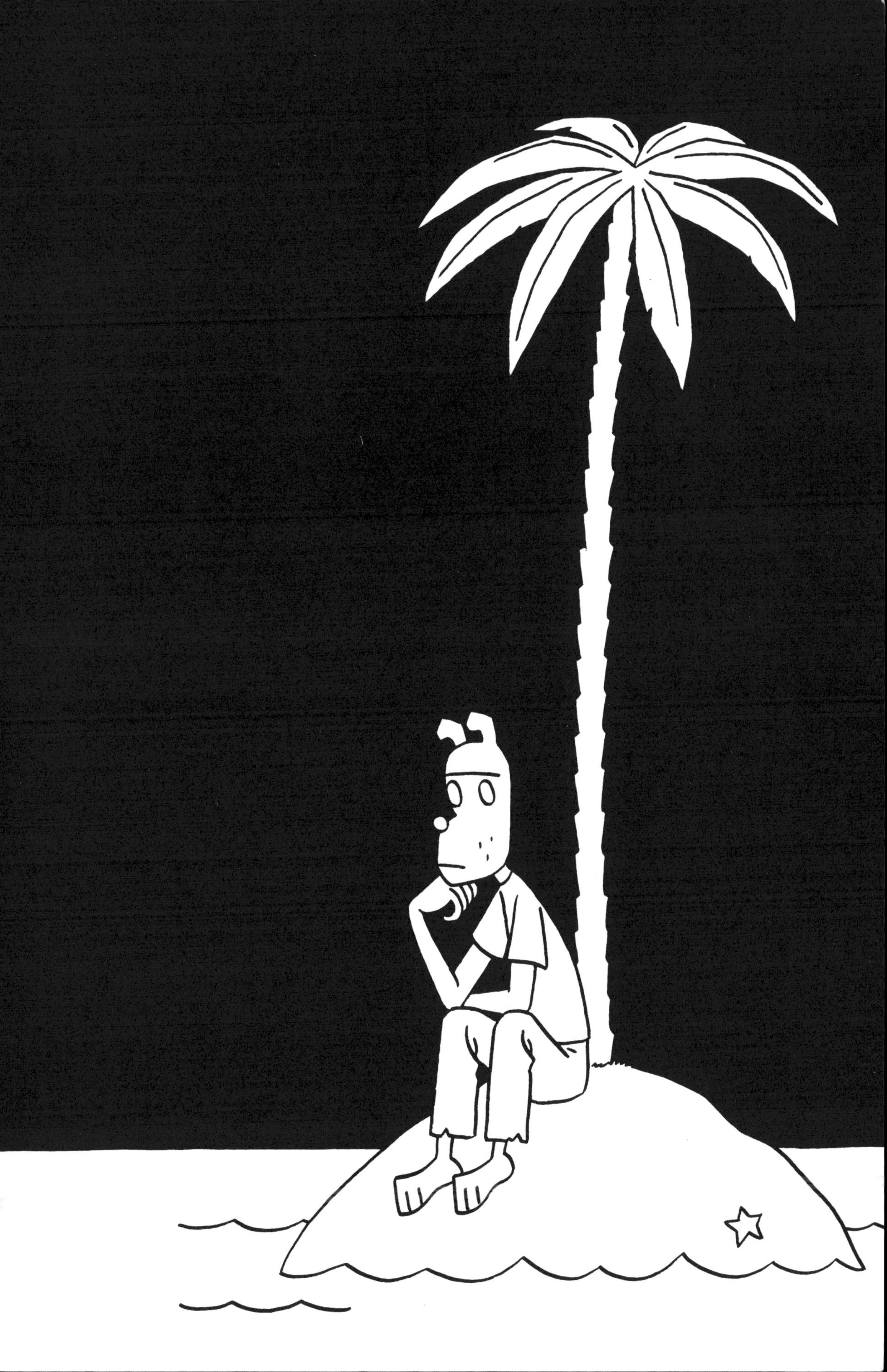

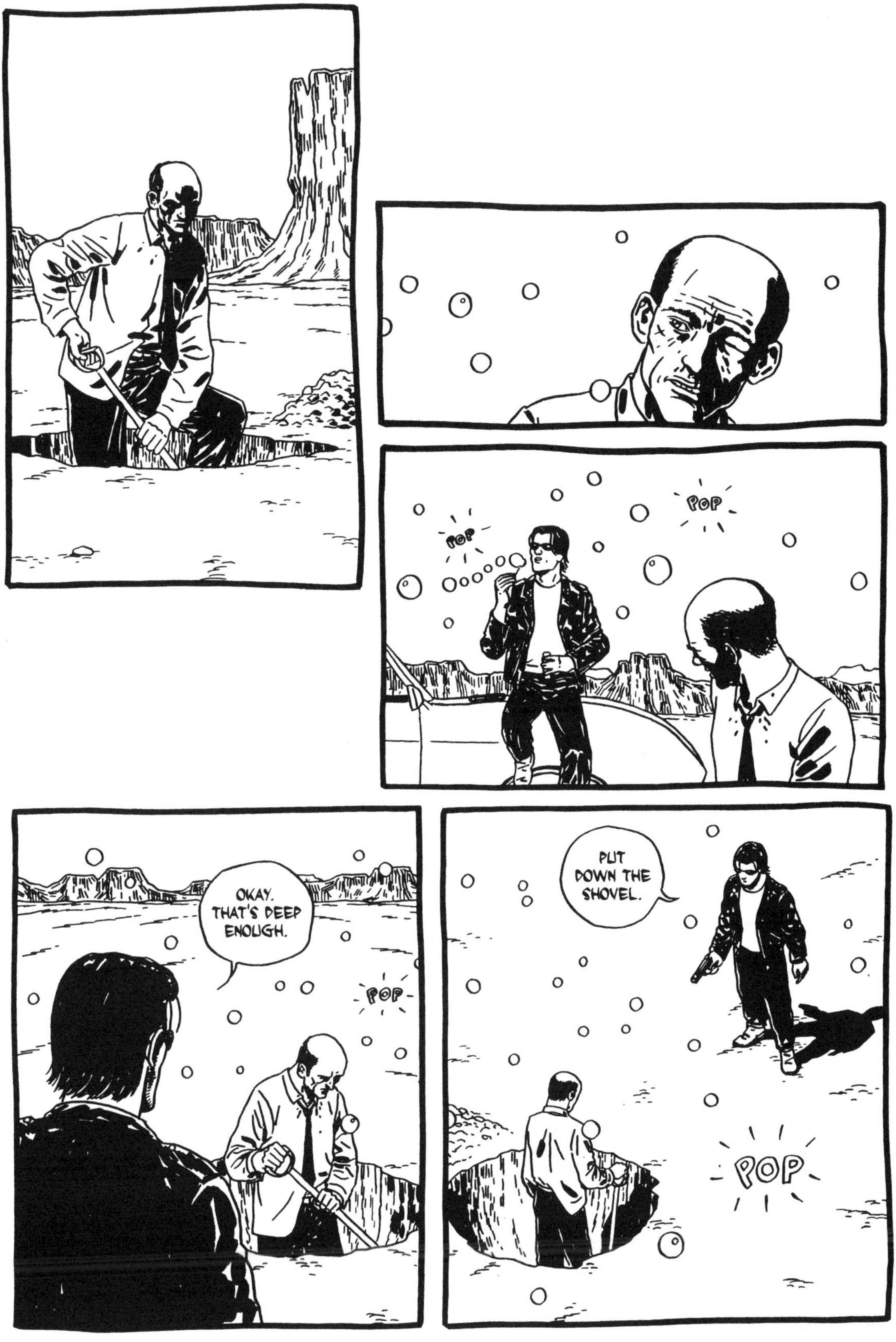
POP
POP
OKAY. THAT'S DEEP ENOUGH.
POP
PUT DOWN THE SHOVEL.
POP

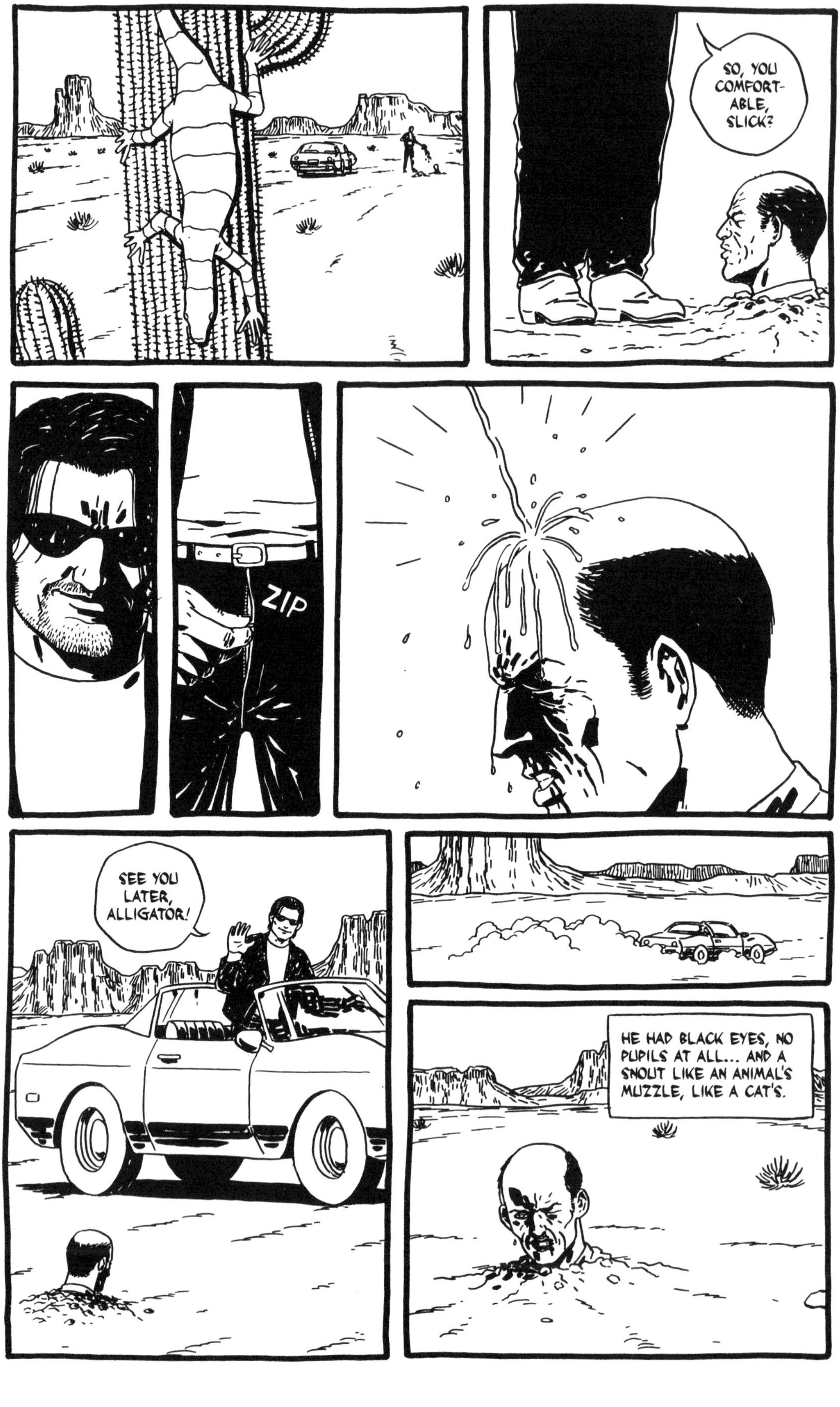
SO, YOU COMFORT-ABLE, SLICK?
ZIP
SEE YOU LATER, ALLIGATOR!
HE HAD BLACK EYES, NO PUPILS AT ALL... AND A SNOUT LIKE AN ANIMAL'S MUZZLE, LIKE A CAT'S.

ON HIS FOREHEAD HE HAD... TWO ANTENNAS, I THINK... THESE LITTLE THINGS THAT STUCK OUT, ANYWAY...

HE WAS QUITE BALD. LONG, POINTY EARS... A LITTLE BIGGER THAN THAT... AND A WIDE MOUTH...

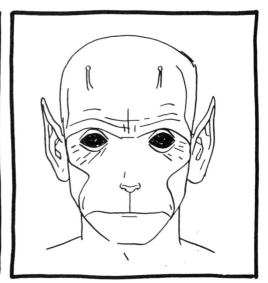

YES, THAT'S EXACTLY WHAT HE LOOKED LIKE! THE CREATURE WHO KNOCKED ME DOWN AND TOOK MY SOCIAL SECURITY CHECK.

WANTED

WANTED

KNOCK KNOCK

KNOCK KNOCK

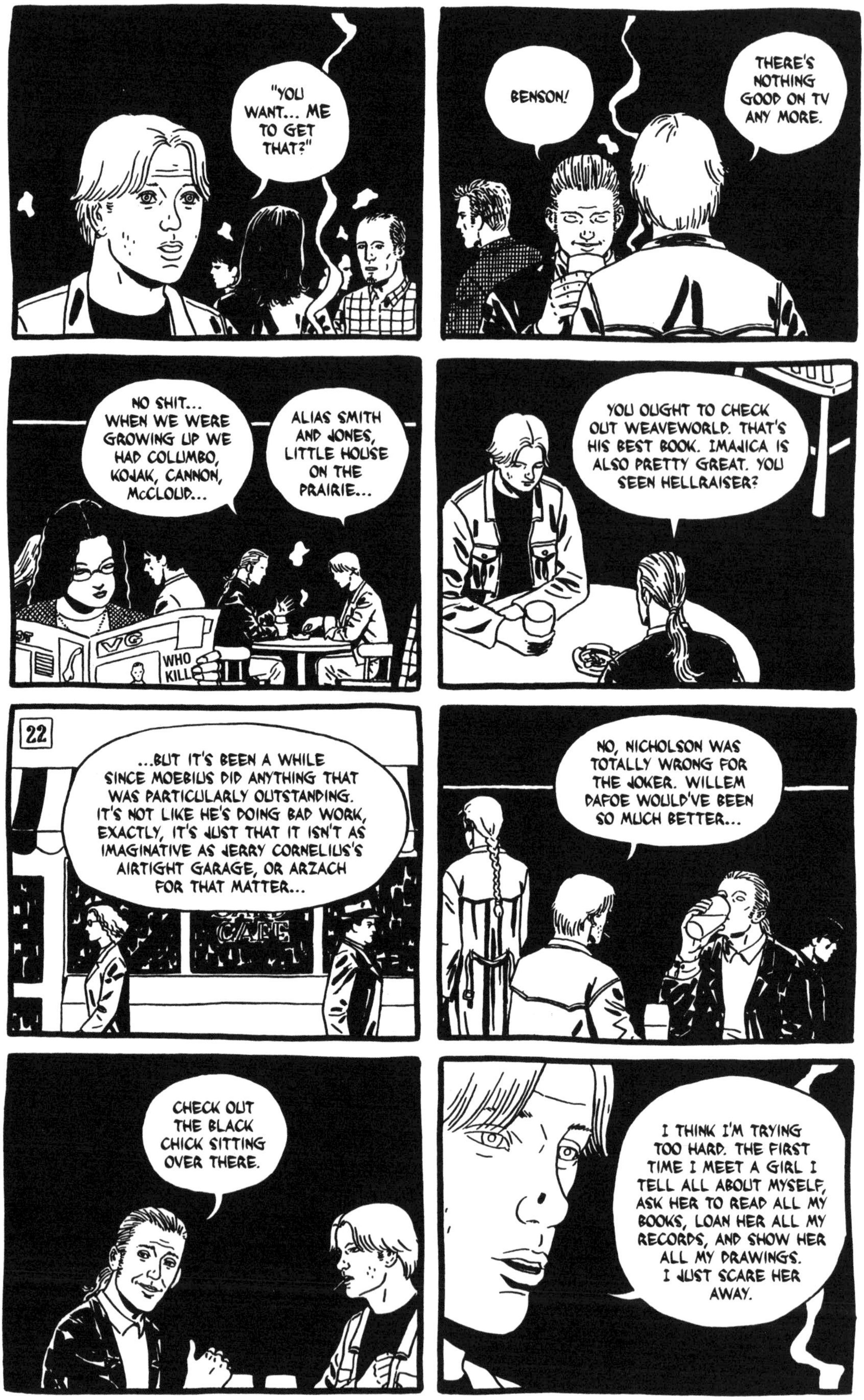
"YOU WANT... ME TO GET THAT?"
BENSON!
THERE'S NOTHING GOOD ON TV ANY MORE.
NO SHIT... WHEN WE WERE GROWING UP WE HAD COLUMBO, KOJAK, CANNON, McCLOUD...
ALIAS SMITH AND JONES, LITTLE HOUSE ON THE PRAIRIE...
VG
WHO KILL
YOU OUGHT TO CHECK OUT WEAVEWORLD. THAT'S HIS BEST BOOK. IMAJICA IS ALSO PRETTY GREAT. YOU SEEN HELLRAISER?
22
...BUT IT'S BEEN A WHILE SINCE MOEBIUS DID ANYTHING THAT WAS PARTICULARLY OUTSTANDING. IT'S NOT LIKE HE'S DOING BAD WORK, EXACTLY, IT'S JUST THAT IT ISN'T AS IMAGINATIVE AS JERRY CORNELIUS'S AIRTIGHT GARAGE, OR ARZACH FOR THAT MATTER...
CAFE
NO, NICHOLSON WAS TOTALLY WRONG FOR THE JOKER. WILLEM DAFOE WOULD'VE BEEN SO MUCH BETTER...
CHECK OUT THE BLACK CHICK SITTING OVER THERE.
I THINK I'M TRYING TOO HARD. THE FIRST TIME I MEET A GIRL I TELL ALL ABOUT MYSELF, ASK HER TO READ ALL MY BOOKS, LOAN HER ALL MY RECORDS, AND SHOW HER ALL MY DRAWINGS. I JUST SCARE HER AWAY.

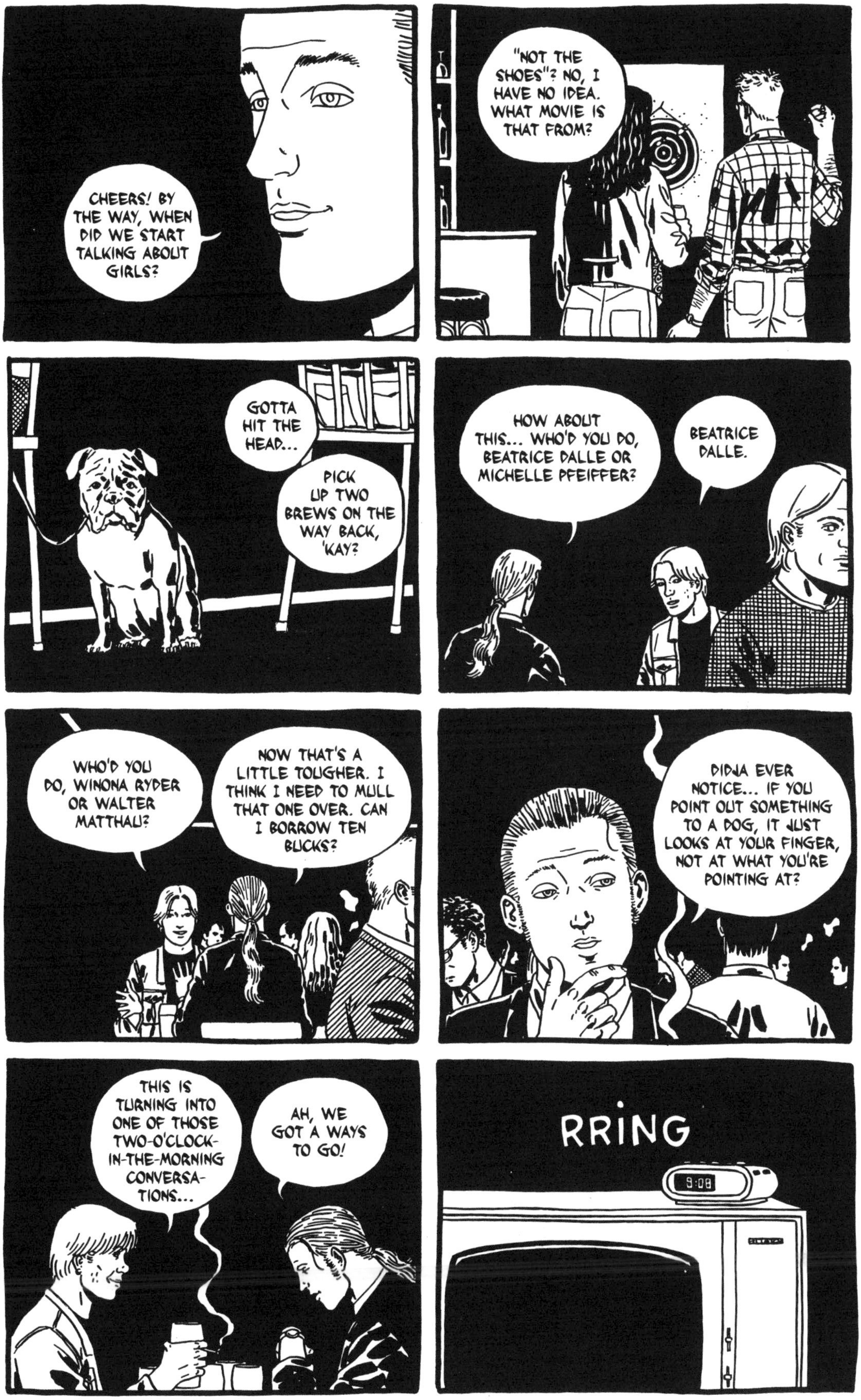
CHEERS! BY THE WAY, WHEN DID WE START TALKING ABOUT GIRLS?
"NOT THE SHOES"? NO, I HAVE NO IDEA. WHAT MOVIE IS THAT FROM?
GOTTA HIT THE HEAD...
PICK UP TWO BREWS ON THE WAY BACK, 'KAY?
HOW ABOUT THIS... WHO'D YOU DO, BEATRICE DALLE OR MICHELLE PFEIFFER?
BEATRICE DALLE.
WHO'D YOU DO, WINONA RYDER OR WALTER MATTHAU?
NOW THAT'S A LITTLE TOUGHER. I THINK I NEED TO MULL THAT ONE OVER. CAN I BORROW TEN BUCKS?
DIDJA EVER NOTICE... IF YOU POINT OUT SOMETHING TO A DOG, IT JUST LOOKS AT YOUR FINGER, NOT AT WHAT YOU'RE POINTING AT?
THIS IS TURNING INTO ONE OF THOSE TWO-O'CLOCK-IN-THE-MORNING CONVERSATIONS...
AH, WE GOT A WAYS TO GO!
RRING
9:08

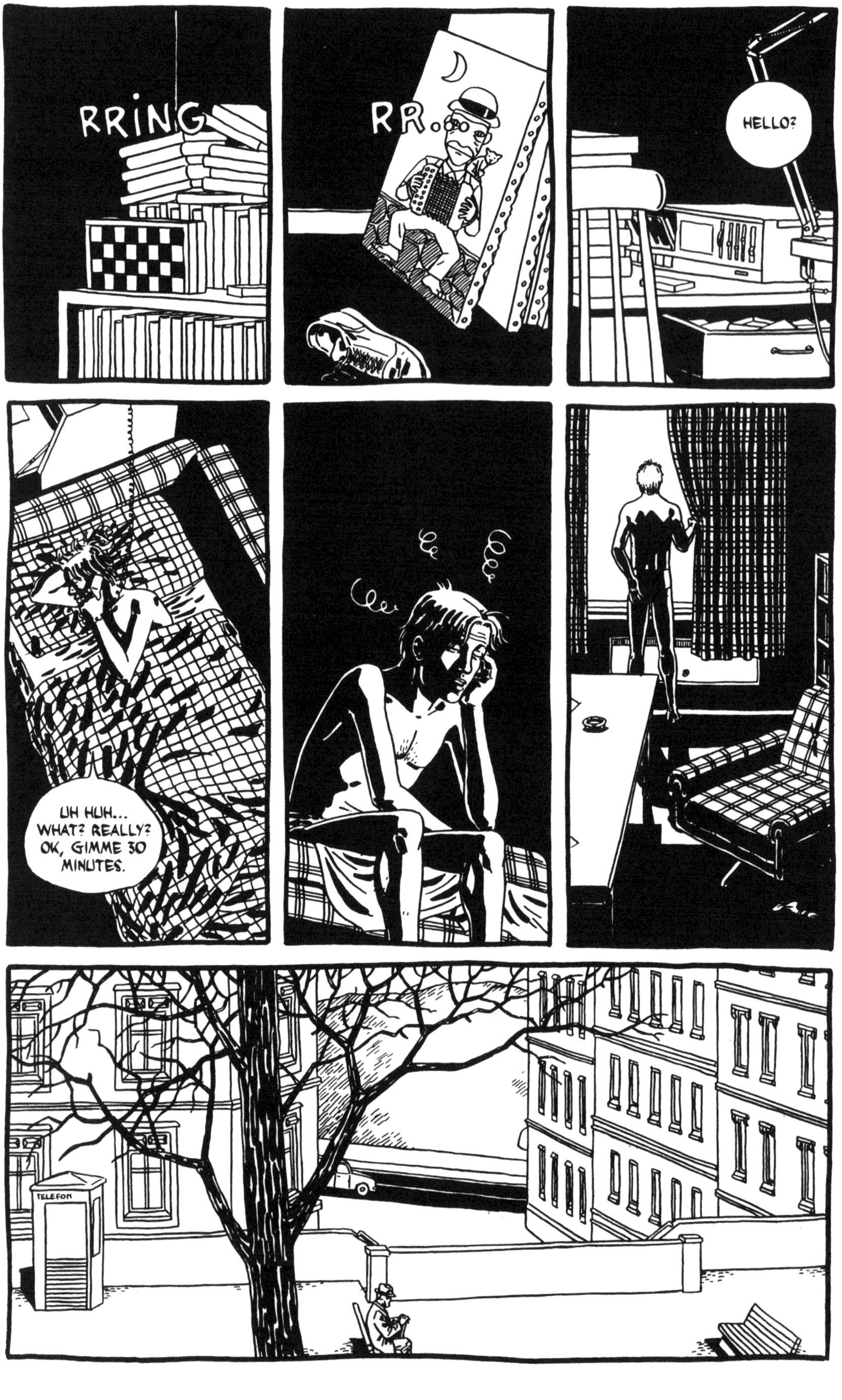
RRING
RR...
HELLO?
UH HUH... WHAT? REALLY? OK, GIMME 30 MINUTES.
TELEFON

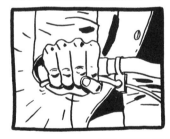

THUD!

ARE YOU HURT? IS EVERYTHING OK?

HELLO?

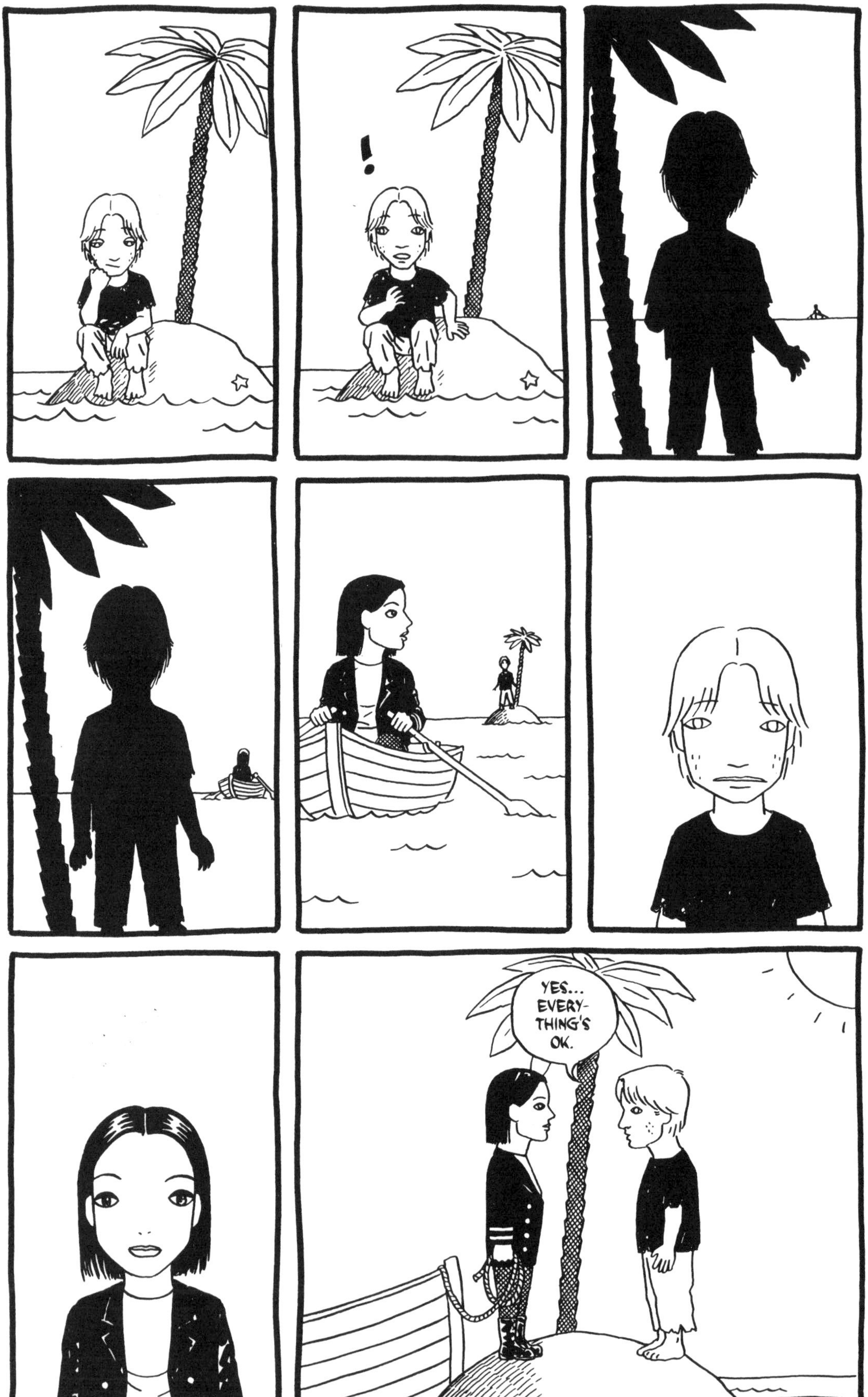
!
YES... EVERY-THING'S OK.

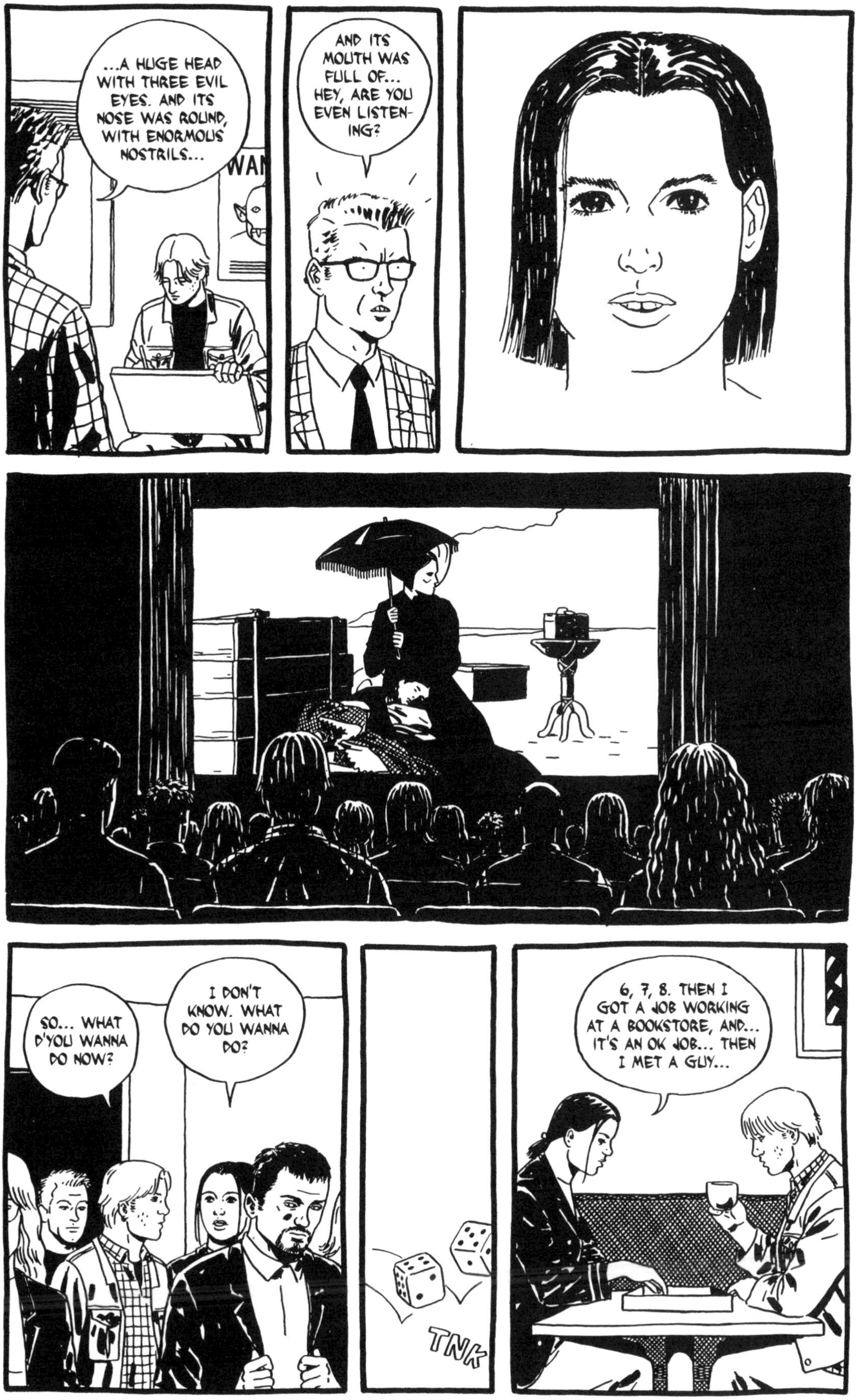
...A HUGE HEAD WITH THREE EVIL EYES. AND ITS NOSE WAS ROUND, WITH ENORMOUS NOSTRILS...
AND ITS MOUTH WAS FULL OF... HEY, ARE YOU EVEN LISTEN-ING?
SO... WHAT D'YOU WANNA DO NOW?
I DON'T KNOW. WHAT DO YOU WANNA DO?
TNK
6, 7, 8. THEN I GOT A JOB WORKING AT A BOOKSTORE, AND... IT'S AN OK JOB... THEN I MET A GUY...

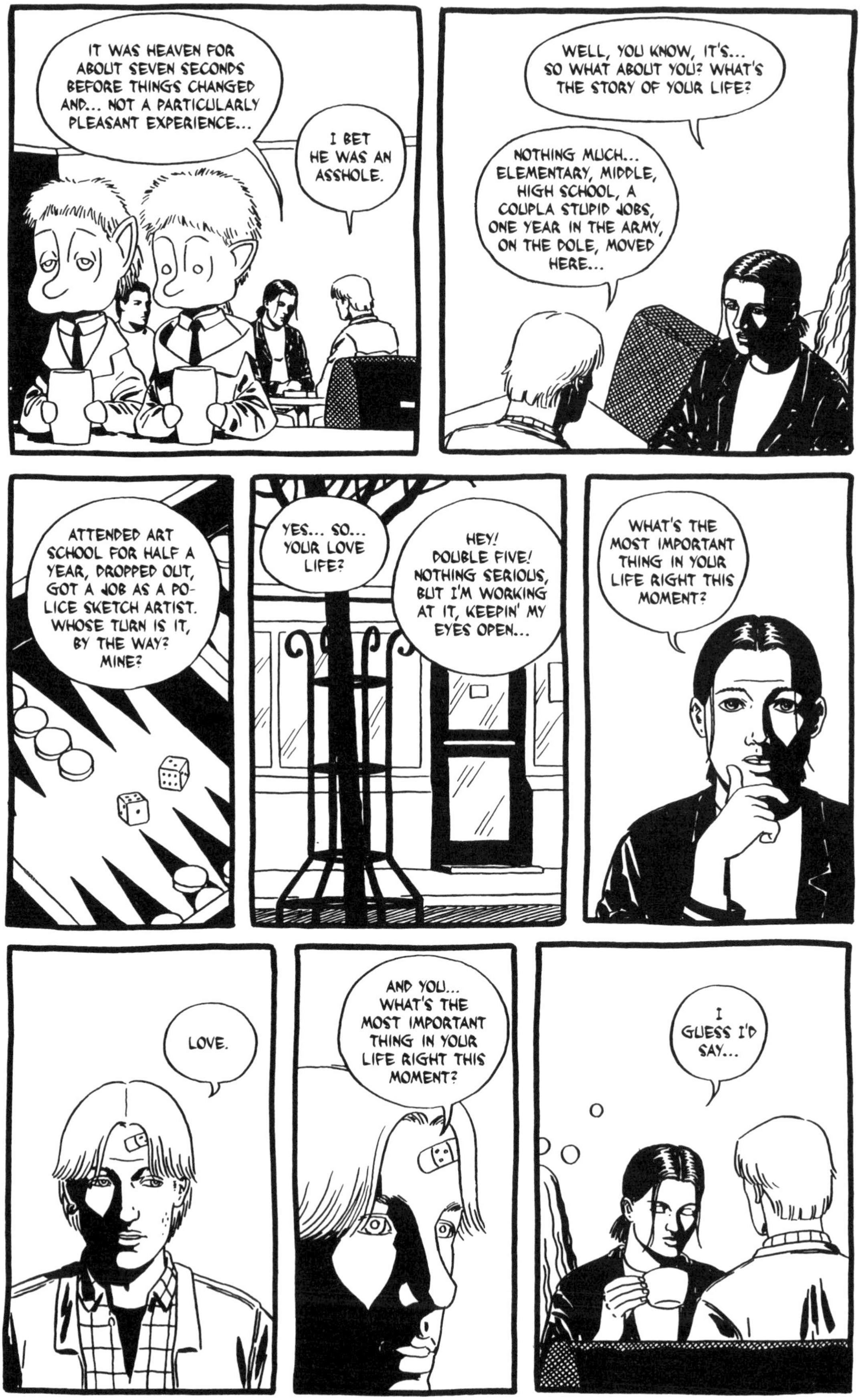
IT WAS HEAVEN FOR ABOUT SEVEN SECONDS BEFORE THINGS CHANGED AND... NOT A PARTICULARLY PLEASANT EXPERIENCE...
I BET HE WAS AN ASSHOLE.
WELL, YOU KNOW, IT'S... SO WHAT ABOUT YOU? WHAT'S THE STORY OF YOUR LIFE?
NOTHING MUCH... ELEMENTARY, MIDDLE, HIGH SCHOOL, A COUPLA STUPID JOBS, ONE YEAR IN THE ARMY, ON THE DOLE, MOVED HERE...
ATTENDED ART SCHOOL FOR HALF A YEAR, DROPPED OUT, GOT A JOB AS A POLICE SKETCH ARTIST. WHOSE TURN IS IT, BY THE WAY? MINE?
YES... SO... YOUR LOVE LIFE?
HEY! DOUBLE FIVE! NOTHING SERIOUS, BUT I'M WORKING AT IT, KEEPIN' MY EYES OPEN...
WHAT'S THE MOST IMPORTANT THING IN YOUR LIFE RIGHT THIS MOMENT?
LOVE.
AND YOU... WHAT'S THE MOST IMPORTANT THING IN YOUR LIFE RIGHT THIS MOMENT?
I GUESS I'D SAY...

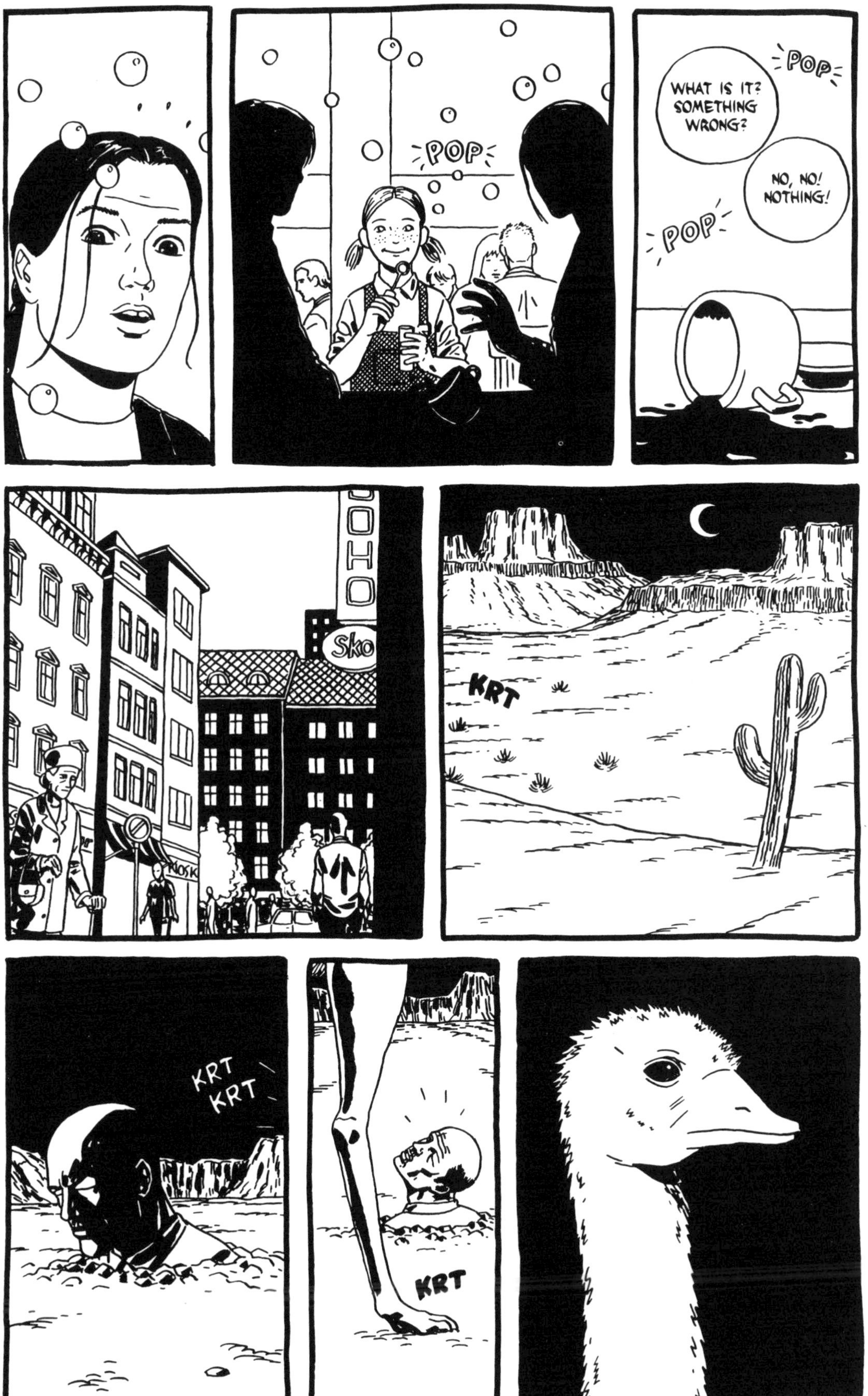
POP
POP
WHAT IS IT? SOMETHING WRONG?
NO, NO! NOTHING!
POP
DOHO
Sko
KIOSK
KRT
KRT KRT
KRT

2231...
HANG ON...
GOT IT!

I CAN NEVER REMEMBER MY OWN NUMBER. HERE YOU GO!

THANKS! I HAVE TO RUN NOW TO CATCH MY BUS.

SEE YA.

14

SEE YA...

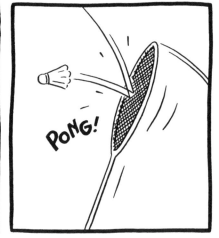

PONG!

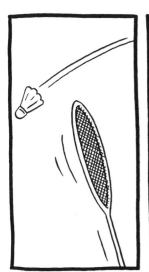

SO WHEN YOU GONNA CALL HER?

I DUNNO. I WANTED TO SEE IF SHE WAS GONNA CALL FIRST.

IF YOU'RE INTERESTED YOU OUGHTA SHOW IT BY CALLING FIRST.

I DON'T WANNA CALL TOO SOON EITHER...

WAS SHE PRETTY?

ALMOST TOO PRETTY. SHE MIGHT BE OUT OF MY LEAGUE.

MAYBE SHE'S GOT AN INCURABLE DISEASE AND ONLY HAS A HALF A YEAR TO LIVE, SO HER STANDARDS AREN'T SO HIGH!

"IS THIS A PIECE OF YOUR BRAIN?"

PONG!

PONG!

FAWLTY TOWERS!

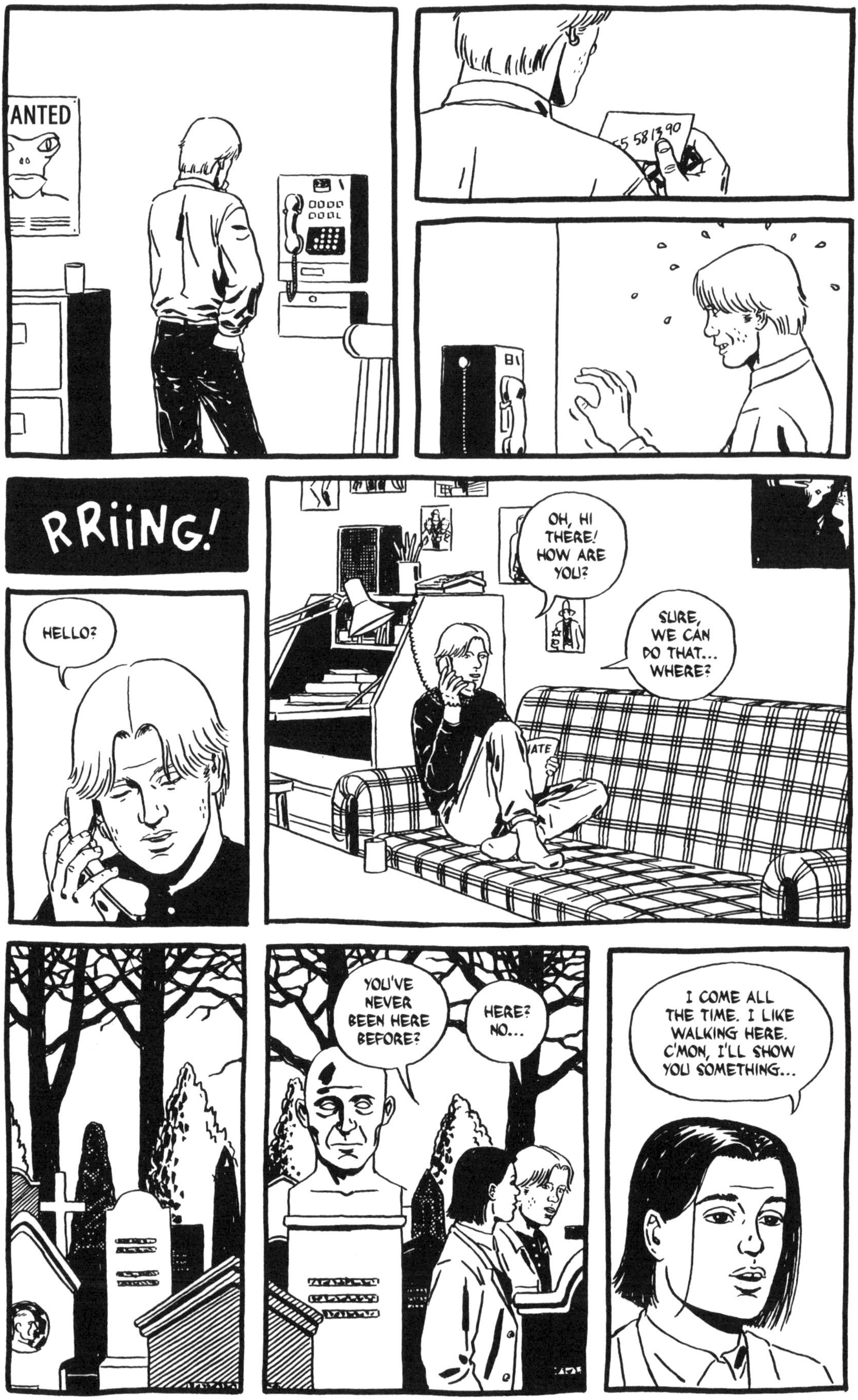
ANTED
RRiiNG!
HELLO?
OH, HI THERE! HOW ARE YOU?
SURE, WE CAN DO THAT... WHERE?
YOU'VE NEVER BEEN HERE BEFORE?
HERE? NO...
I COME ALL THE TIME. I LIKE WALKING HERE. C'MON, I'LL SHOW YOU SOMETHING...

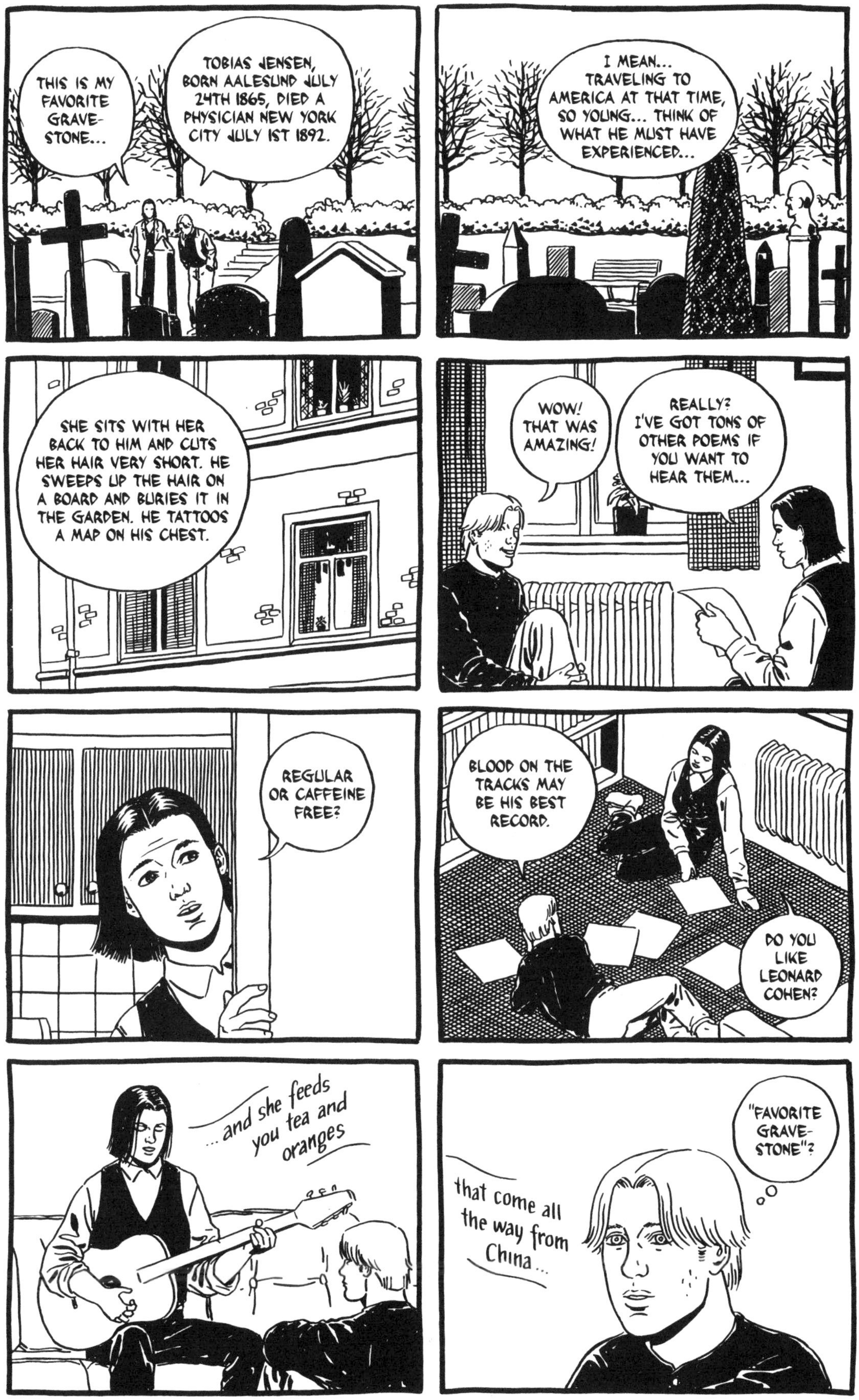

THIS IS MY FAVORITE GRAVE-STONE...
TOBIAS JENSEN, BORN AALESUND JULY 24TH 1865, DIED A PHYSICIAN NEW YORK CITY JULY 1ST 1892.
I MEAN... TRAVELING TO AMERICA AT THAT TIME, SO YOUNG... THINK OF WHAT HE MUST HAVE EXPERIENCED...
SHE SITS WITH HER BACK TO HIM AND CUTS HER HAIR VERY SHORT. HE SWEEPS UP THE HAIR ON A BOARD AND BURIES IT IN THE GARDEN. HE TATTOOS A MAP ON HIS CHEST.
WOW! THAT WAS AMAZING!
REALLY? I'VE GOT TONS OF OTHER POEMS IF YOU WANT TO HEAR THEM...
REGULAR OR CAFFEINE FREE?
BLOOD ON THE TRACKS MAY BE HIS BEST RECORD.
DO YOU LIKE LEONARD COHEN?
...and she feeds you tea and oranges
that come all the way from China...
"FAVORITE GRAVE-STONE"?

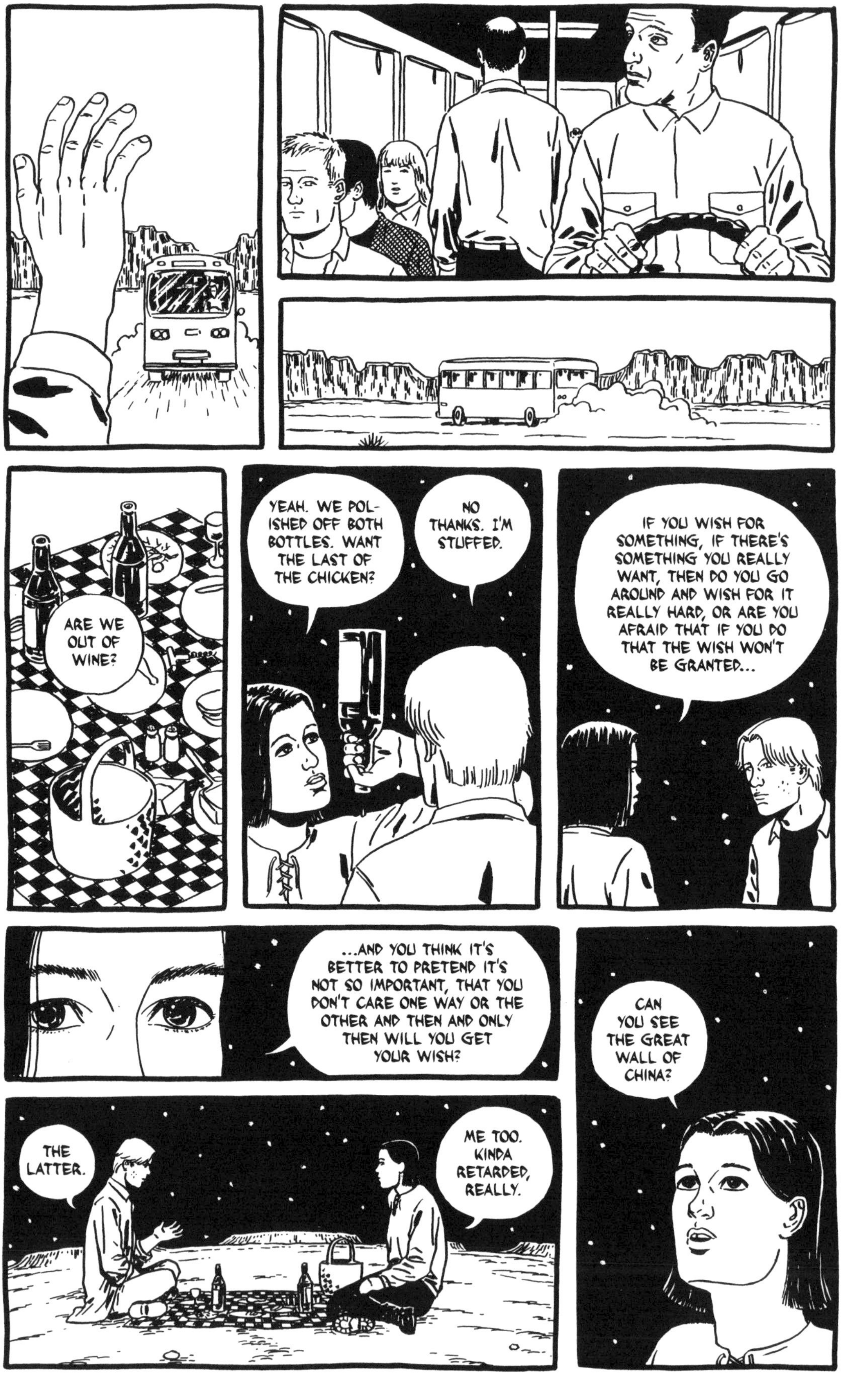
ARE WE OUT OF WINE?
YEAH. WE POLISHED OFF BOTH BOTTLES. WANT THE LAST OF THE CHICKEN?
NO THANKS. I'M STUFFED.
IF YOU WISH FOR SOMETHING, IF THERE'S SOMETHING YOU REALLY WANT, THEN DO YOU GO AROUND AND WISH FOR IT REALLY HARD, OR ARE YOU AFRAID THAT IF YOU DO THAT THE WISH WON'T BE GRANTED...
...AND YOU THINK IT'S BETTER TO PRETEND IT'S NOT SO IMPORTANT, THAT YOU DON'T CARE ONE WAY OR THE OTHER AND THEN AND ONLY THEN WILL YOU GET YOUR WISH?
THE LATTER.
ME TOO. KINDA RETARDED, REALLY.
CAN YOU SEE THE GREAT WALL OF CHINA?

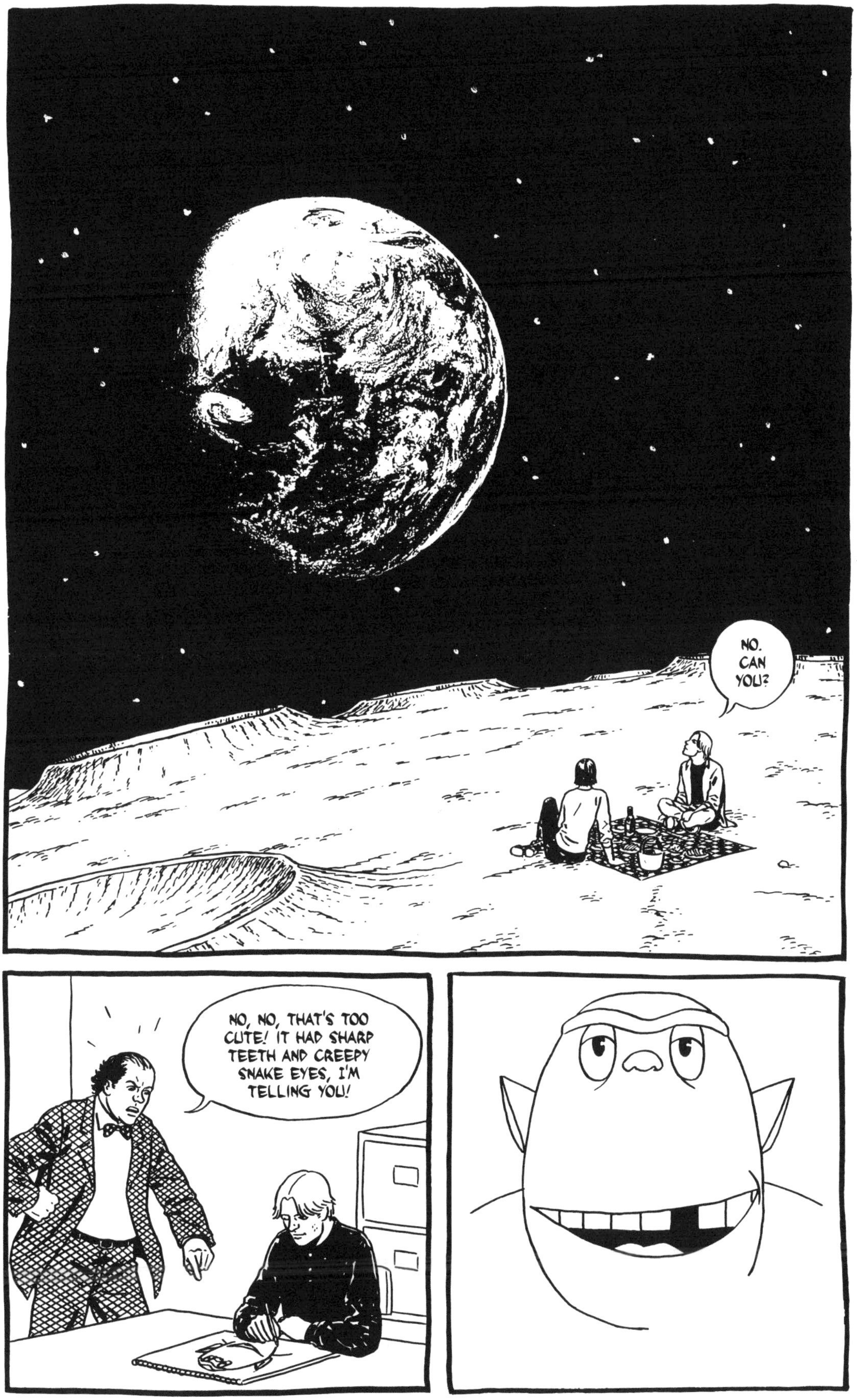
NO. CAN YOU?
NO, NO, THAT'S TOO CUTE! IT HAD SHARP TEETH AND CREEPY SNAKE EYES, I'M TELLING YOU!

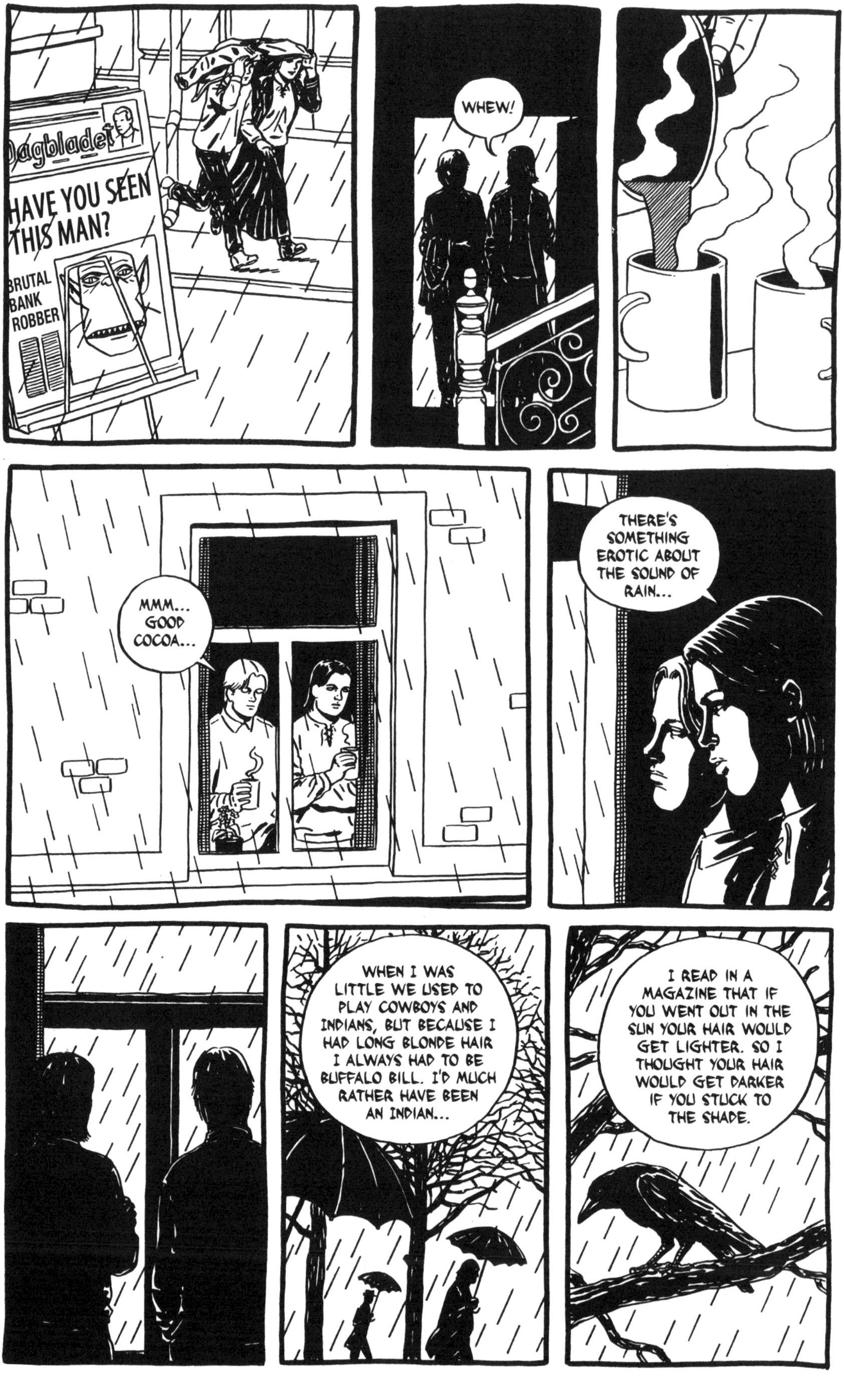
Dagbladet
HAVE YOU SEEN THIS MAN?
BRUTAL BANK ROBBER
WHEW!
MMM... GOOD COCOA...
THERE'S SOMETHING EROTIC ABOUT THE SOUND OF RAIN...
WHEN I WAS LITTLE WE USED TO PLAY COWBOYS AND INDIANS, BUT BECAUSE I HAD LONG BLONDE HAIR I ALWAYS HAD TO BE BUFFALO BILL. I'D MUCH RATHER HAVE BEEN AN INDIAN...
I READ IN A MAGAZINE THAT IF YOU WENT OUT IN THE SUN YOUR HAIR WOULD GET LIGHTER. SO I THOUGHT YOUR HAIR WOULD GET DARKER IF YOU STUCK TO THE SHADE.

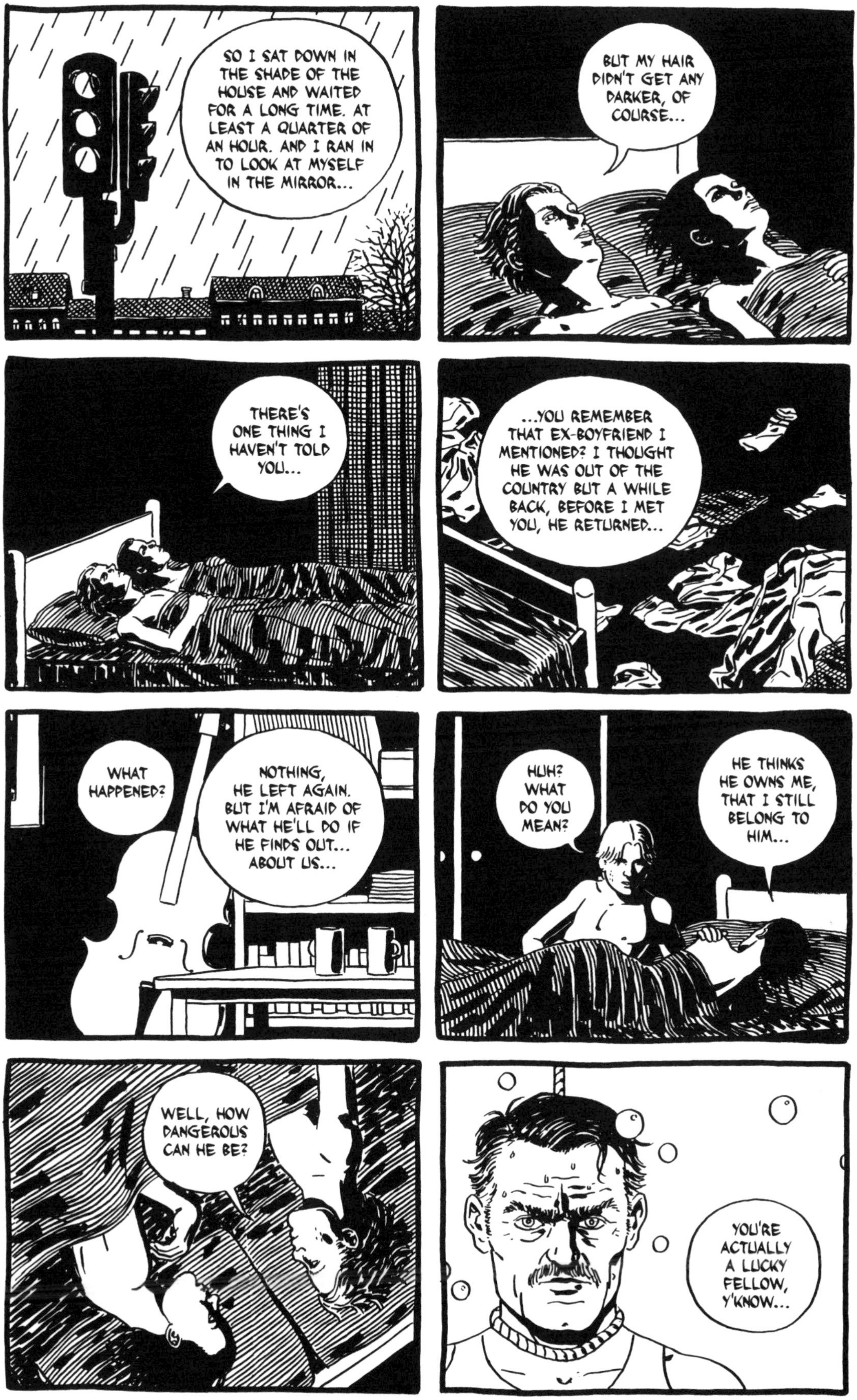
SO I SAT DOWN IN THE SHADE OF THE HOUSE AND WAITED FOR A LONG TIME. AT LEAST A QUARTER OF AN HOUR. AND I RAN IN TO LOOK AT MYSELF IN THE MIRROR...
BUT MY HAIR DIDN'T GET ANY DARKER, OF COURSE...
THERE'S ONE THING I HAVEN'T TOLD YOU...
...YOU REMEMBER THAT EX-BOYFRIEND I MENTIONED? I THOUGHT HE WAS OUT OF THE COUNTRY BUT A WHILE BACK, BEFORE I MET YOU, HE RETURNED...
WHAT HAPPENED?
NOTHING, HE LEFT AGAIN. BUT I'M AFRAID OF WHAT HE'LL DO IF HE FINDS OUT... ABOUT US...
HUH? WHAT DO YOU MEAN?
HE THINKS HE OWNS ME, THAT I STILL BELONG TO HIM...
WELL, HOW DANGEROUS CAN HE BE?
YOU'RE ACTUALLY A LUCKY FELLOW, Y'KNOW...

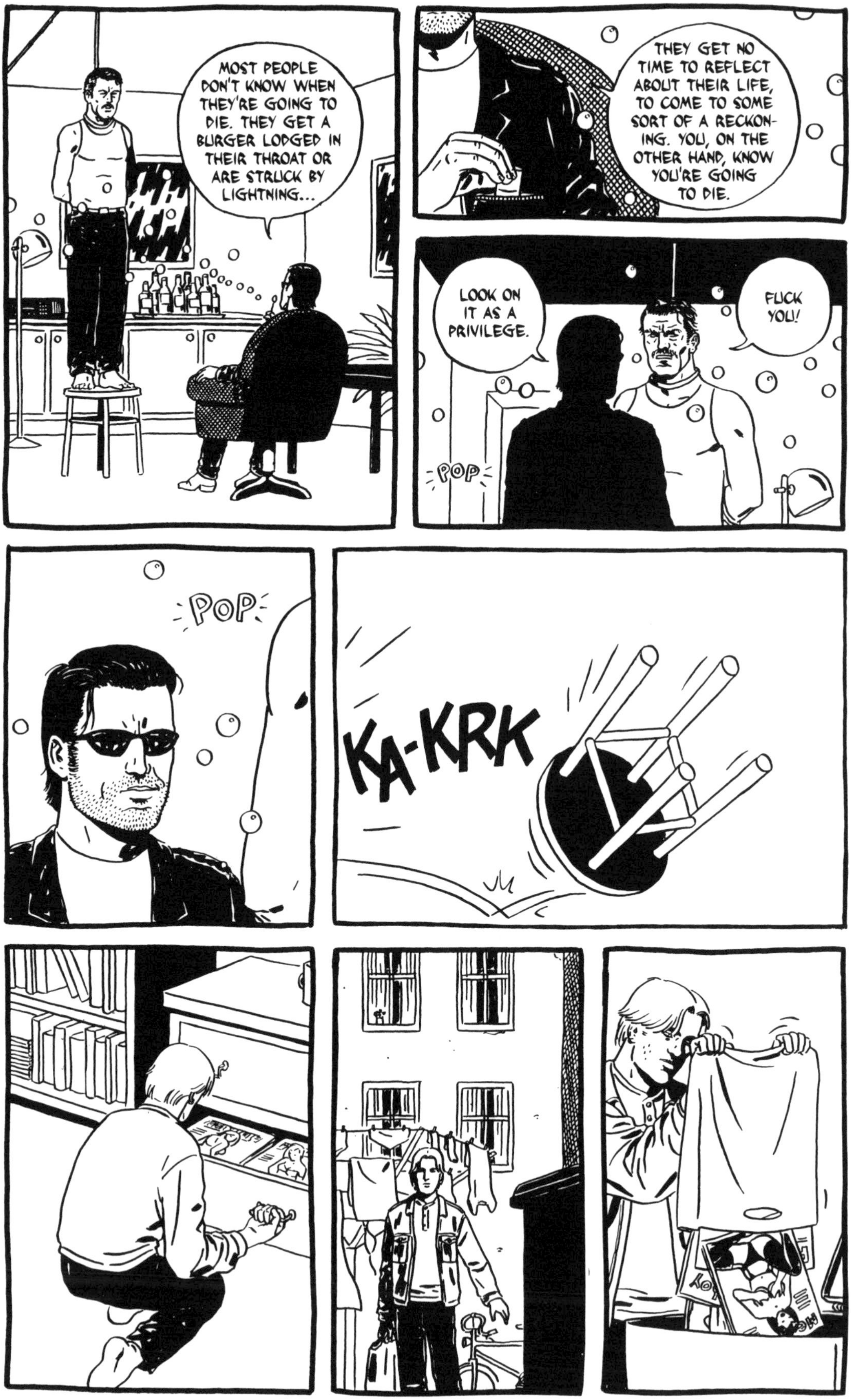
MOST PEOPLE DON'T KNOW WHEN THEY'RE GOING TO DIE. THEY GET A BURGER LODGED IN THEIR THROAT OR ARE STRUCK BY LIGHTNING...
THEY GET NO TIME TO REFLECT ABOUT THEIR LIFE, TO COME TO SOME SORT OF A RECKONING. YOU, ON THE OTHER HAND, KNOW YOU'RE GOING TO DIE.
LOOK ON IT AS A PRIVILEGE.
FUCK YOU!
POP
POP
KA-KRK

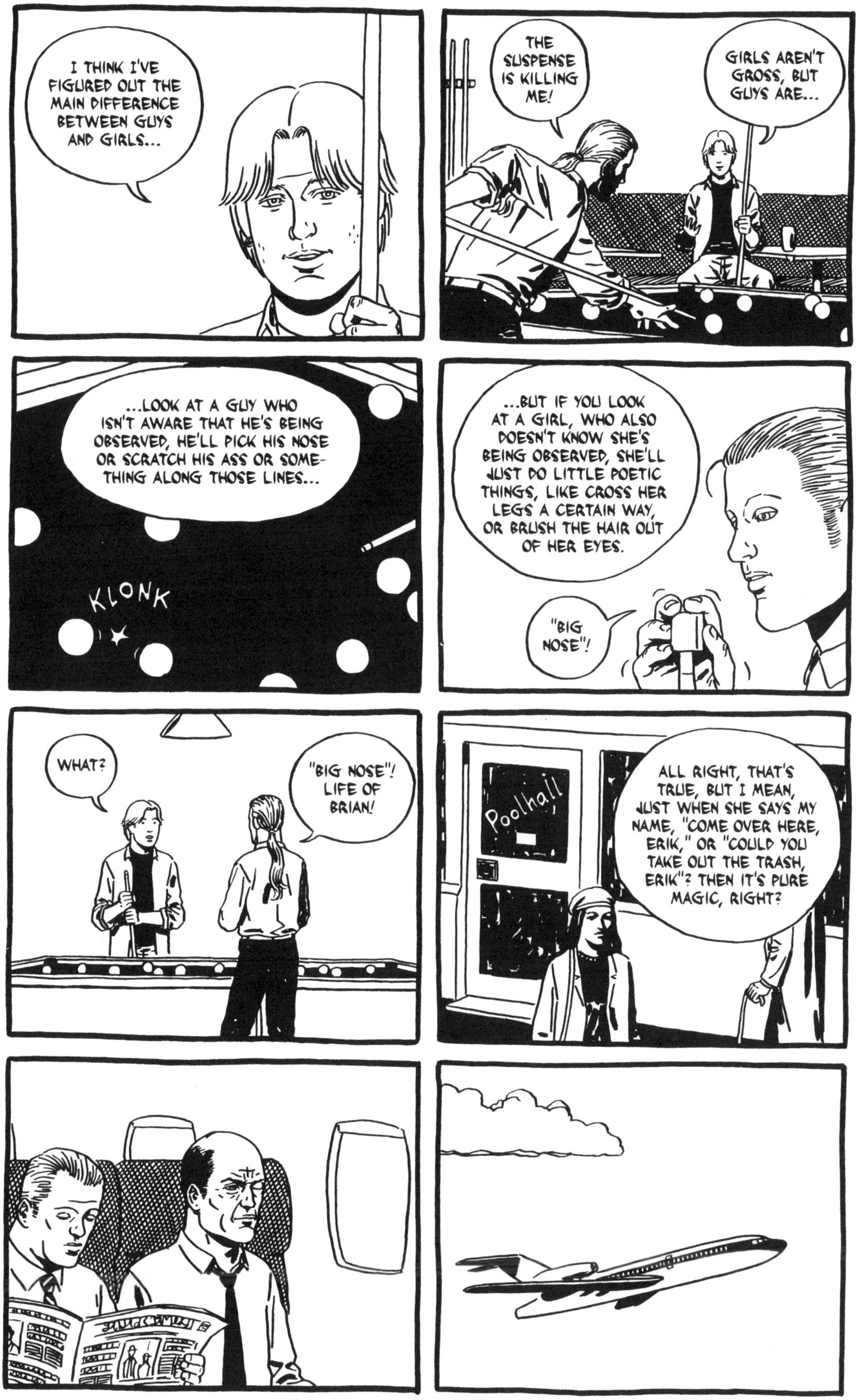
I THINK I'VE FIGURED OUT THE MAIN DIFFERENCE BETWEEN GUYS AND GIRLS...
THE SUSPENSE IS KILLING ME!
GIRLS AREN'T GROSS, BUT GUYS ARE...
...LOOK AT A GUY WHO ISN'T AWARE THAT HE'S BEING OBSERVED, HE'LL PICK HIS NOSE OR SCRATCH HIS ASS OR SOMETHING ALONG THOSE LINES...
KLONK
...BUT IF YOU LOOK AT A GIRL, WHO ALSO DOESN'T KNOW SHE'S BEING OBSERVED, SHE'LL JUST DO LITTLE POETIC THINGS, LIKE CROSS HER LEGS A CERTAIN WAY, OR BRUSH THE HAIR OUT OF HER EYES.
"BIG NOSE"!
WHAT?
"BIG NOSE"! LIFE OF BRIAN!
Poolhall
ALL RIGHT, THAT'S TRUE, BUT I MEAN, JUST WHEN SHE SAYS MY NAME, "COME OVER HERE, ERIK," OR "COULD YOU TAKE OUT THE TRASH, ERIK"? THEN IT'S PURE MAGIC, RIGHT?

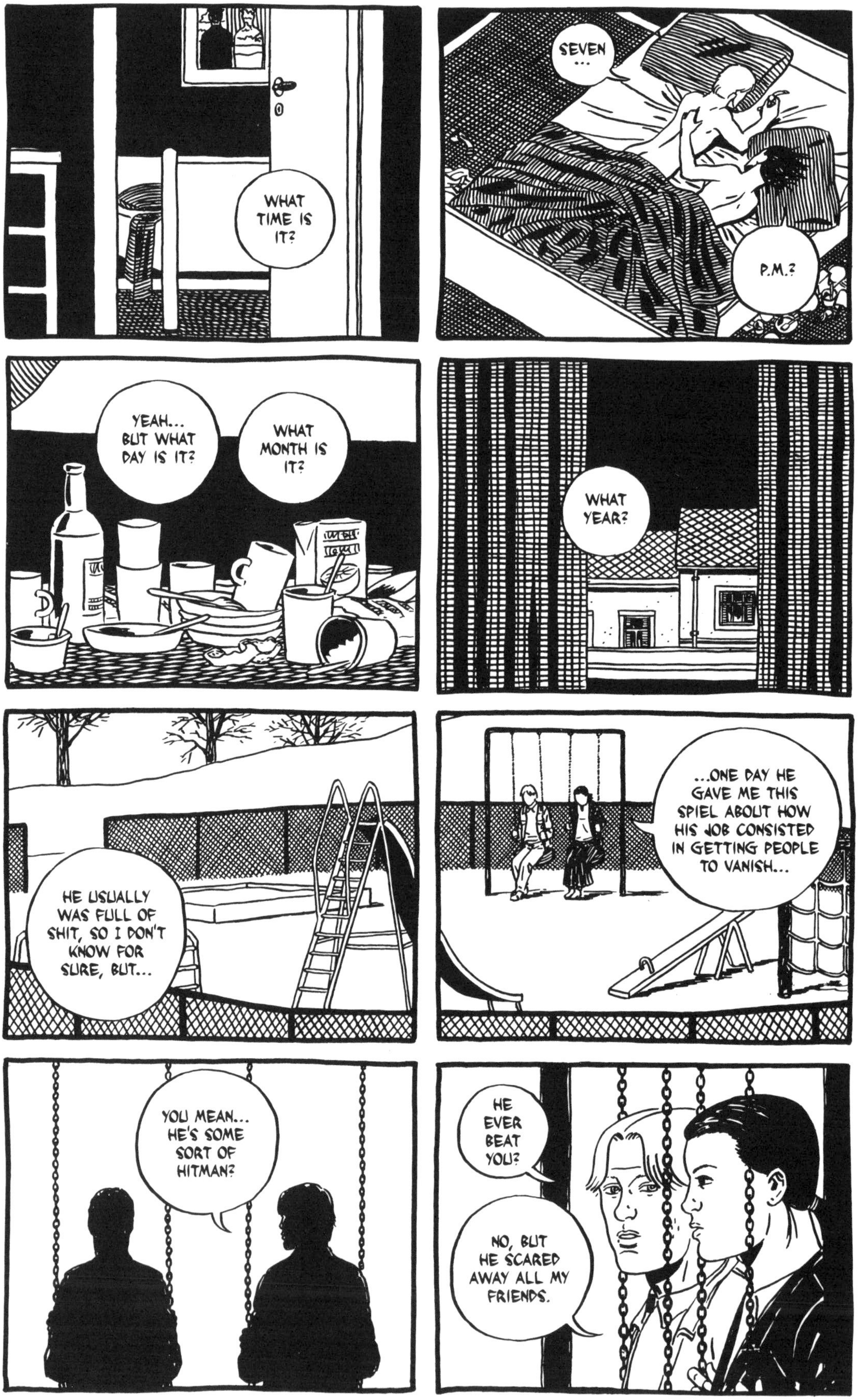
WHAT TIME IS IT?
SEVEN...
P.M.?
YEAH... BUT WHAT DAY IS IT?
WHAT MONTH IS IT?
WHAT YEAR?
HE USUALLY WAS FULL OF SHIT, SO I DON'T KNOW FOR SURE, BUT...
...ONE DAY HE GAVE ME THIS SPIEL ABOUT HOW HIS JOB CONSISTED IN GETTING PEOPLE TO VANISH...
YOU MEAN... HE'S SOME SORT OF HITMAN?
HE EVER BEAT YOU?
NO, BUT HE SCARED AWAY ALL MY FRIENDS.

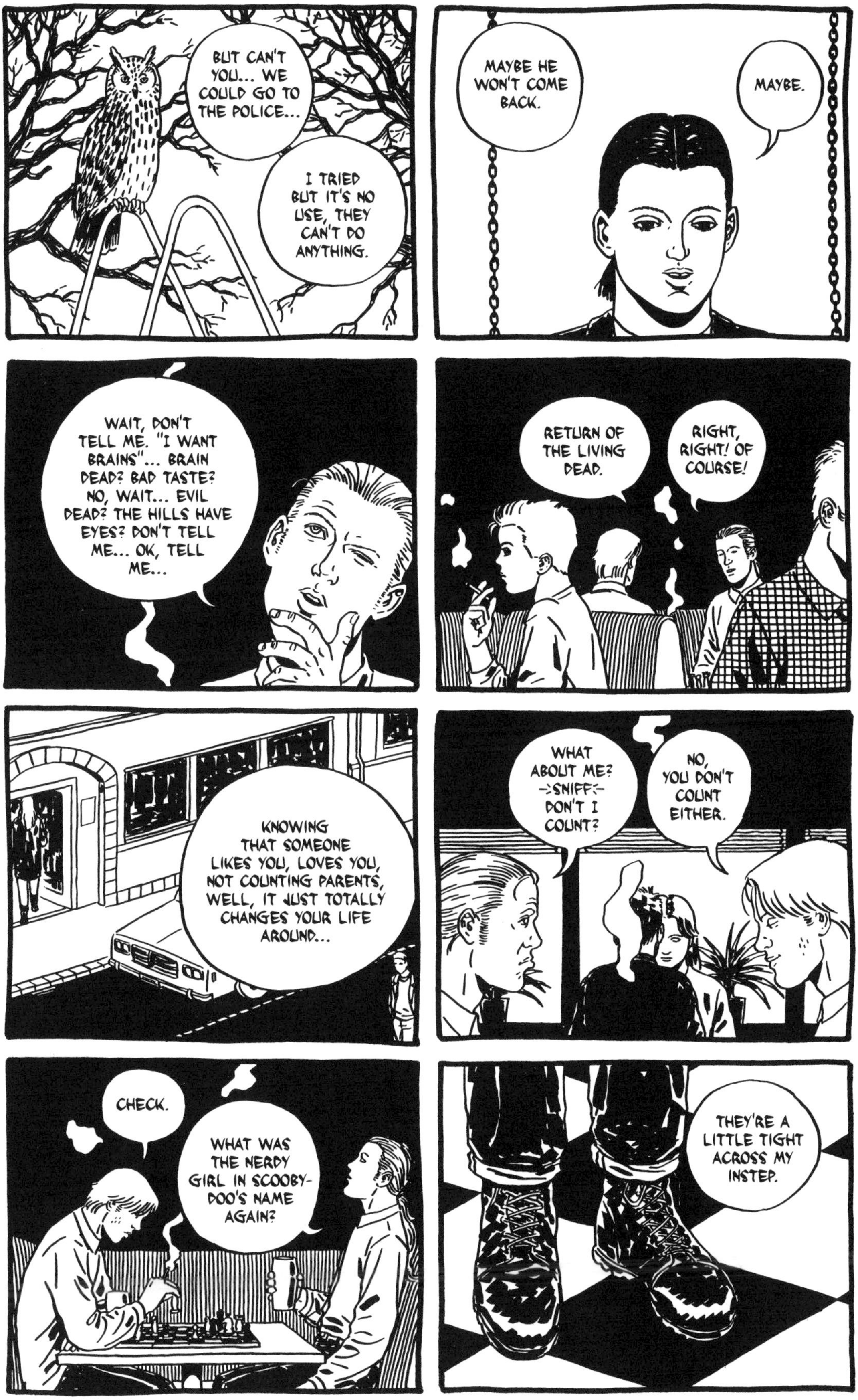
BUT CAN'T YOU... WE COULD GO TO THE POLICE...
I TRIED BUT IT'S NO USE, THEY CAN'T DO ANYTHING.
MAYBE HE WON'T COME BACK.
MAYBE.
WAIT, DON'T TELL ME. "I WANT BRAINS"... BRAIN DEAD? BAD TASTE? NO, WAIT... EVIL DEAD? THE HILLS HAVE EYES? DON'T TELL ME... OK, TELL ME...
RETURN OF THE LIVING DEAD.
RIGHT, RIGHT! OF COURSE!
KNOWING THAT SOMEONE LIKES YOU, LOVES YOU, NOT COUNTING PARENTS, WELL, IT JUST TOTALLY CHANGES YOUR LIFE AROUND...
WHAT ABOUT ME? -SNIFF- DON'T I COUNT?
NO, YOU DON'T COUNT EITHER.
CHECK.
WHAT WAS THE NERDY GIRL IN SCOOBY-DOO'S NAME AGAIN?
THEY'RE A LITTLE TIGHT ACROSS MY INSTEP.

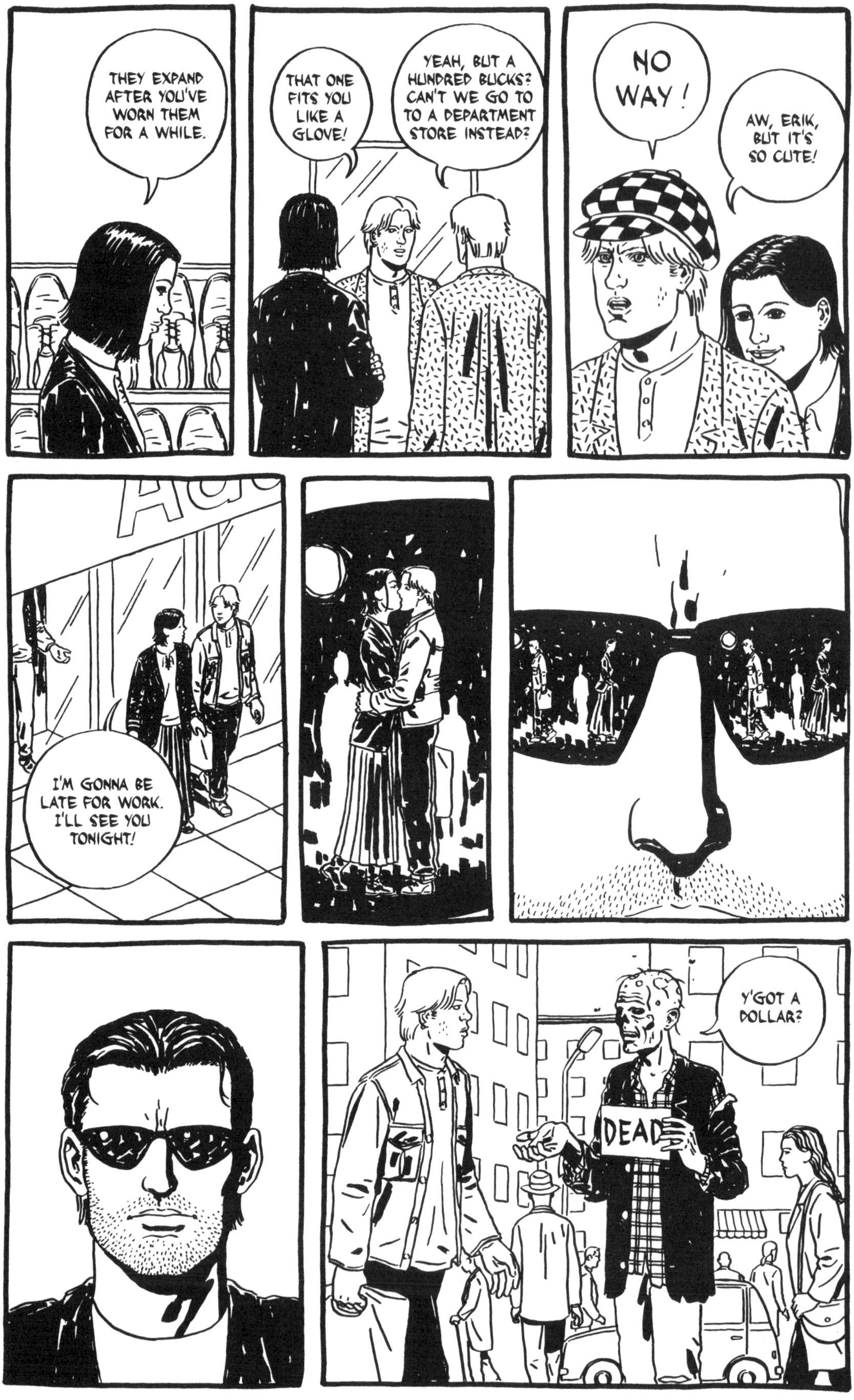
THEY EXPAND AFTER YOU'VE WORN THEM FOR A WHILE.
THAT ONE FITS YOU LIKE A GLOVE!
YEAH, BUT A HUNDRED BUCKS? CAN'T WE GO TO TO A DEPARTMENT STORE INSTEAD?
NO WAY!
AW, ERIK, BUT IT'S SO CUTE!
I'M GONNA BE LATE FOR WORK. I'LL SEE YOU TONIGHT!
Y'GOT A DOLLAR?
DEAD

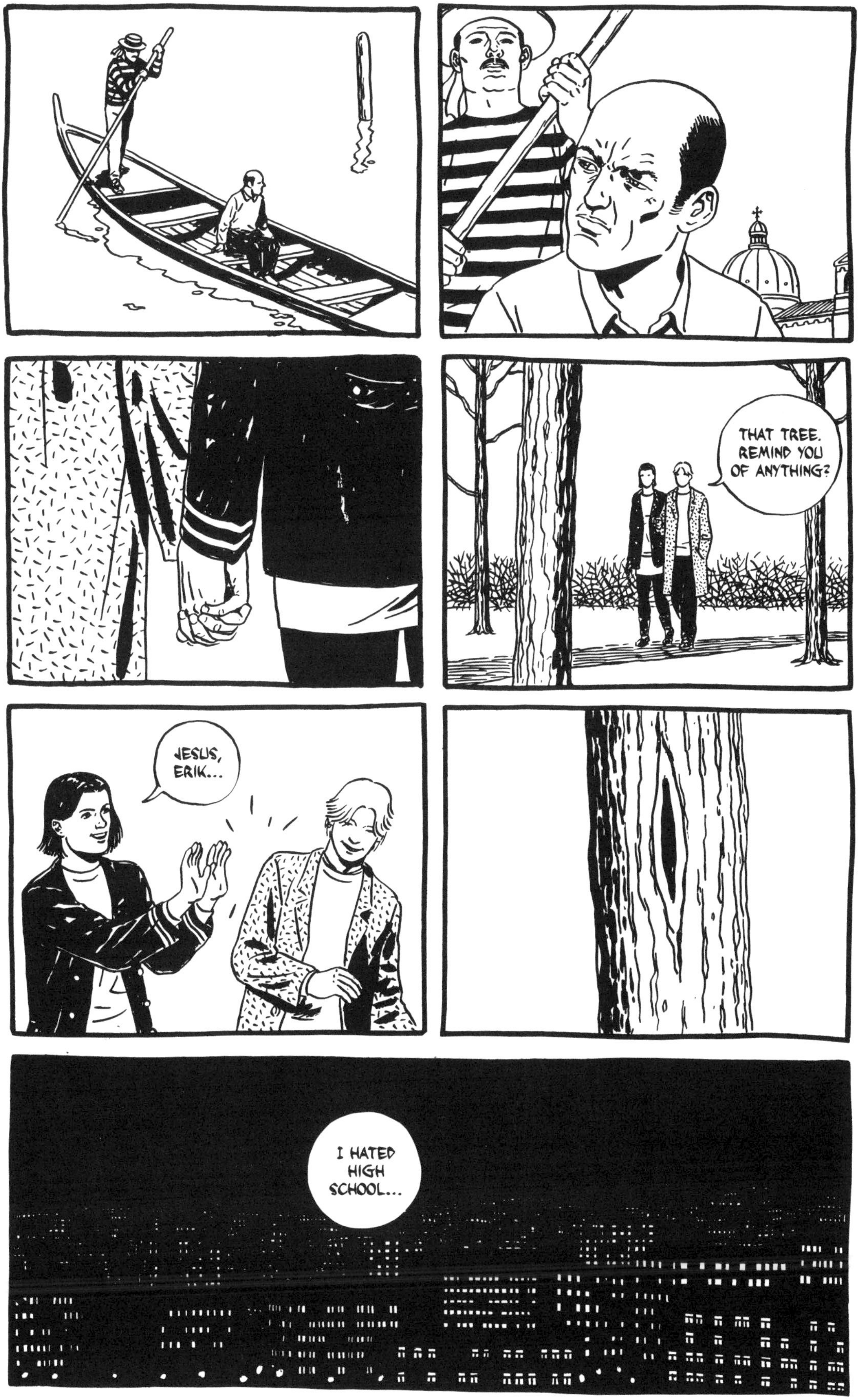
THAT TREE. REMIND YOU OF ANYTHING?
JESUS, ERIK...
I HATED HIGH SCHOOL...

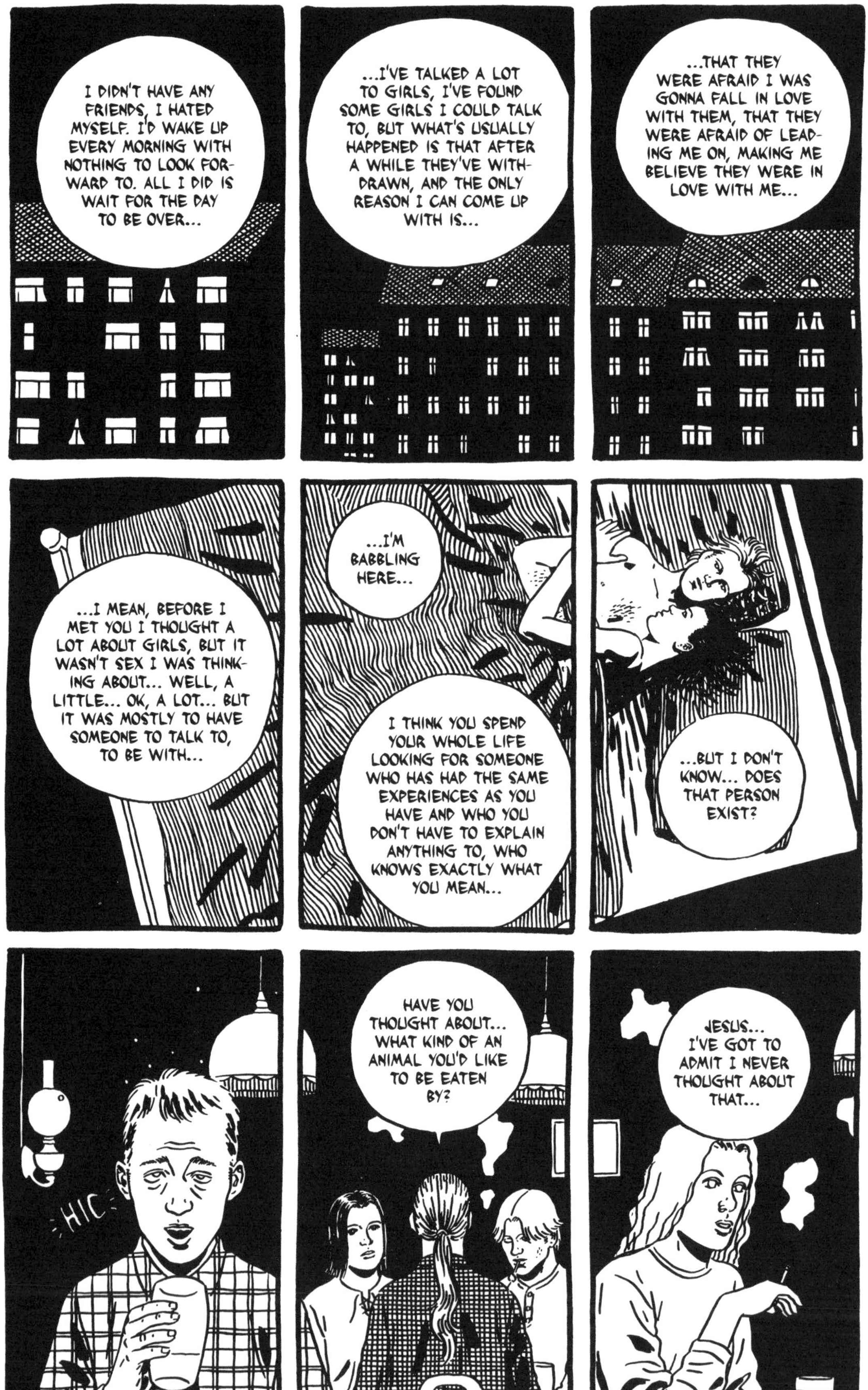
I DIDN'T HAVE ANY FRIENDS, I HATED MYSELF. I'D WAKE UP EVERY MORNING WITH NOTHING TO LOOK FORWARD TO. ALL I DID IS WAIT FOR THE DAY TO BE OVER...
...I'VE TALKED A LOT TO GIRLS, I'VE FOUND SOME GIRLS I COULD TALK TO, BUT WHAT'S USUALLY HAPPENED IS THAT AFTER A WHILE THEY'VE WITHDRAWN, AND THE ONLY REASON I CAN COME UP WITH IS...
...THAT THEY WERE AFRAID I WAS GONNA FALL IN LOVE WITH THEM, THAT THEY WERE AFRAID OF LEADING ME ON, MAKING ME BELIEVE THEY WERE IN LOVE WITH ME...
...I MEAN, BEFORE I MET YOU I THOUGHT A LOT ABOUT GIRLS, BUT IT WASN'T SEX I WAS THINKING ABOUT... WELL, A LITTLE... OK, A LOT... BUT IT WAS MOSTLY TO HAVE SOMEONE TO TALK TO, TO BE WITH...
...I'M BABBLING HERE...
I THINK YOU SPEND YOUR WHOLE LIFE LOOKING FOR SOMEONE WHO HAS HAD THE SAME EXPERIENCES AS YOU HAVE AND WHO YOU DON'T HAVE TO EXPLAIN ANYTHING TO, WHO KNOWS EXACTLY WHAT YOU MEAN...
...BUT I DON'T KNOW... DOES THAT PERSON EXIST?
HIC
HAVE YOU THOUGHT ABOUT... WHAT KIND OF AN ANIMAL YOU'D LIKE TO BE EATEN BY?
JESUS... I'VE GOT TO ADMIT I NEVER THOUGHT ABOUT THAT...

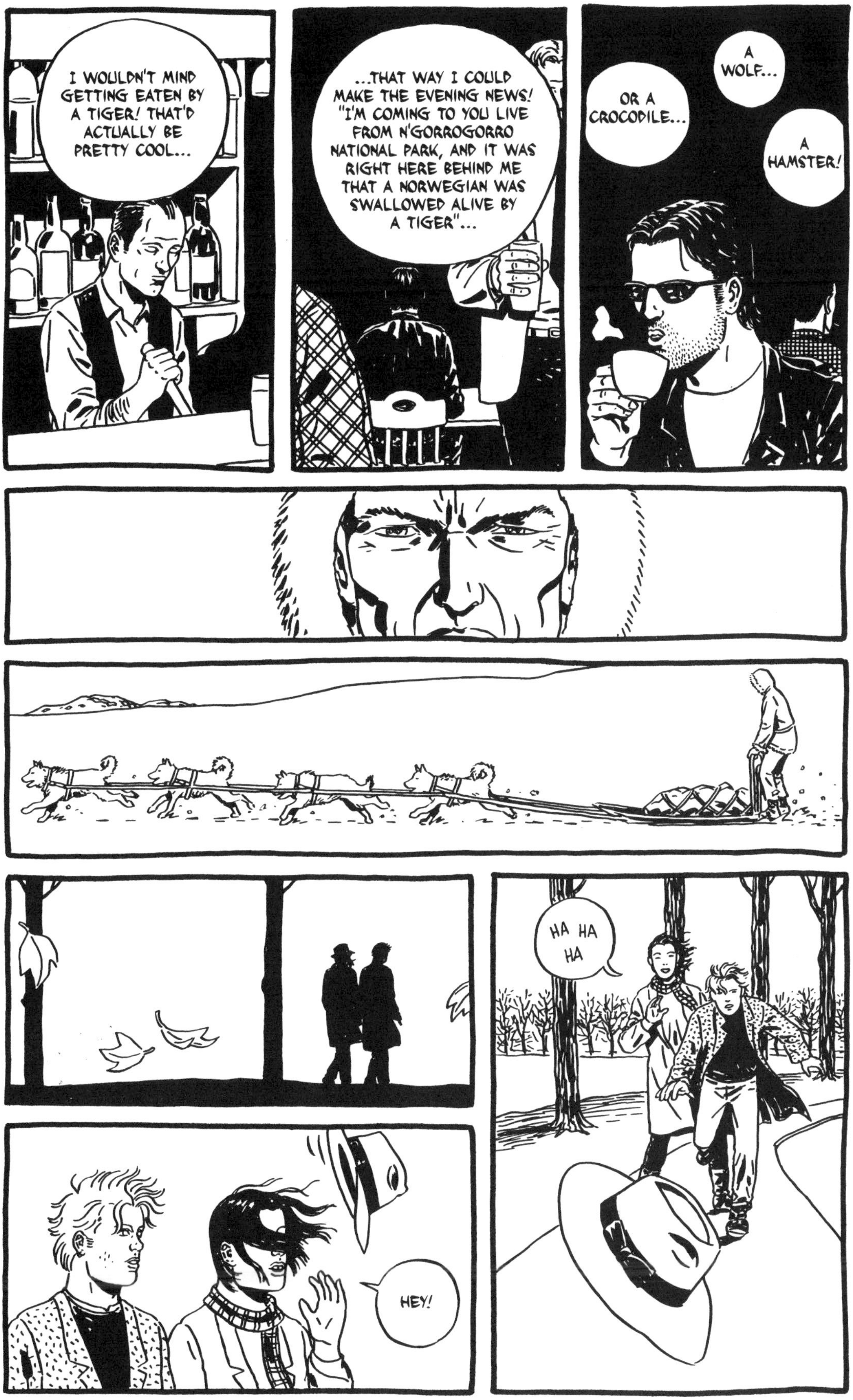
I WOULDN'T MIND GETTING EATEN BY A TIGER! THAT'D ACTUALLY BE PRETTY COOL...
...THAT WAY I COULD MAKE THE EVENING NEWS! "I'M COMING TO YOU LIVE FROM N'GORROGORRO NATIONAL PARK, AND IT WAS RIGHT HERE BEHIND ME THAT A NORWEGIAN WAS SWALLOWED ALIVE BY A TIGER"...
OR A CROCODILE...
A WOLF...
A HAMSTER!
HEY!
HA HA HA

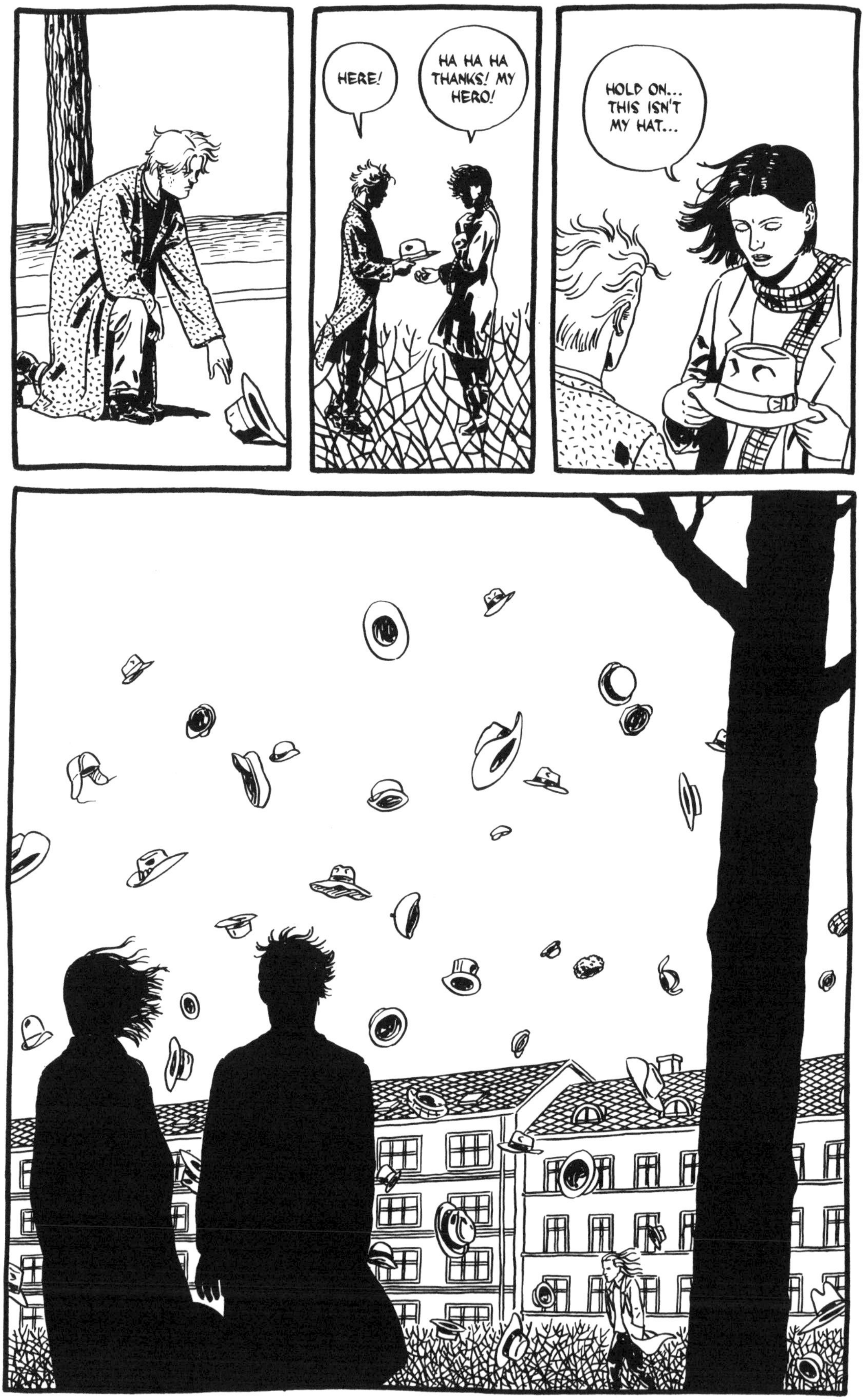
HERE!
HA HA HA THANKS! MY HERO!
HOLD ON... THIS ISN'T MY HAT...

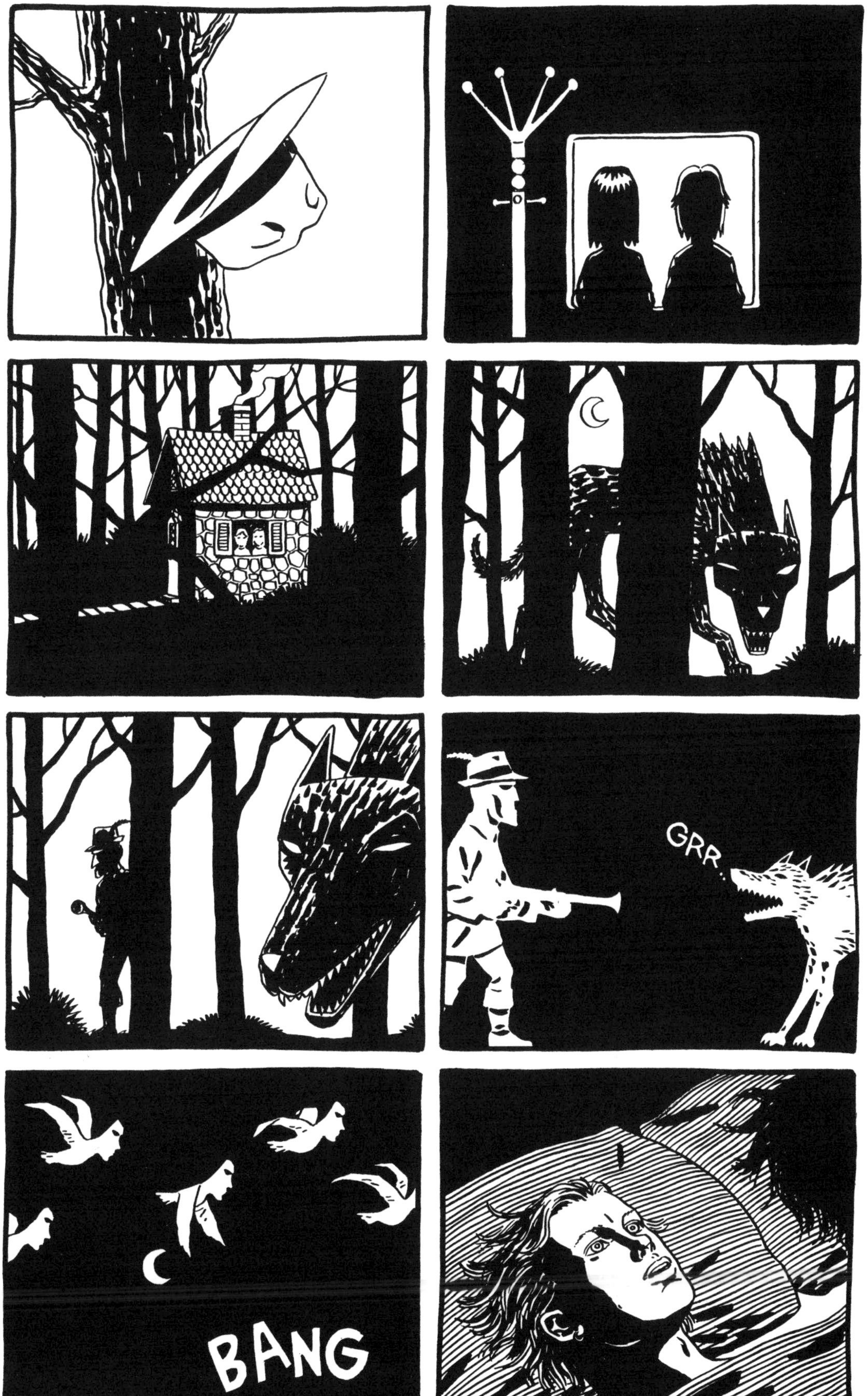
GRR...
BANG

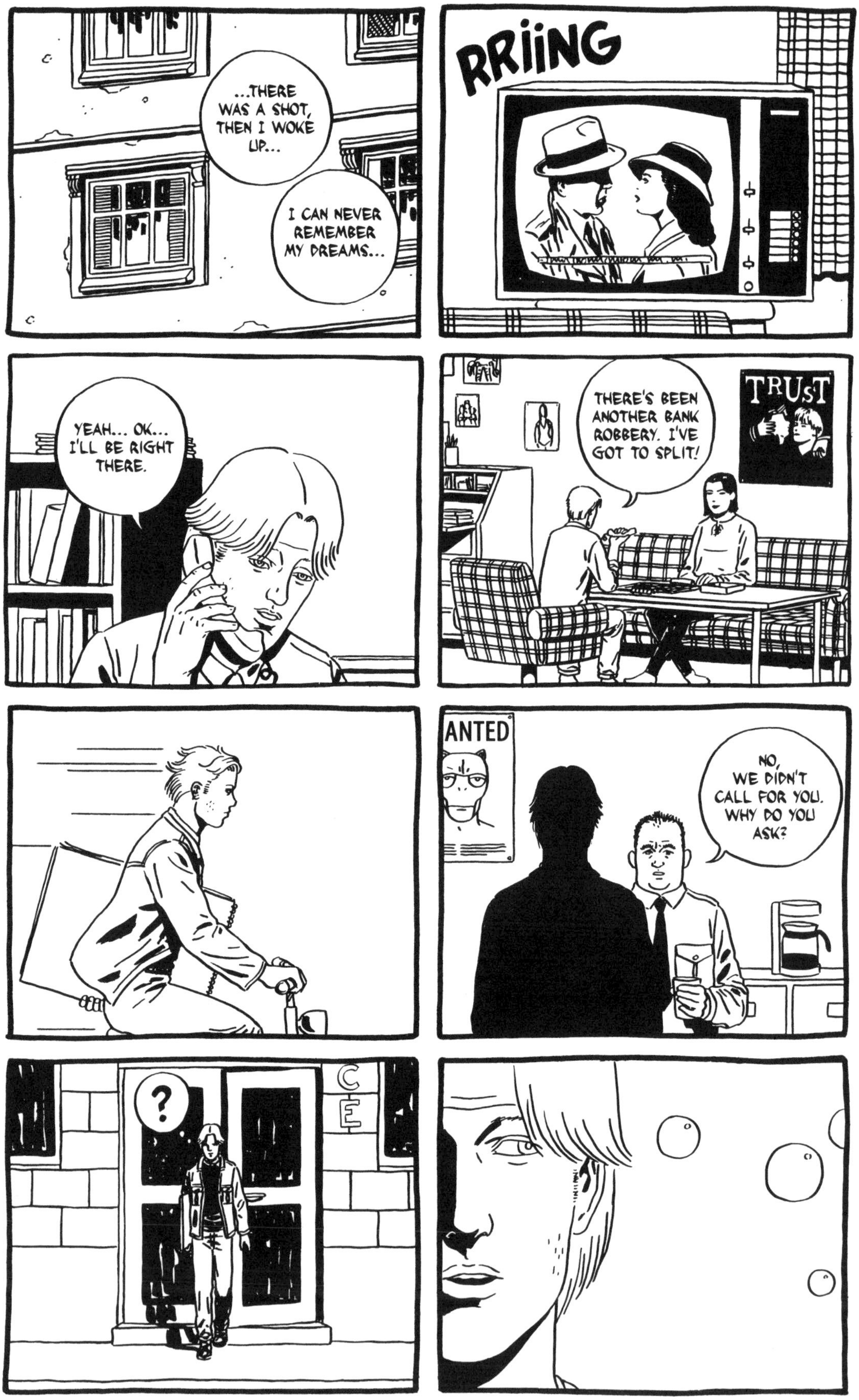
...THERE WAS A SHOT, THEN I WOKE UP...
I CAN NEVER REMEMBER MY DREAMS...
RRiiNG
YEAH... OK... I'LL BE RIGHT THERE.
THERE'S BEEN ANOTHER BANK ROBBERY. I'VE GOT TO SPLIT!
TRUST
ANTED
NO, WE DIDN'T CALL FOR YOU. WHY DO YOU ASK?
?
C
E

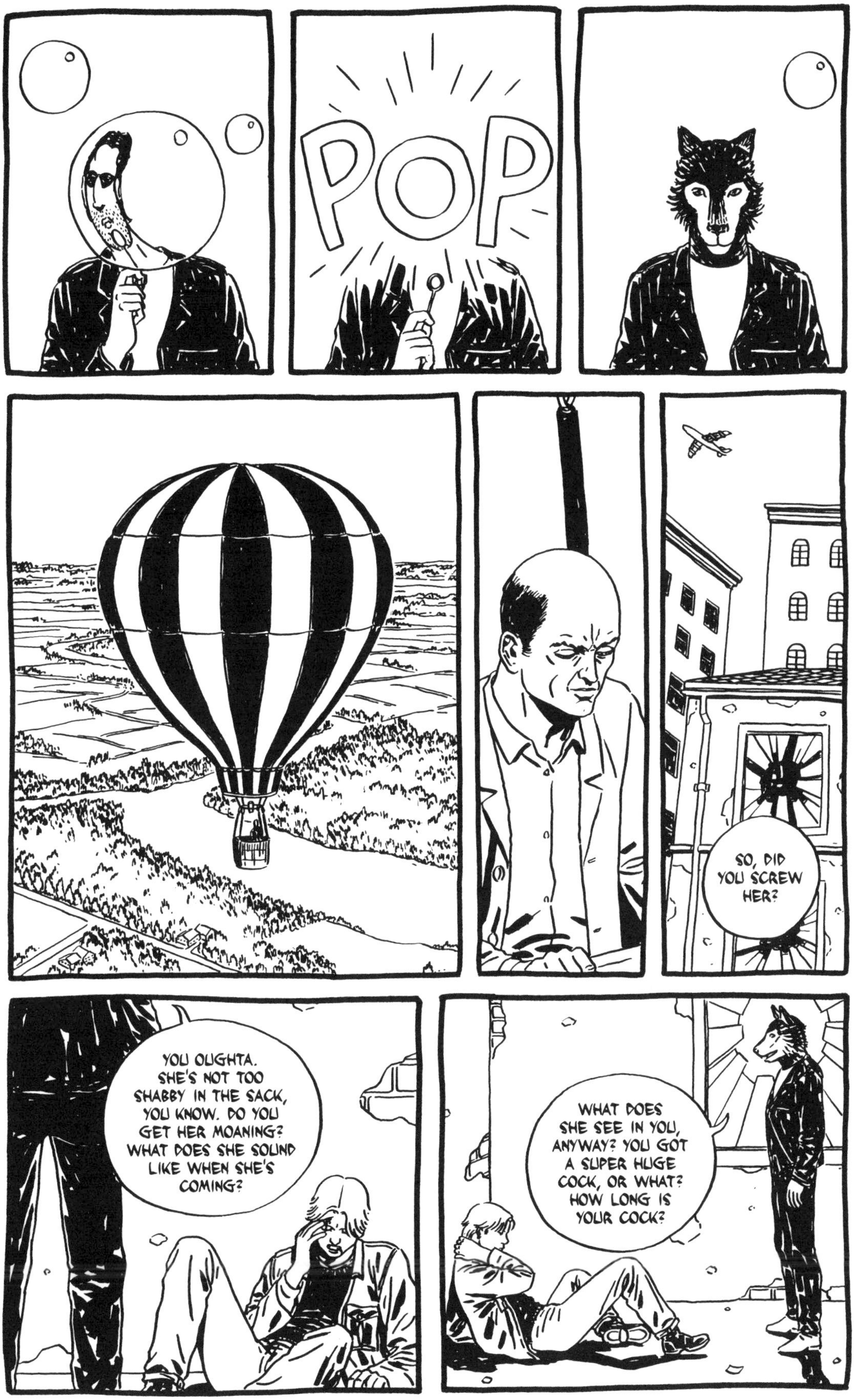
POP
SO, DID YOU SCREW HER?
YOU OUGHTA. SHE'S NOT TOO SHABBY IN THE SACK, YOU KNOW. DO YOU GET HER MOANING? WHAT DOES SHE SOUND LIKE WHEN SHE'S COMING?
WHAT DOES SHE SEE IN YOU, ANYWAY? YOU GOT A SUPER HUGE COCK, OR WHAT? HOW LONG IS YOUR COCK?

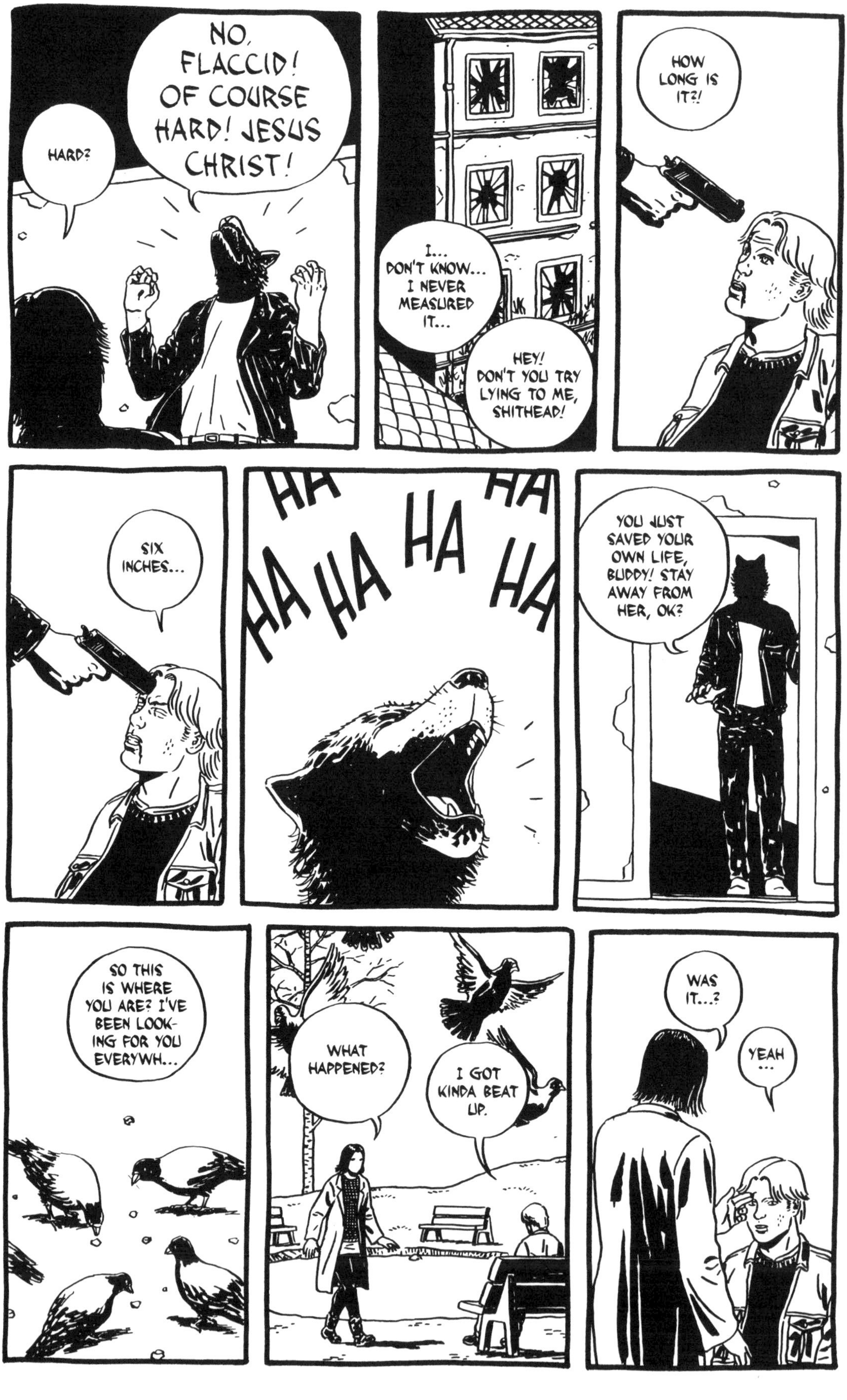
HARD?
NO, FLACCID! OF COURSE HARD! JESUS CHRIST!
I... DON'T KNOW... I NEVER MEASURED IT...
HEY! DON'T YOU TRY LYING TO ME, SHITHEAD!
HOW LONG IS IT?!
SIX INCHES...
HA HA HA HA HA HA HA
YOU JUST SAVED YOUR OWN LIFE, BUDDY! STAY AWAY FROM HER, OK?
SO THIS IS WHERE YOU ARE? I'VE BEEN LOOK-ING FOR YOU EVERYWH...
WHAT HAPPENED?
I GOT KINDA BEAT UP.
WAS IT...?
YEAH...

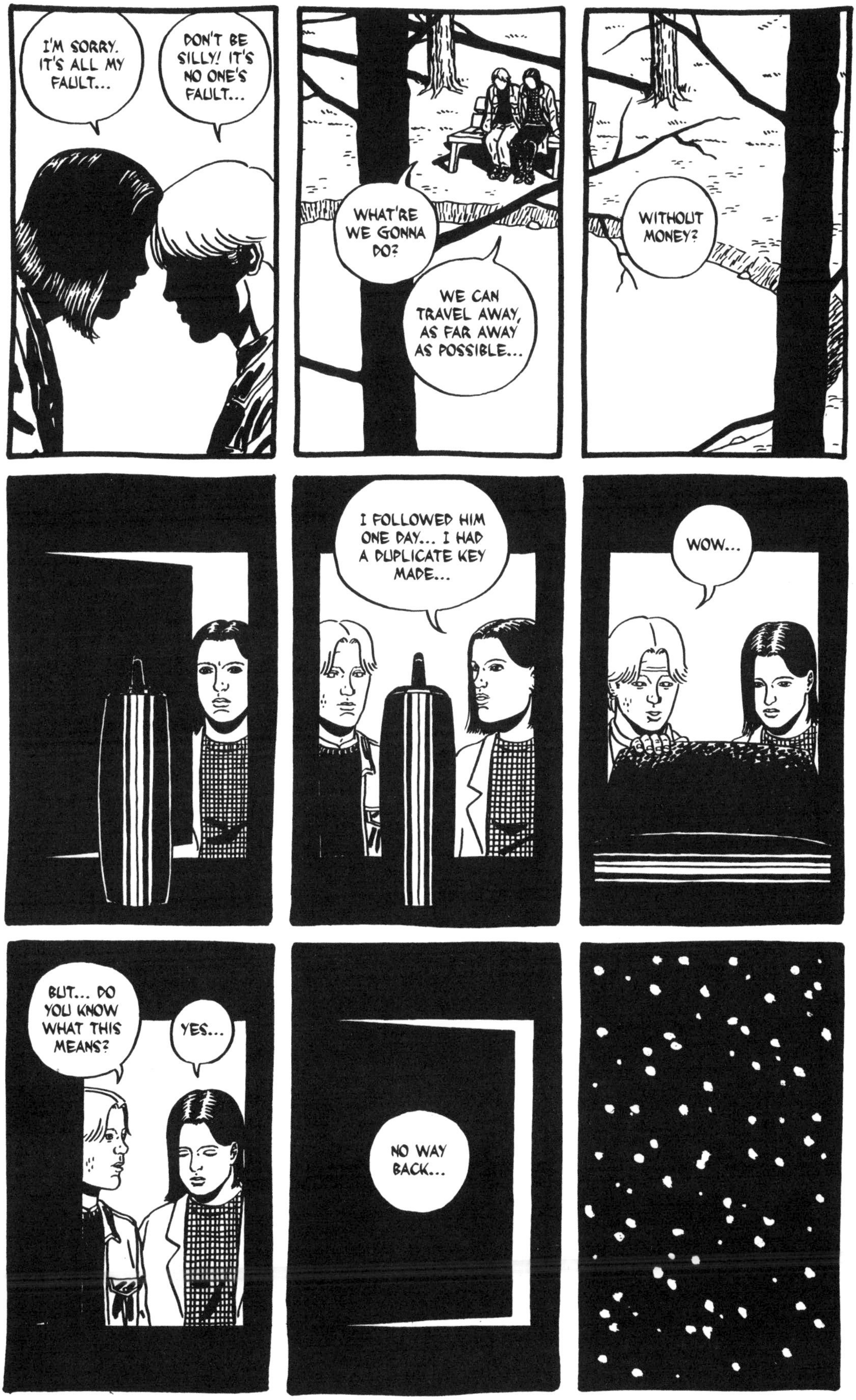
I'M SORRY. IT'S ALL MY FAULT...
DON'T BE SILLY! IT'S NO ONE'S FAULT...
WHAT'RE WE GONNA DO?
WE CAN TRAVEL AWAY, AS FAR AWAY AS POSSIBLE...
WITHOUT MONEY?
I FOLLOWED HIM ONE DAY... I HAD A DUPLICATE KEY MADE...
WOW...
BUT... DO YOU KNOW WHAT THIS MEANS?
YES...
NO WAY BACK...

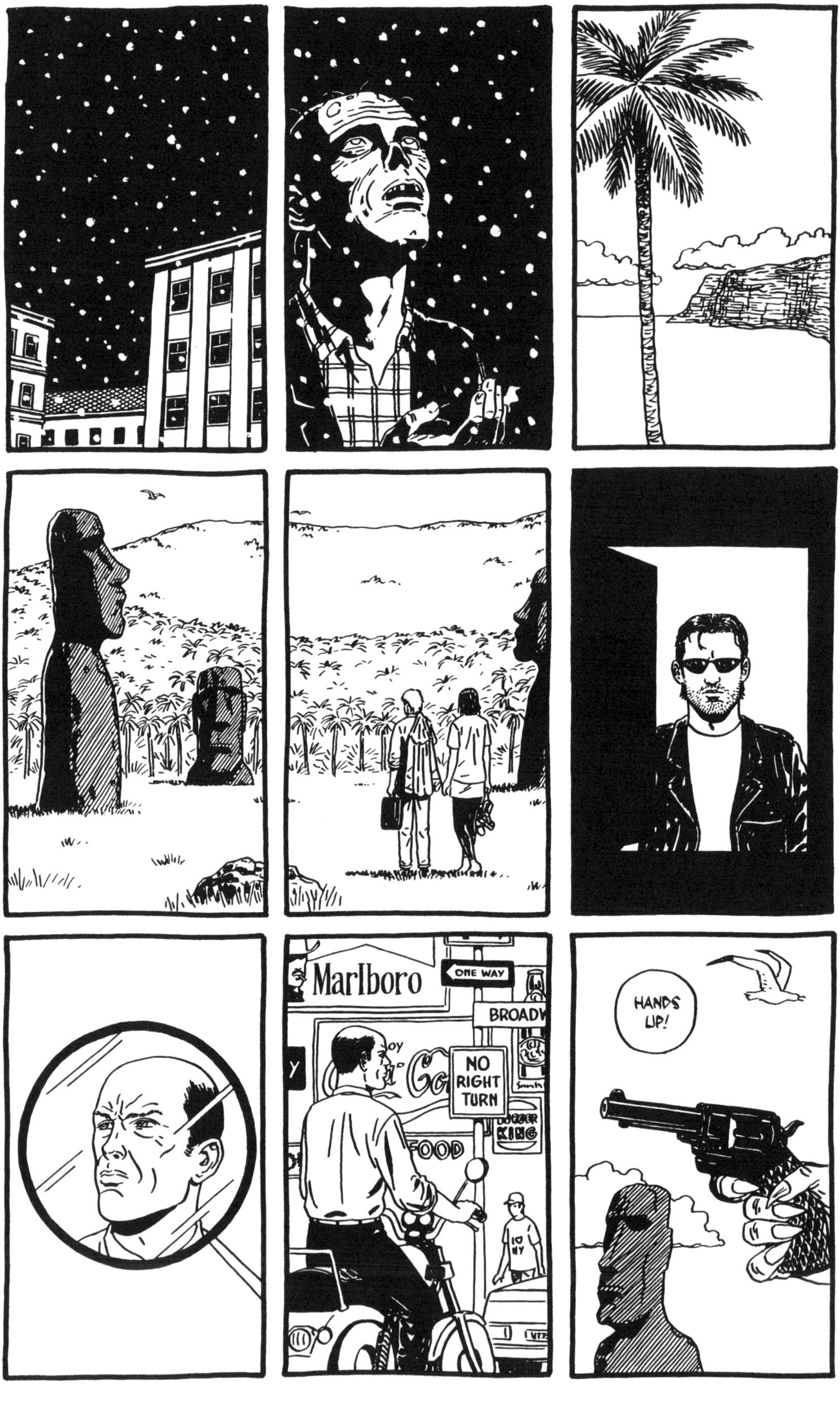
Marlboro
ONE WAY
BROADW
NO RIGHT TURN
KING
FOOD
HANDS UP!

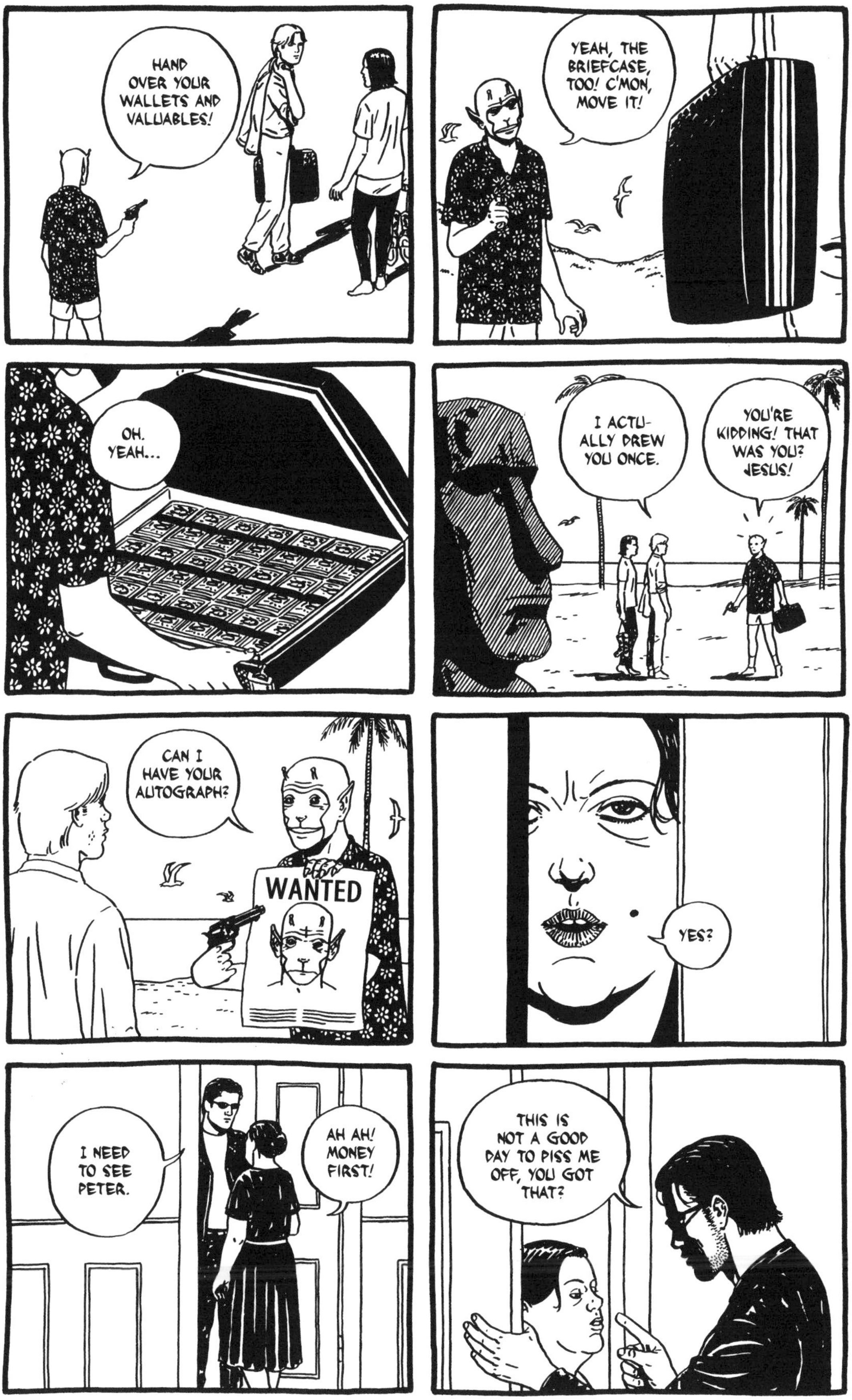
HAND OVER YOUR WALLETS AND VALUABLES!
YEAH, THE BRIEFCASE, TOO! C'MON, MOVE IT!
OH. YEAH...
I ACTUALLY DREW YOU ONCE.
YOU'RE KIDDING! THAT WAS YOU? JESUS!
CAN I HAVE YOUR AUTOGRAPH?
WANTED
YES?
I NEED TO SEE PETER.
AH AH! MONEY FIRST!
THIS IS NOT A GOOD DAY TO PISS ME OFF, YOU GOT THAT?

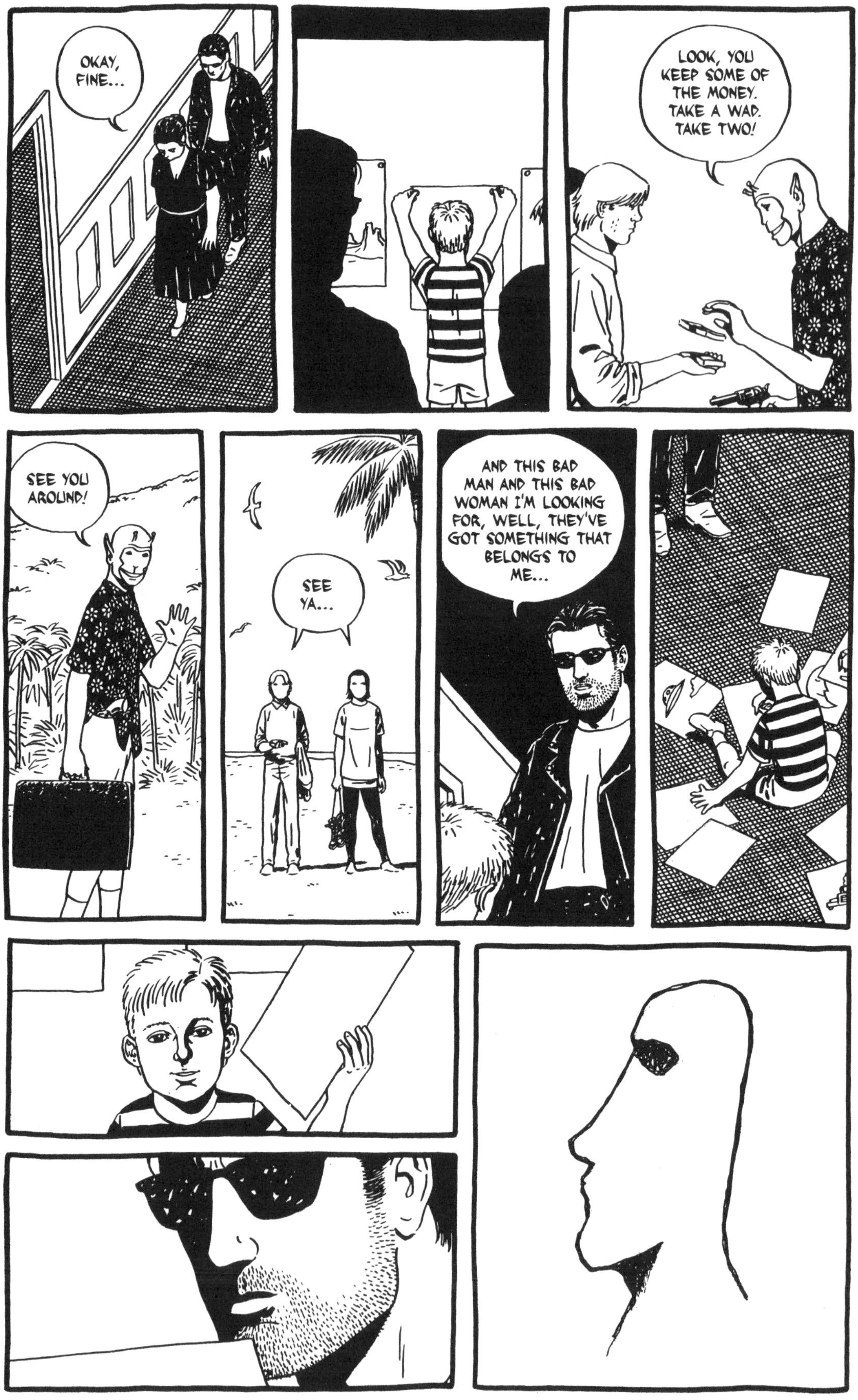
OKAY, FINE...
LOOK, YOU KEEP SOME OF THE MONEY. TAKE A WAD. TAKE TWO!
SEE YOU AROUND!
SEE YA...
AND THIS BAD MAN AND THIS BAD WOMAN I'M LOOKING FOR, WELL, THEY'VE GOT SOMETHING THAT BELONGS TO ME...

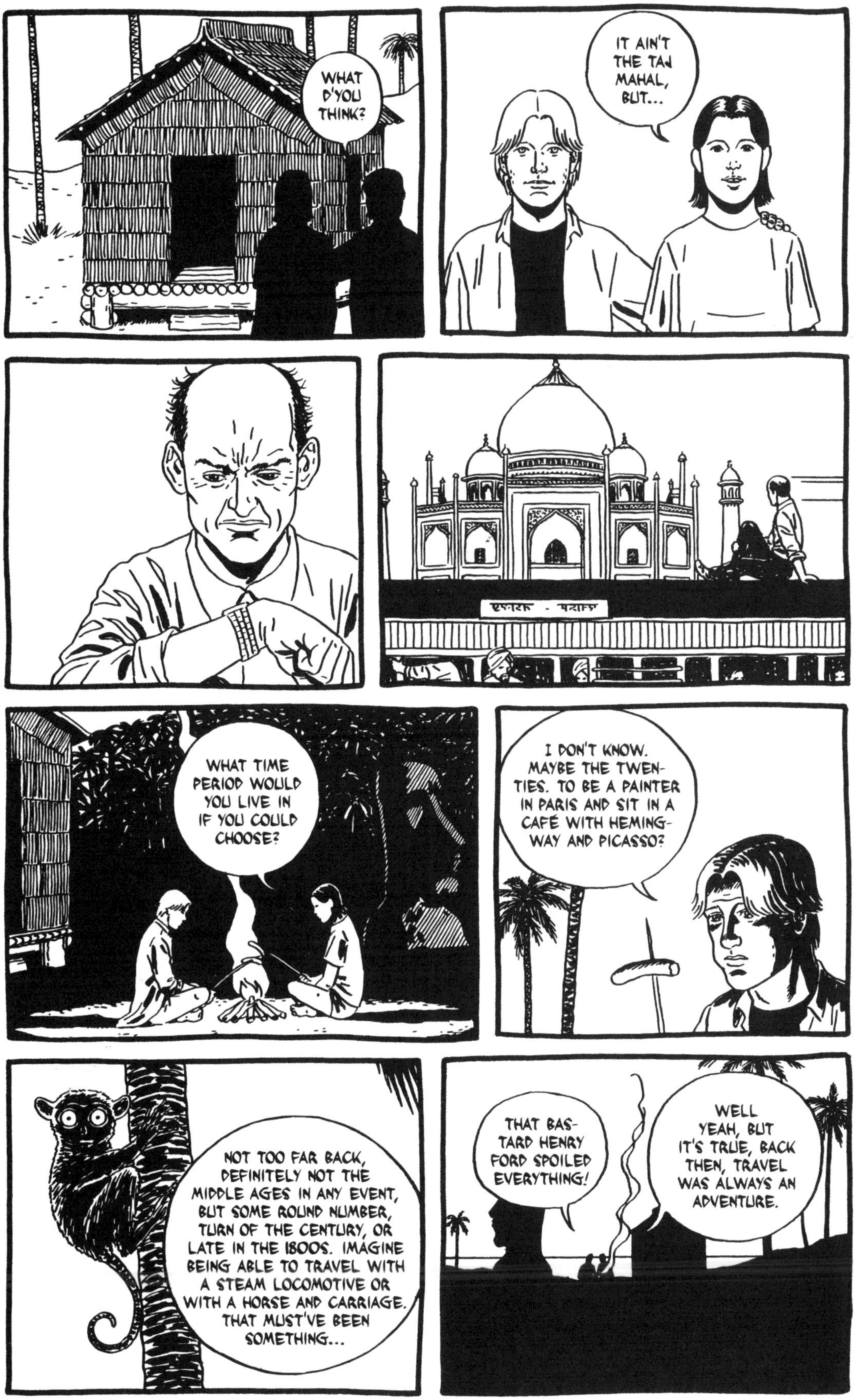
WHAT D'YOU THINK?
IT AIN'T THE TAJ MAHAL, BUT...
WHAT TIME PERIOD WOULD YOU LIVE IN IF YOU COULD CHOOSE?
I DON'T KNOW. MAYBE THE TWEN-TIES. TO BE A PAINTER IN PARIS AND SIT IN A CAFÉ WITH HEMING-WAY AND PICASSO?
NOT TOO FAR BACK, DEFINITELY NOT THE MIDDLE AGES IN ANY EVENT, BUT SOME ROUND NUMBER, TURN OF THE CENTURY, OR LATE IN THE 1800S. IMAGINE BEING ABLE TO TRAVEL WITH A STEAM LOCOMOTIVE OR WITH A HORSE AND CARRIAGE. THAT MUST'VE BEEN SOMETHING...
WELL YEAH, BUT IT'S TRUE, BACK THEN, TRAVEL WAS ALWAYS AN ADVENTURE.
THAT BAS-TARD HENRY FORD SPOILED EVERYTHING!

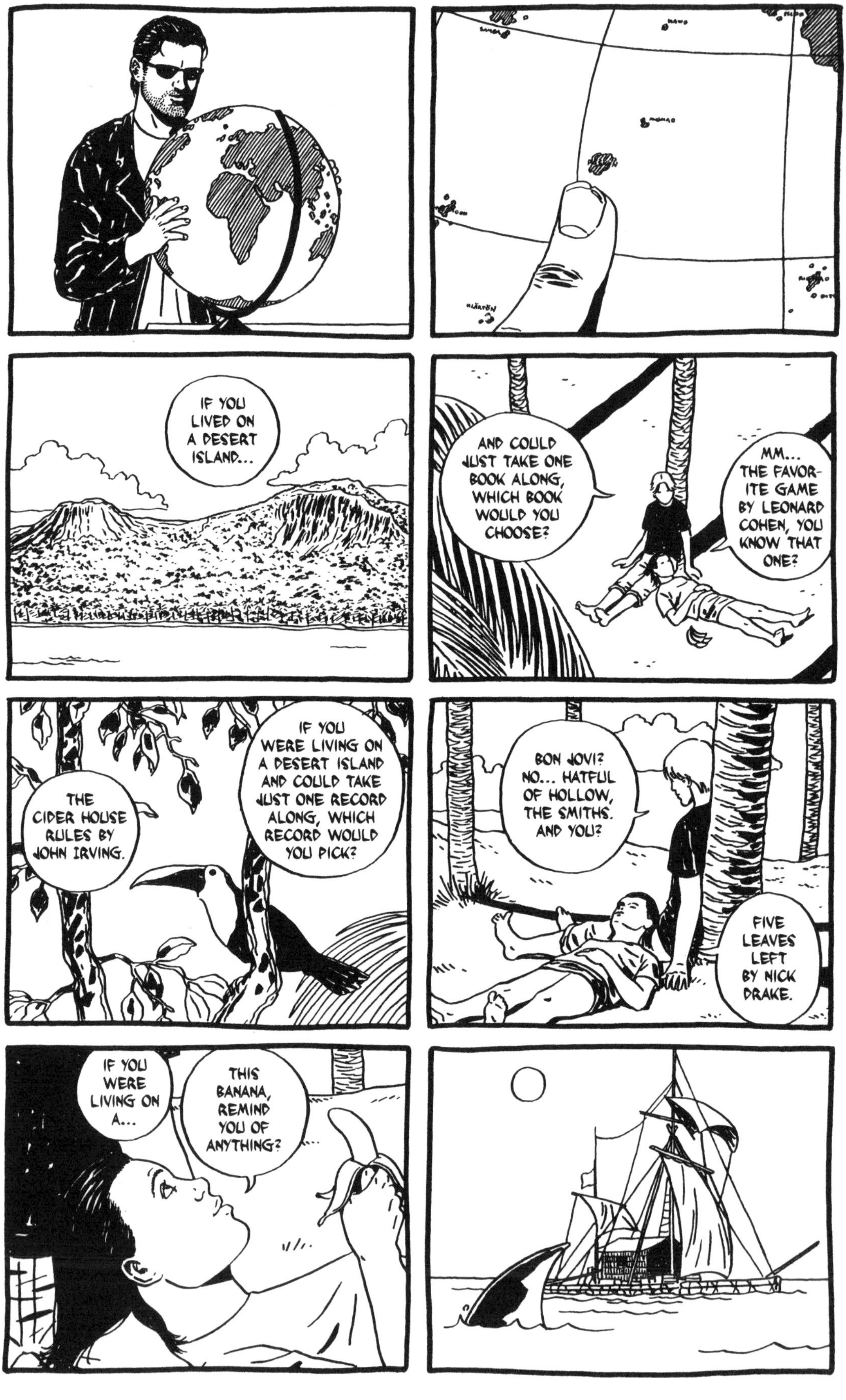
IF YOU LIVED ON A DESERT ISLAND...
AND COULD JUST TAKE ONE BOOK ALONG, WHICH BOOK WOULD YOU CHOOSE?
MM... THE FAVORITE GAME BY LEONARD COHEN, YOU KNOW THAT ONE?
THE CIDER HOUSE RULES BY JOHN IRVING.
IF YOU WERE LIVING ON A DESERT ISLAND AND COULD TAKE JUST ONE RECORD ALONG, WHICH RECORD WOULD YOU PICK?
BON JOVI? NO... HATFUL OF HOLLOW, THE SMITHS. AND YOU?
FIVE LEAVES LEFT BY NICK DRAKE.
IF YOU WERE LIVING ON A...
THIS BANANA, REMIND YOU OF ANYTHING?

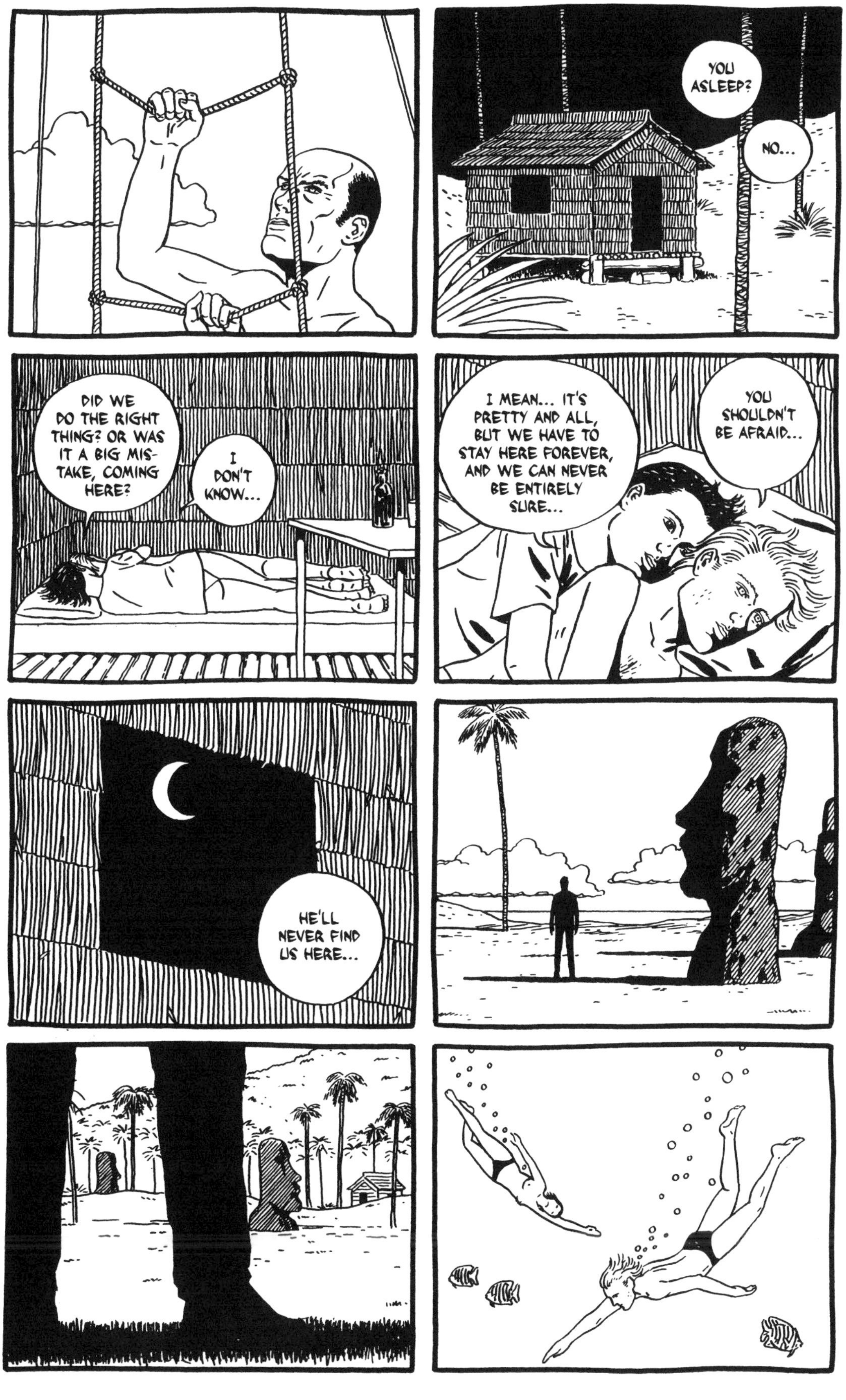
YOU ASLEEP?
NO...
DID WE DO THE RIGHT THING? OR WAS IT A BIG MISTAKE, COMING HERE?
I DON'T KNOW...
I MEAN... IT'S PRETTY AND ALL, BUT WE HAVE TO STAY HERE FOREVER, AND WE CAN NEVER BE ENTIRELY SURE...
YOU SHOULDN'T BE AFRAID...
HE'LL NEVER FIND US HERE...

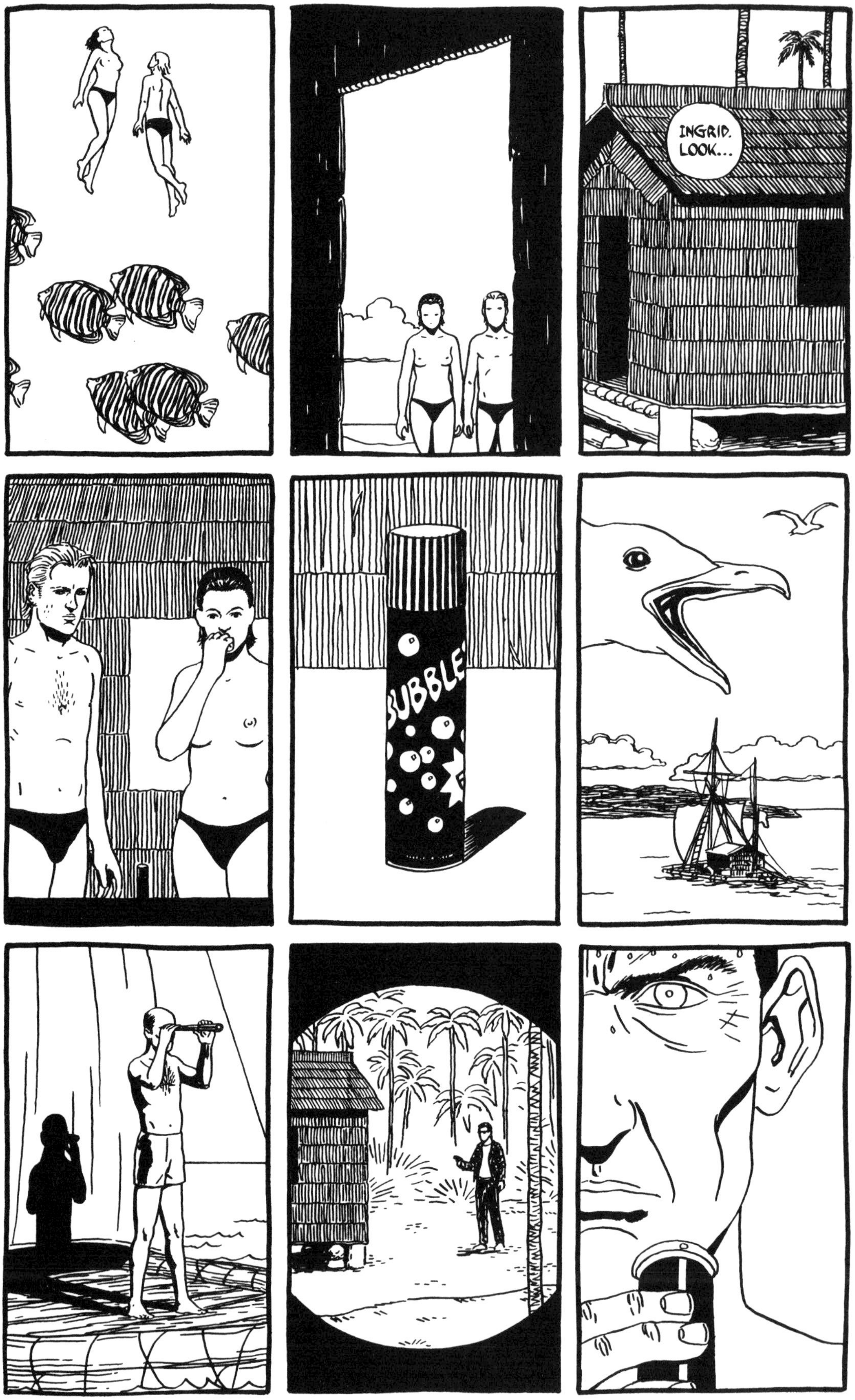
INGRID. LOOK...
BUBBLES

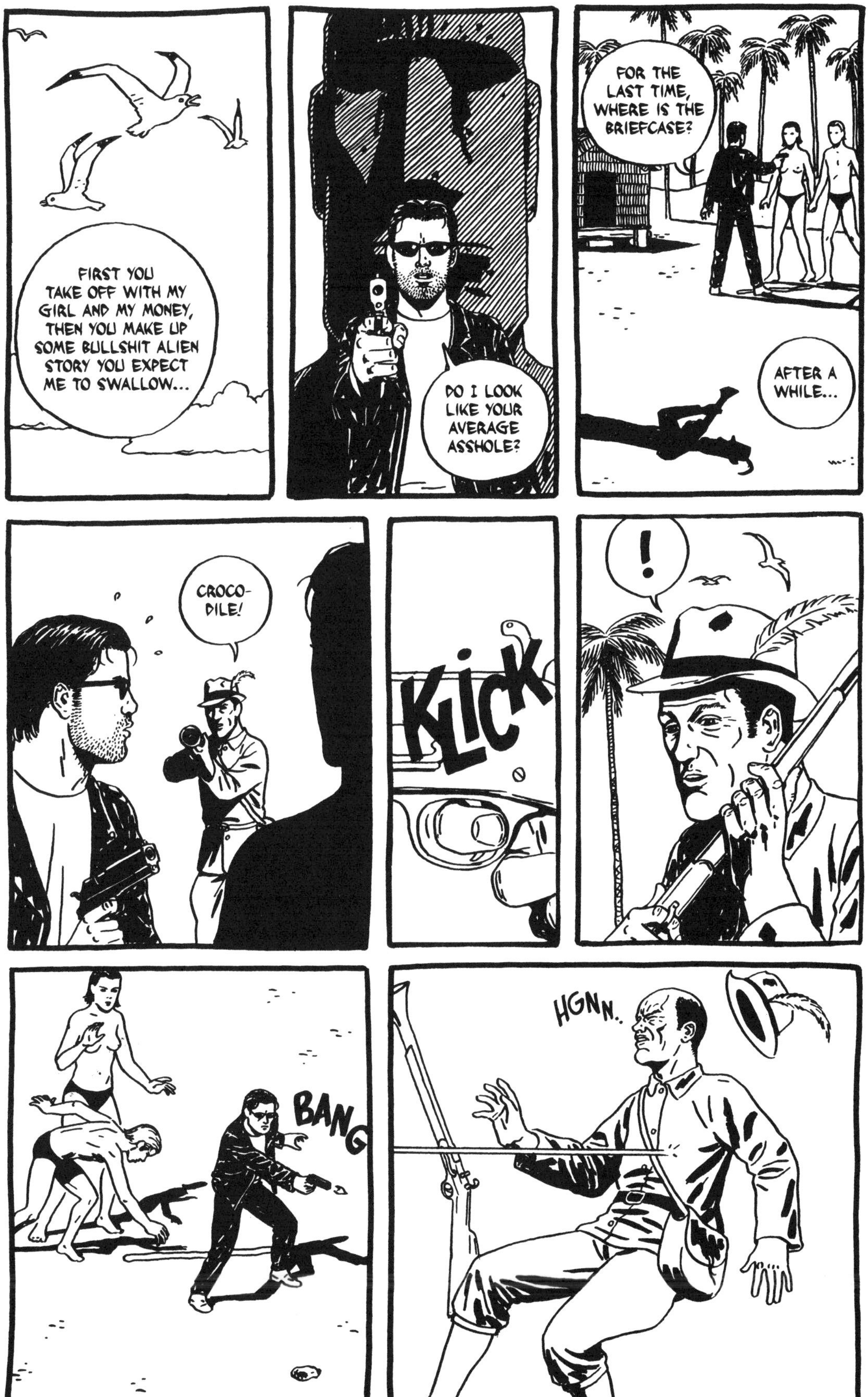
FIRST YOU TAKE OFF WITH MY GIRL AND MY MONEY, THEN YOU MAKE UP SOME BULLSHIT ALIEN STORY YOU EXPECT ME TO SWALLOW...
DO I LOOK LIKE YOUR AVERAGE ASSHOLE?
FOR THE LAST TIME, WHERE IS THE BRIEFCASE?
AFTER A WHILE...
CROCO-DILE!
KLICK
!
BANG
HGNN..

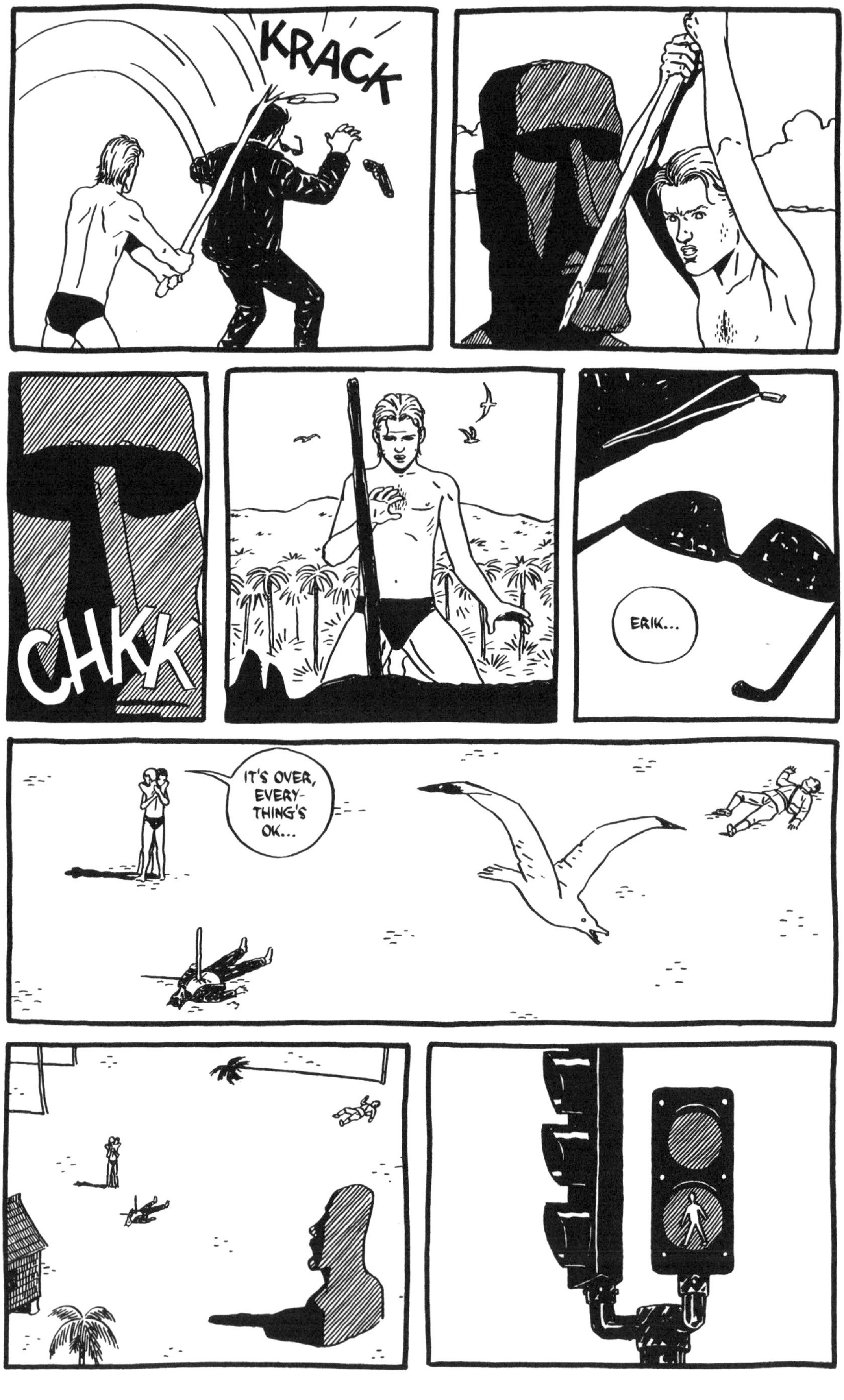
KRACK
CHKK
ERIK...
IT'S OVER, EVERY-THING'S OK...

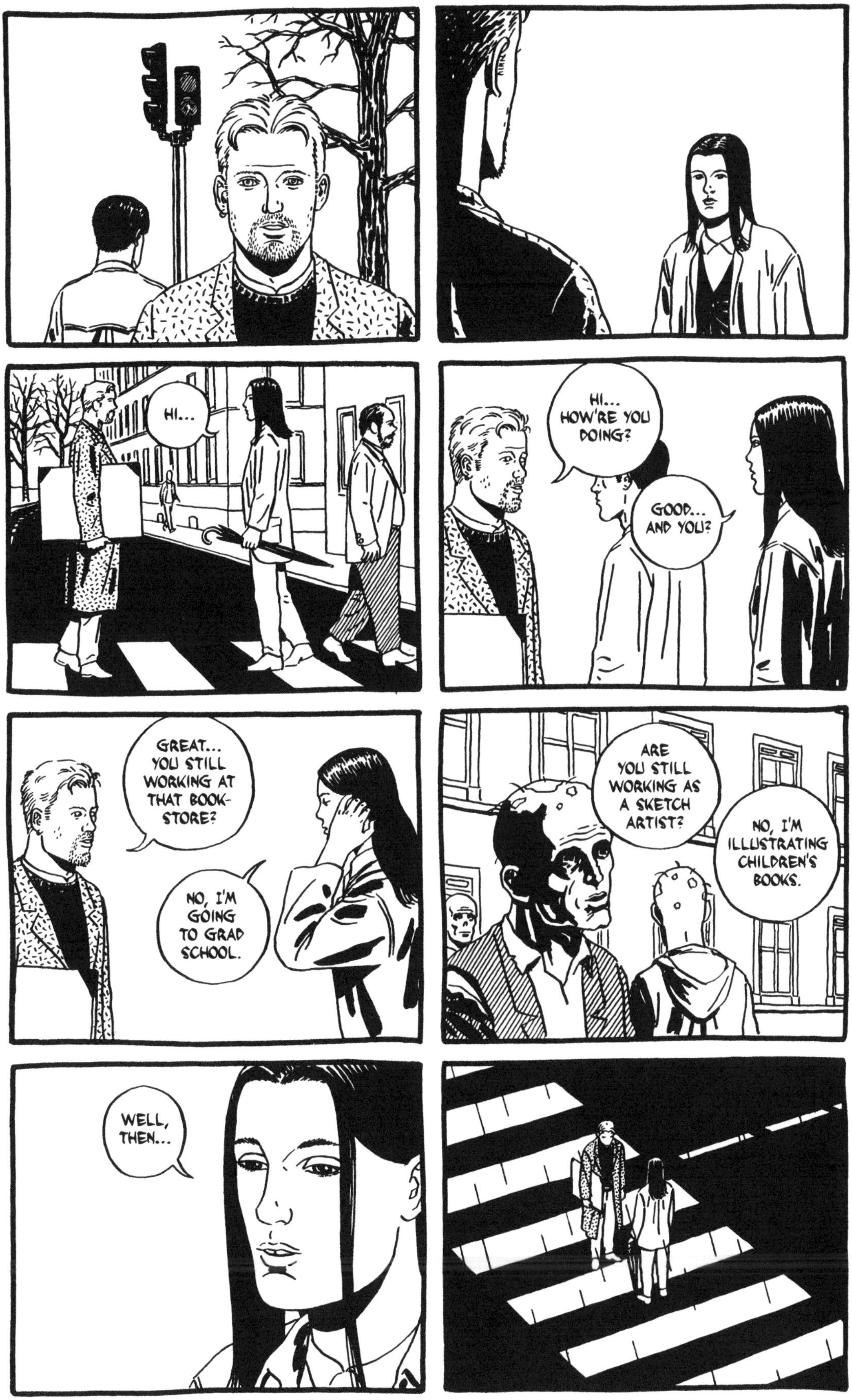
HI...
HI... HOW'RE YOU DOING?
GOOD... AND YOU?
GREAT... YOU STILL WORKING AT THAT BOOK-STORE?
NO, I'M GOING TO GRAD SCHOOL.
ARE YOU STILL WORKING AS A SKETCH ARTIST?
NO, I'M ILLUSTRATING CHILDREN'S BOOKS.
WELL, THEN...

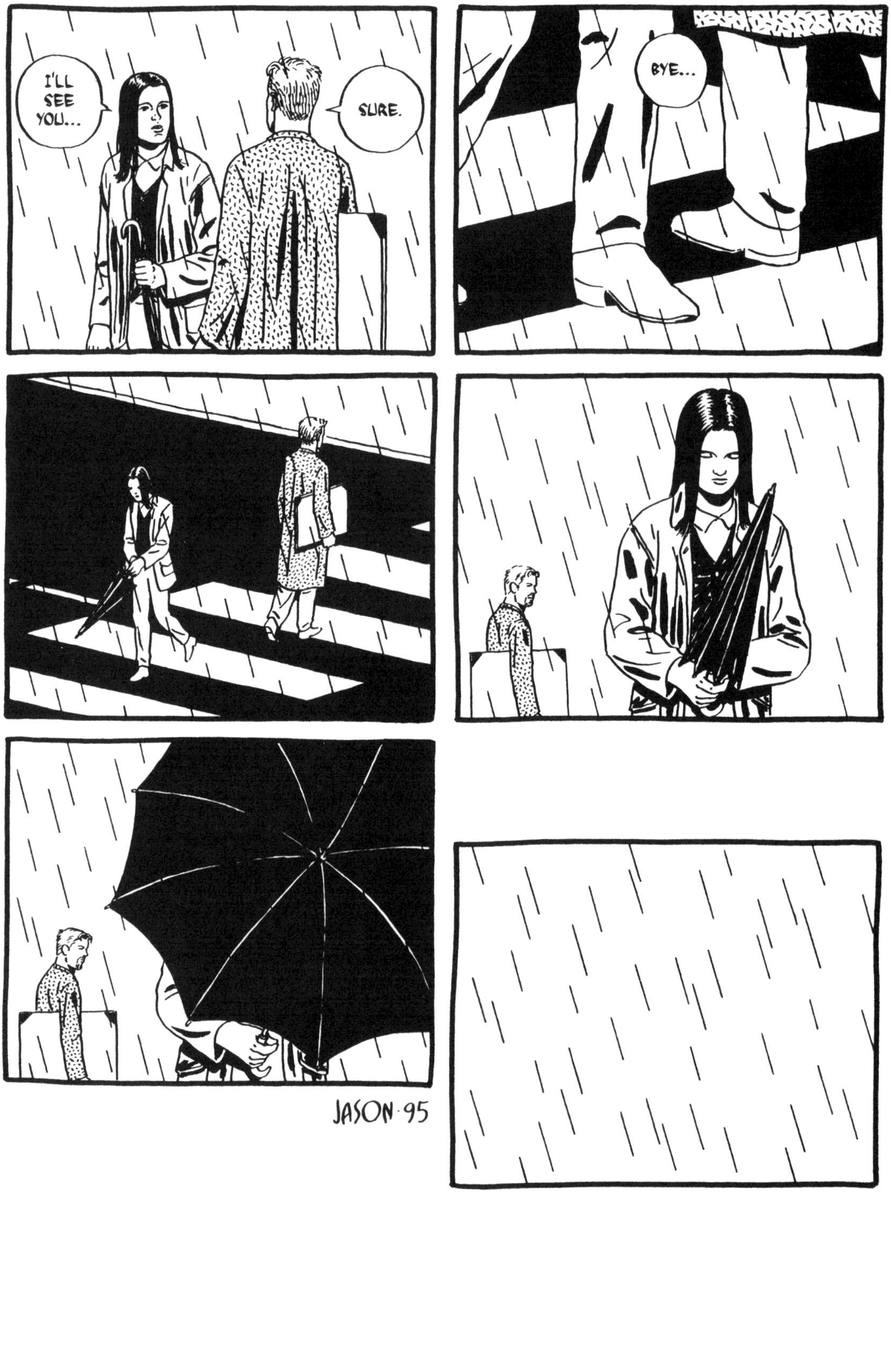
I'LL SEE YOU...
SURE.
BYE...
JASON·95

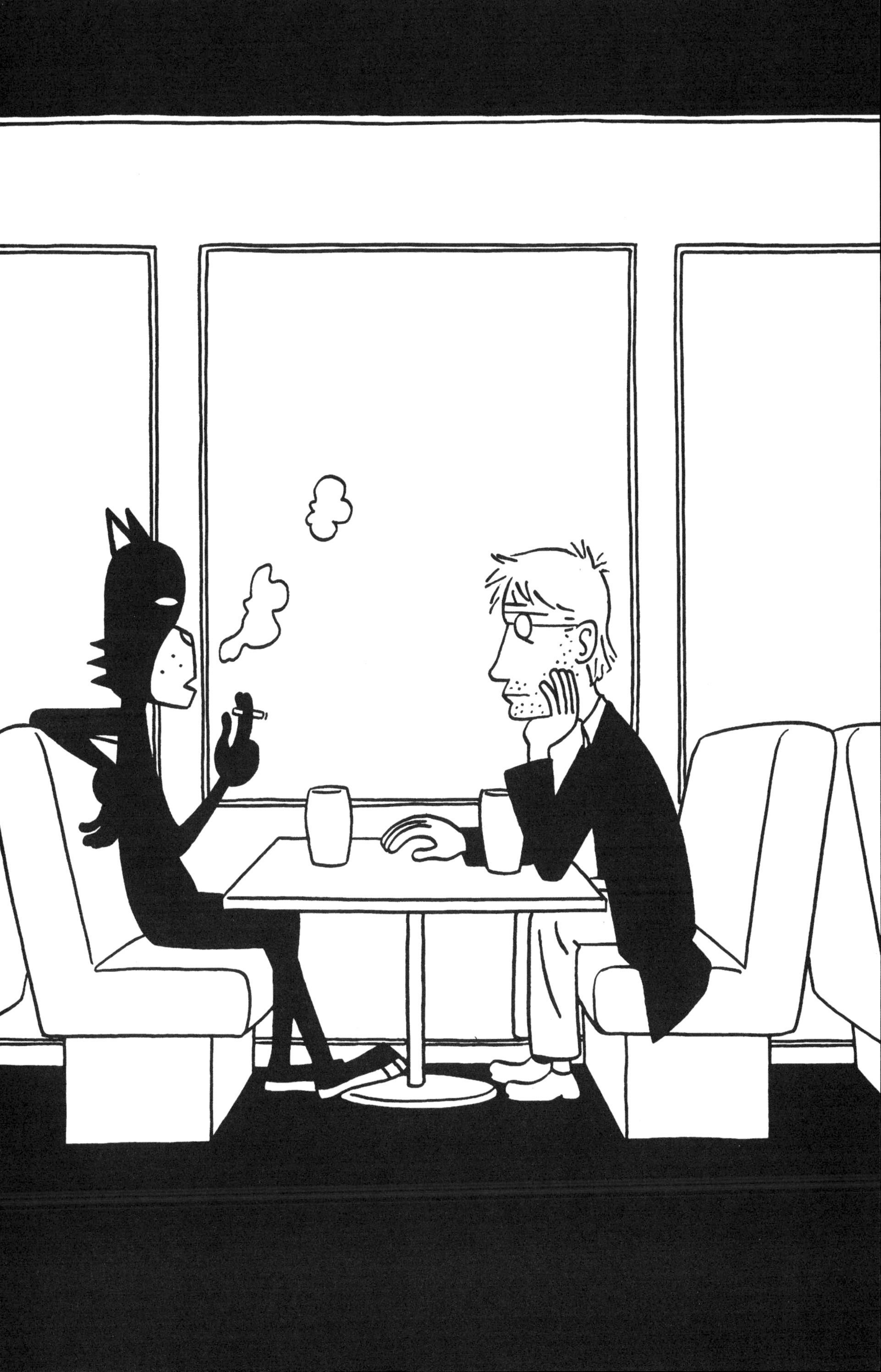

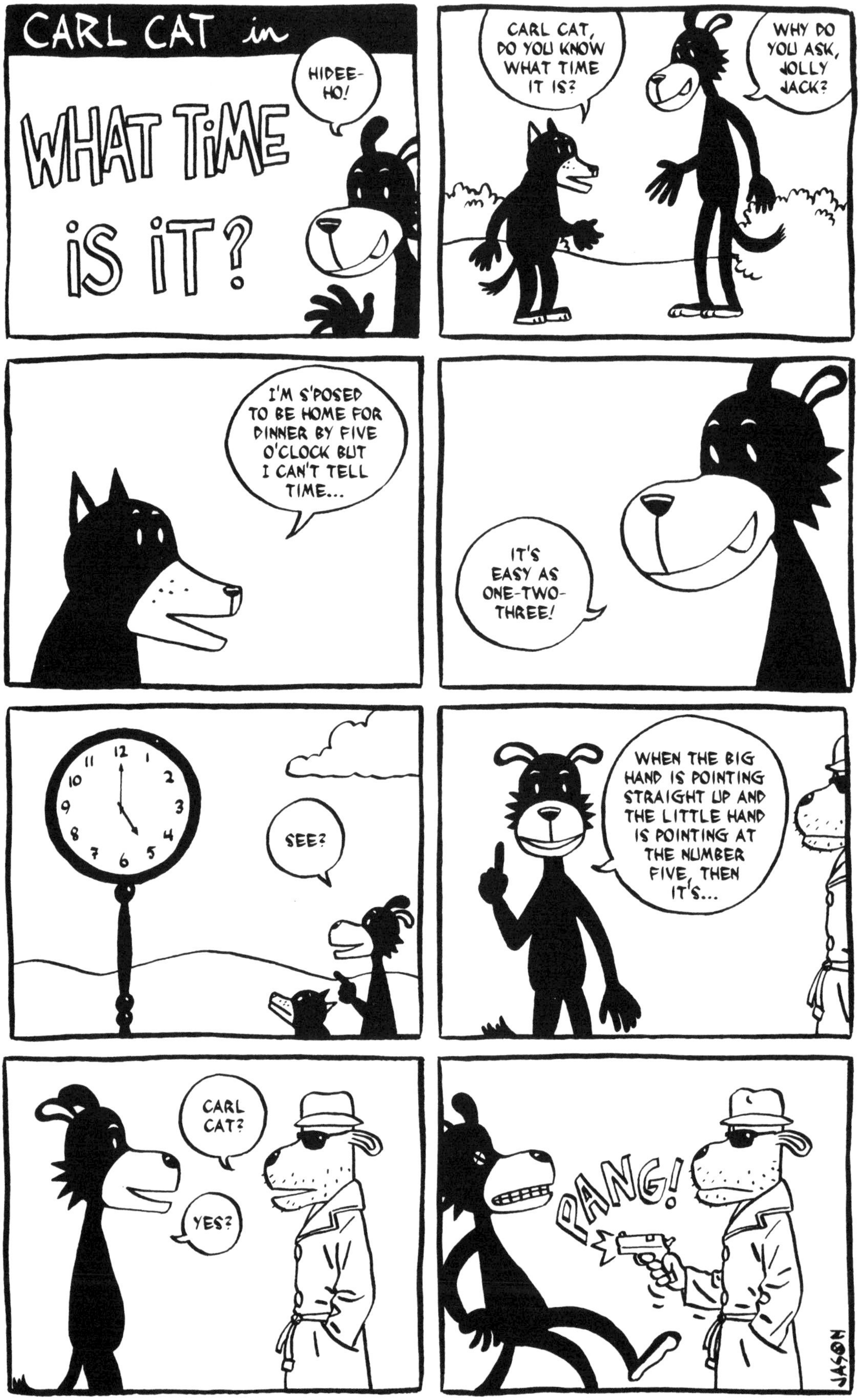
CARL CAT in
WHAT TIME IS IT?
HIDEE-HO!
CARL CAT, DO YOU KNOW WHAT TIME IT IS?
WHY DO YOU ASK, JOLLY JACK?
I'M S'POSED TO BE HOME FOR DINNER BY FIVE O'CLOCK BUT I CAN'T TELL TIME...
IT'S EASY AS ONE-TWO-THREE!
SEE?
WHEN THE BIG HAND IS POINTING STRAIGHT UP AND THE LITTLE HAND IS POINTING AT THE NUMBER FIVE, THEN IT'S...
CARL CAT?
YES?
PANG!
JASON

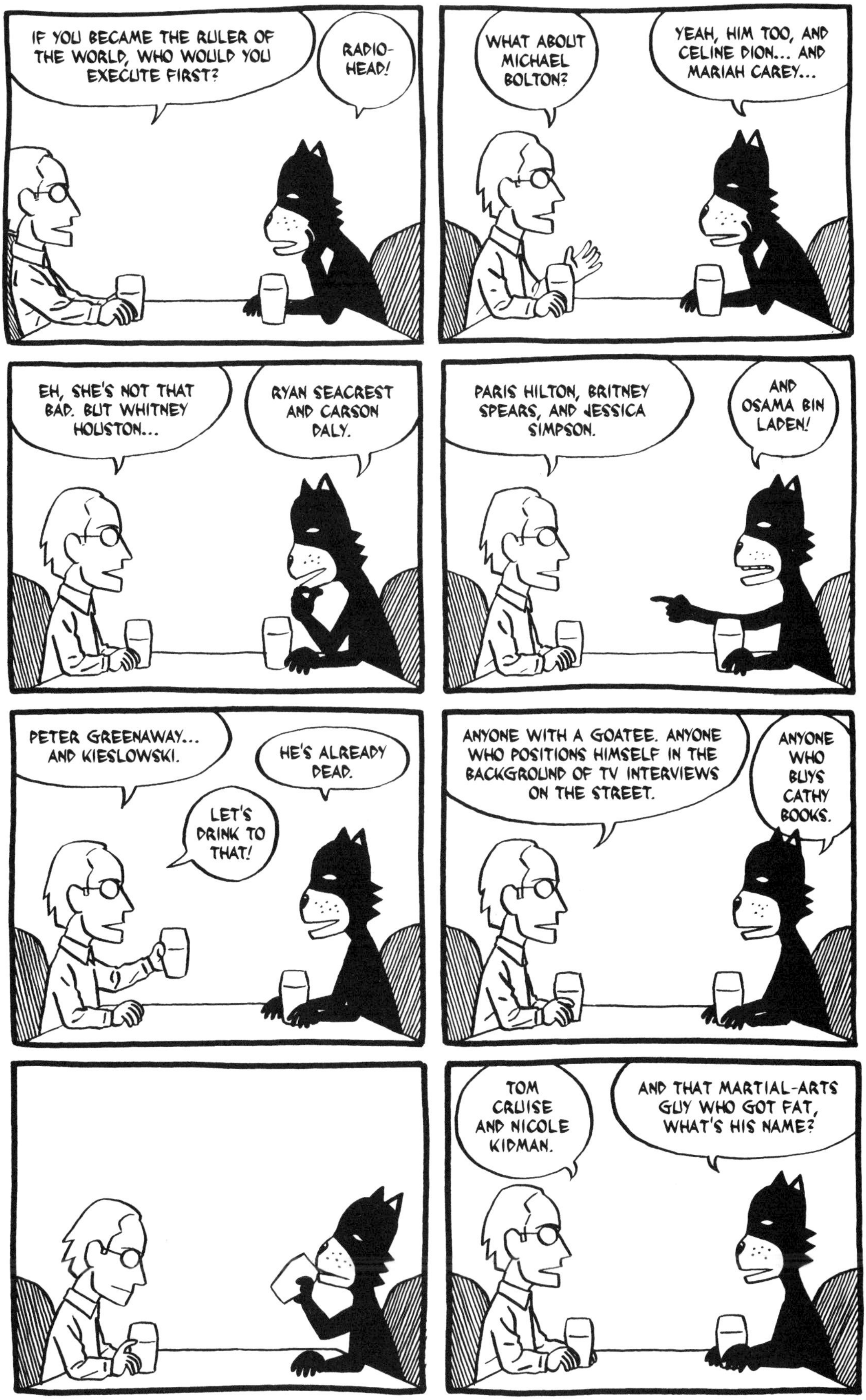
IF YOU BECAME THE RULER OF THE WORLD, WHO WOULD YOU EXECUTE FIRST?
RADIO-HEAD!
WHAT ABOUT MICHAEL BOLTON?
YEAH, HIM TOO, AND CELINE DION... AND MARIAH CAREY...
EH, SHE'S NOT THAT BAD. BUT WHITNEY HOUSTON...
RYAN SEACREST AND CARSON DALY.
PARIS HILTON, BRITNEY SPEARS, AND JESSICA SIMPSON.
AND OSAMA BIN LADEN!
PETER GREENAWAY... AND KIESLOWSKI.
HE'S ALREADY DEAD.
LET'S DRINK TO THAT!
ANYONE WITH A GOATEE. ANYONE WHO POSITIONS HIMSELF IN THE BACKGROUND OF TV INTERVIEWS ON THE STREET.
ANYONE WHO BUYS CATHY BOOKS.
TOM CRUISE AND NICOLE KIDMAN.
AND THAT MARTIAL-ARTS GUY WHO GOT FAT, WHAT'S HIS NAME?

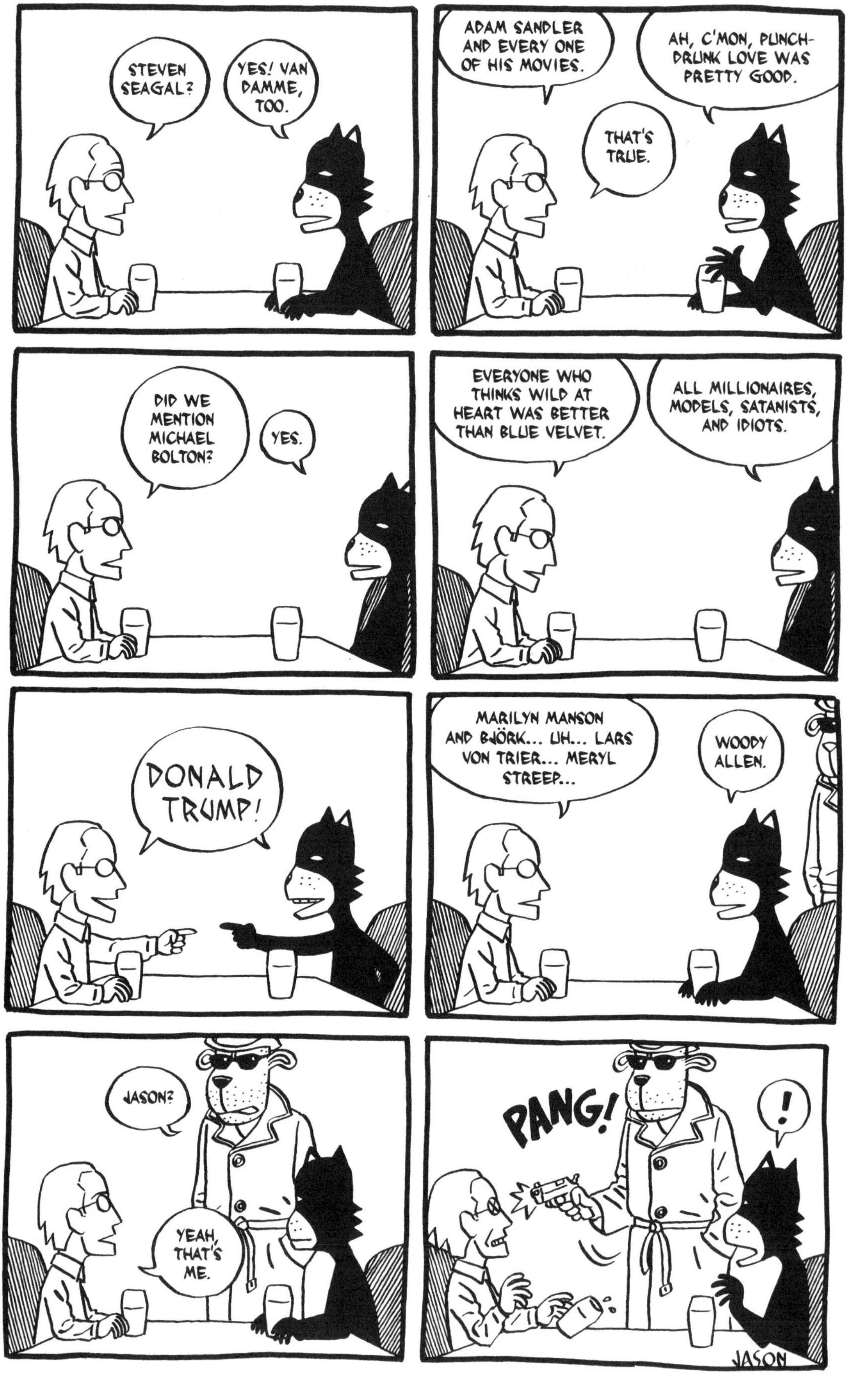
STEVEN SEAGAL?
YES! VAN DAMME, TOO.
ADAM SANDLER AND EVERY ONE OF HIS MOVIES.
AH, C'MON, PUNCH-DRUNK LOVE WAS PRETTY GOOD.
THAT'S TRUE.
DID WE MENTION MICHAEL BOLTON?
YES.
EVERYONE WHO THINKS WILD AT HEART WAS BETTER THAN BLUE VELVET.
ALL MILLIONAIRES, MODELS, SATANISTS, AND IDIOTS.
DONALD TRUMP!
MARILYN MANSON AND BJÖRK... UH... LARS VON TRIER... MERYL STREEP...
WOODY ALLEN.
JASON?
YEAH, THAT'S ME.
PANG!
!
JASON

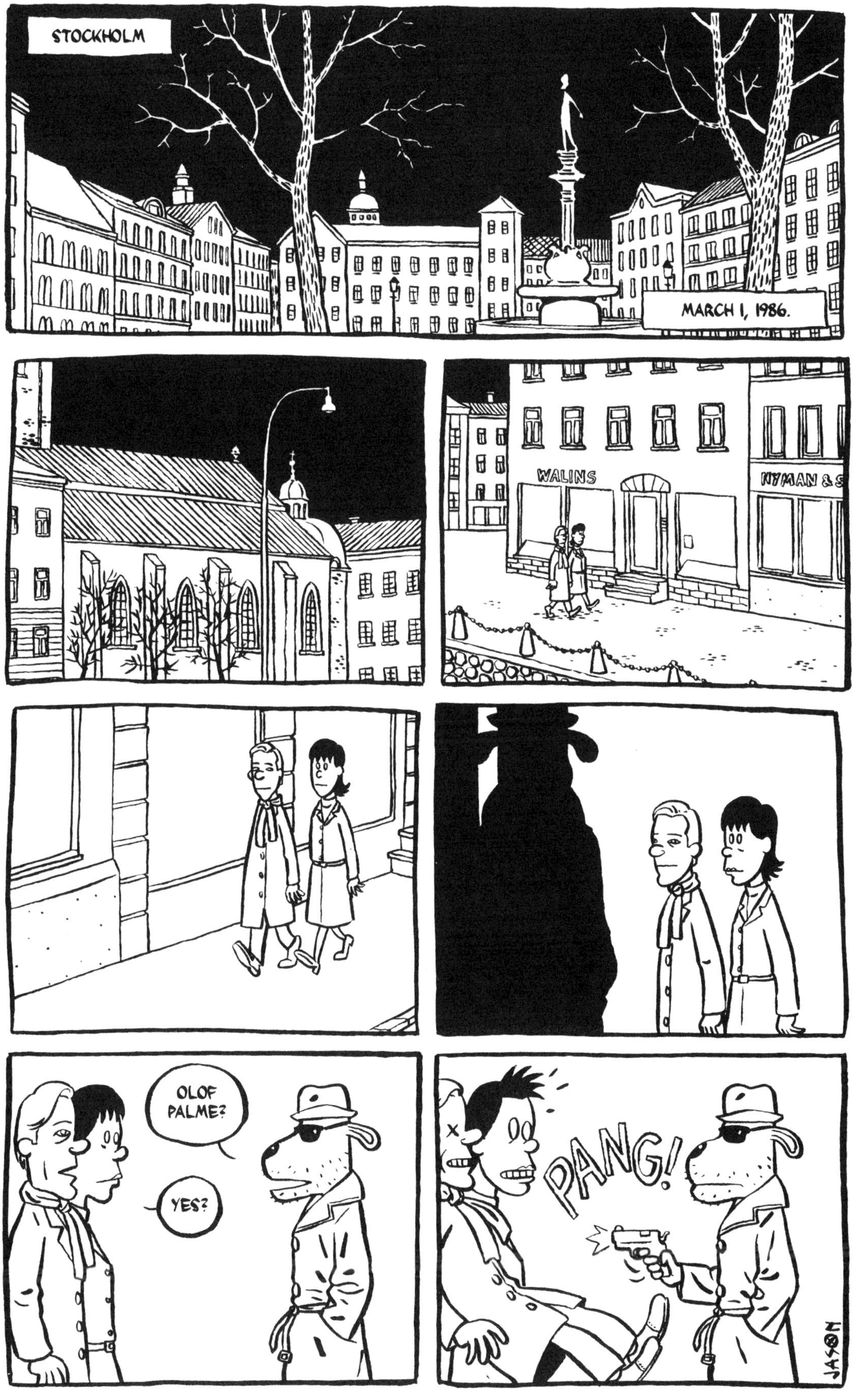
STOCKHOLM
MARCH 1, 1986.
WALINS
NYMAN & S
OLOF PALME?
YES?
PANG!
JASON

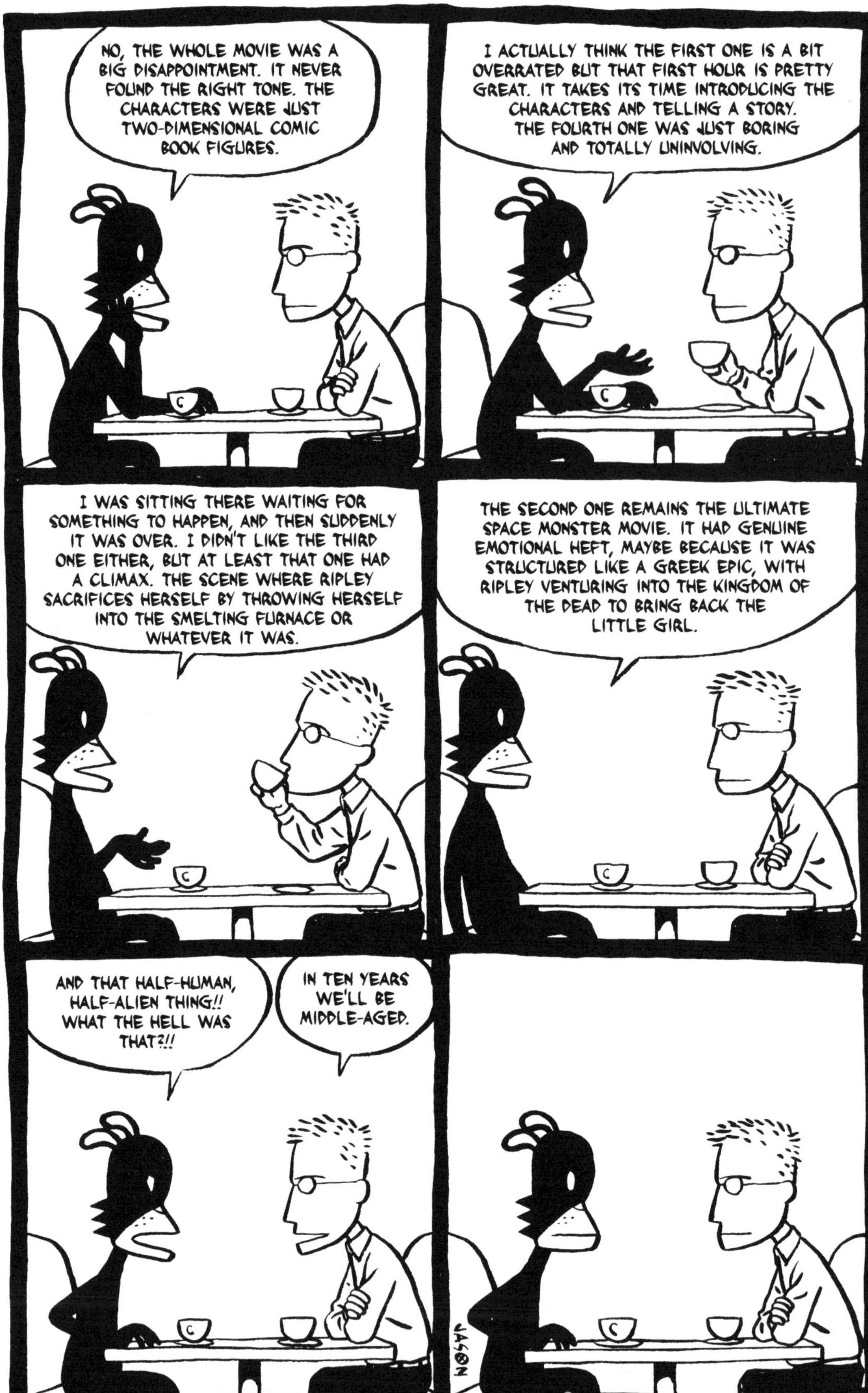
NO, THE WHOLE MOVIE WAS A BIG DISAPPOINTMENT. IT NEVER FOUND THE RIGHT TONE. THE CHARACTERS WERE JUST TWO-DIMENSIONAL COMIC BOOK FIGURES.
I ACTUALLY THINK THE FIRST ONE IS A BIT OVERRATED BUT THAT FIRST HOUR IS PRETTY GREAT. IT TAKES ITS TIME INTRODUCING THE CHARACTERS AND TELLING A STORY. THE FOURTH ONE WAS JUST BORING AND TOTALLY UNINVOLVING.
I WAS SITTING THERE WAITING FOR SOMETHING TO HAPPEN, AND THEN SUDDENLY IT WAS OVER. I DIDN'T LIKE THE THIRD ONE EITHER, BUT AT LEAST THAT ONE HAD A CLIMAX. THE SCENE WHERE RIPLEY SACRIFICES HERSELF BY THROWING HERSELF INTO THE SMELTING FURNACE OR WHATEVER IT WAS.
THE SECOND ONE REMAINS THE ULTIMATE SPACE MONSTER MOVIE. IT HAD GENUINE EMOTIONAL HEFT, MAYBE BECAUSE IT WAS STRUCTURED LIKE A GREEK EPIC, WITH RIPLEY VENTURING INTO THE KINGDOM OF THE DEAD TO BRING BACK THE LITTLE GIRL.
AND THAT HALF-HUMAN, HALF-ALIEN THING!! WHAT THE HELL WAS THAT?!!
IN TEN YEARS WE'LL BE MIDDLE-AGED.
JASON

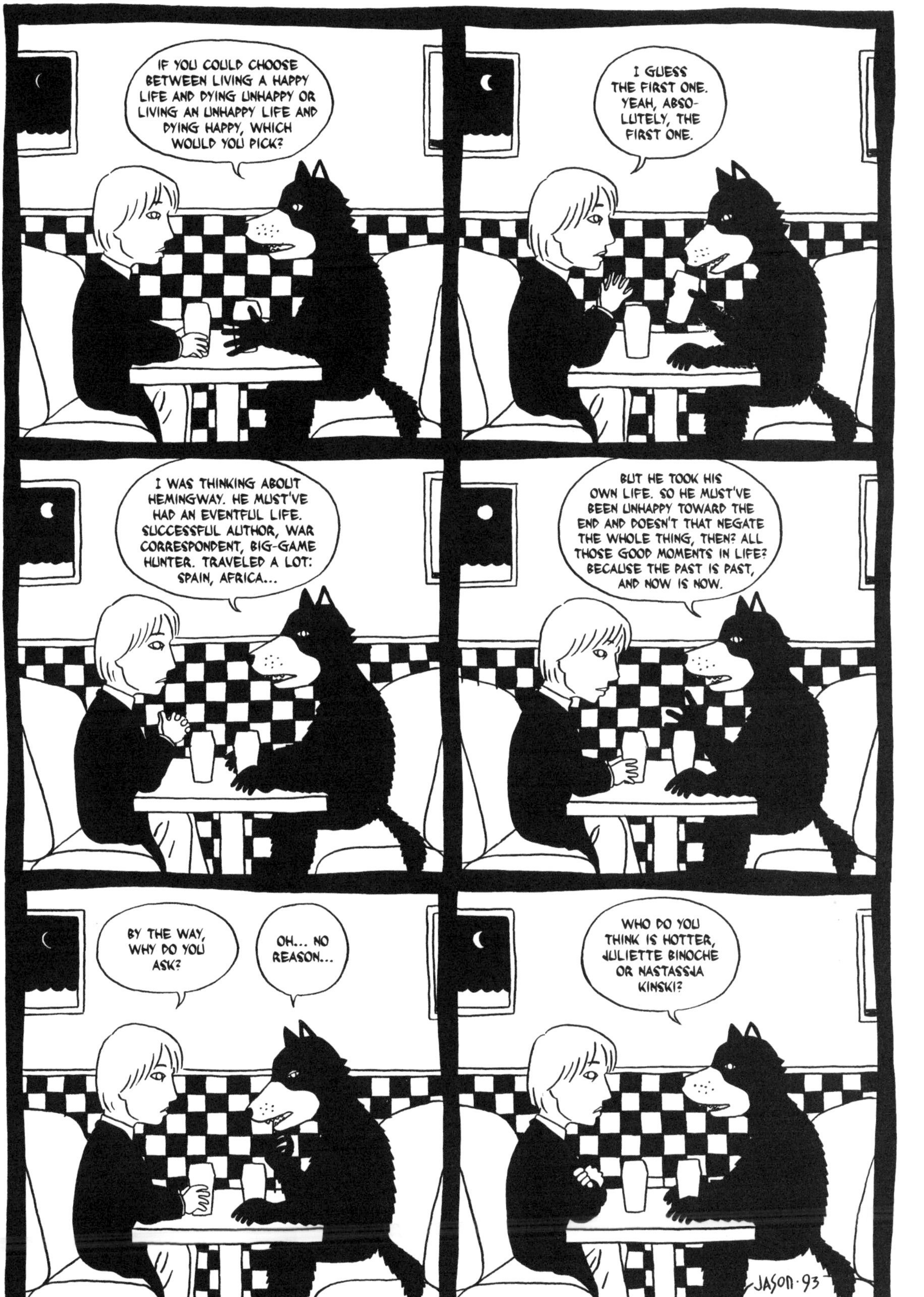
IF YOU COULD CHOOSE BETWEEN LIVING A HAPPY LIFE AND DYING UNHAPPY OR LIVING AN UNHAPPY LIFE AND DYING HAPPY, WHICH WOULD YOU PICK?
I GUESS THE FIRST ONE. YEAH, ABSO-LUTELY, THE FIRST ONE.
I WAS THINKING ABOUT HEMINGWAY. HE MUST'VE HAD AN EVENTFUL LIFE. SUCCESSFUL AUTHOR, WAR CORRESPONDENT, BIG-GAME HUNTER. TRAVELED A LOT: SPAIN, AFRICA...
BUT HE TOOK HIS OWN LIFE. SO HE MUST'VE BEEN UNHAPPY TOWARD THE END AND DOESN'T THAT NEGATE THE WHOLE THING, THEN? ALL THOSE GOOD MOMENTS IN LIFE? BECAUSE THE PAST IS PAST, AND NOW IS NOW.
BY THE WAY, WHY DO YOU ASK?
OH... NO REASON...
WHO DO YOU THINK IS HOTTER, JULIETTE BINOCHE OR NASTASSJA KINSKI?
JASON · 93

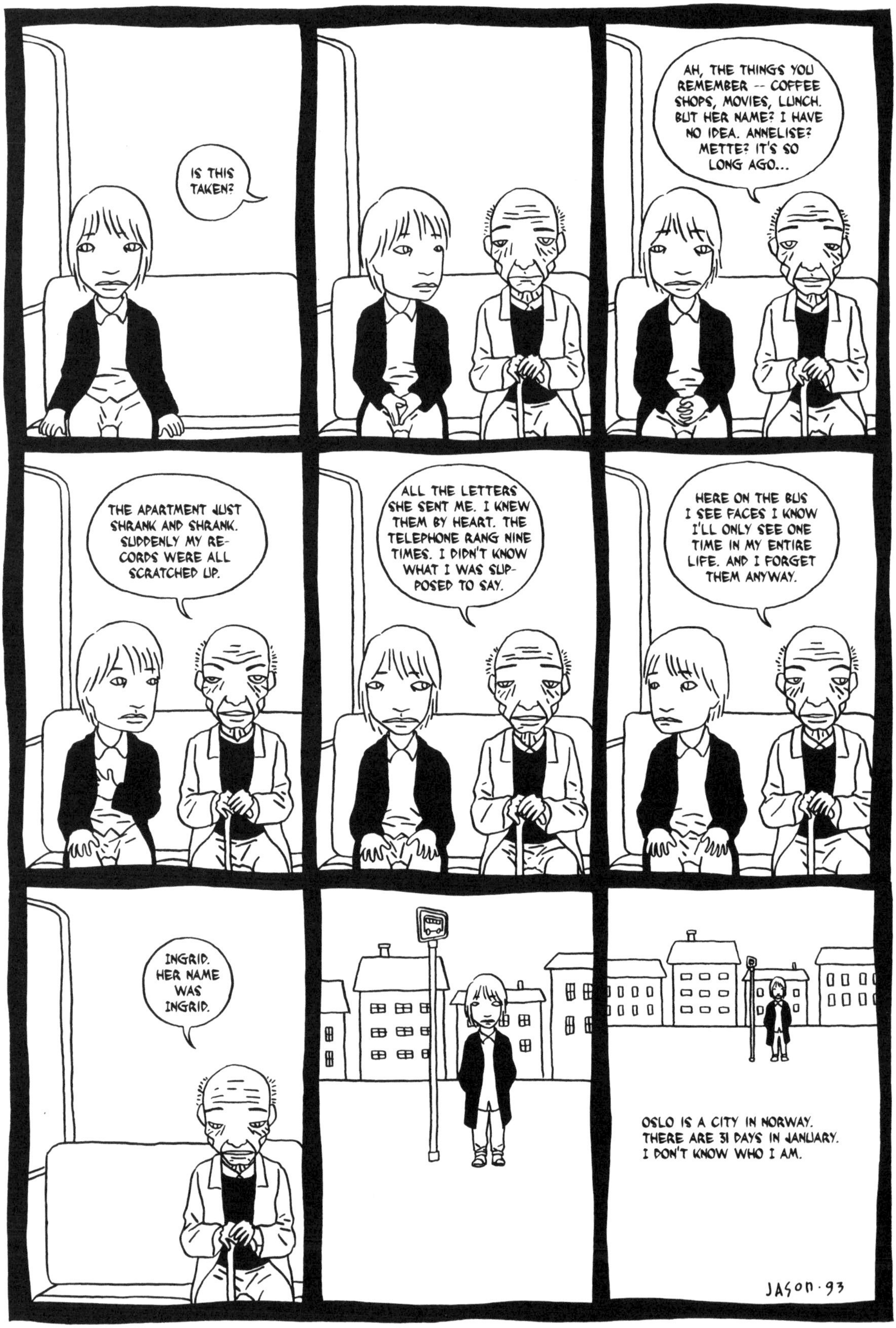
IS THIS TAKEN?
AH, THE THINGS YOU REMEMBER -- COFFEE SHOPS, MOVIES, LUNCH. BUT HER NAME? I HAVE NO IDEA. ANNELISE? METTE? IT'S SO LONG AGO...
THE APARTMENT JUST SHRANK AND SHRANK. SUDDENLY MY RE-CORDS WERE ALL SCRATCHED UP.
ALL THE LETTERS SHE SENT ME. I KNEW THEM BY HEART. THE TELEPHONE RANG NINE TIMES. I DIDN'T KNOW WHAT I WAS SUP-POSED TO SAY.
HERE ON THE BUS I SEE FACES I KNOW I'LL ONLY SEE ONE TIME IN MY ENTIRE LIFE. AND I FORGET THEM ANYWAY.
INGRID. HER NAME WAS INGRID.
OSLO IS A CITY IN NORWAY. THERE ARE 31 DAYS IN JANUARY. I DON'T KNOW WHO I AM.
JASON · 93

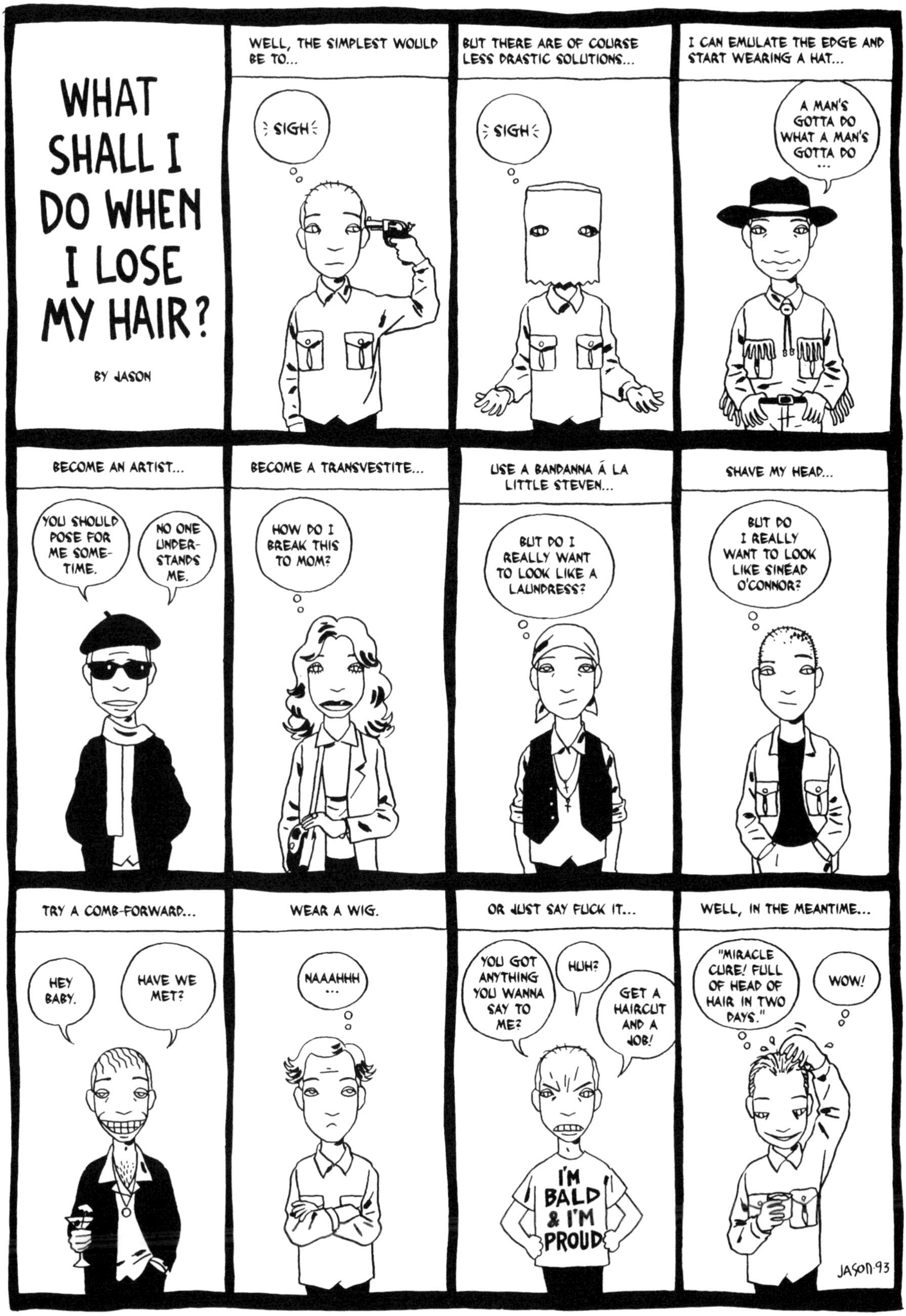
WHAT SHALL I DO WHEN I LOSE MY HAIR?
BY JASON
WELL, THE SIMPLEST WOULD BE TO...
SIGH
BUT THERE ARE OF COURSE LESS DRASTIC SOLUTIONS...
SIGH
I CAN EMULATE THE EDGE AND START WEARING A HAT...
A MAN'S GOTTA DO WHAT A MAN'S GOTTA DO ...
BECOME AN ARTIST...
YOU SHOULD POSE FOR ME SOME-TIME.
NO ONE UNDER-STANDS ME.
BECOME A TRANSVESTITE...
HOW DO I BREAK THIS TO MOM?
USE A BANDANNA Á LA LITTLE STEVEN...
BUT DO I REALLY WANT TO LOOK LIKE A LAUNDRESS?
SHAVE MY HEAD...
BUT DO I REALLY WANT TO LOOK LIKE SINEAD O'CONNOR?
TRY A COMB-FORWARD...
HEY BABY.
HAVE WE MET?
WEAR A WIG.
NAAAHHH ...
OR JUST SAY FUCK IT...
YOU GOT ANYTHING YOU WANNA SAY TO ME?
HUH?
GET A HAIRCUT AND A JOB!
I'M BALD & I'M PROUD
WELL, IN THE MEANTIME...
"MIRACLE CURE! FULL OF HEAD OF HAIR IN TWO DAYS."
WOW!
JASON·93

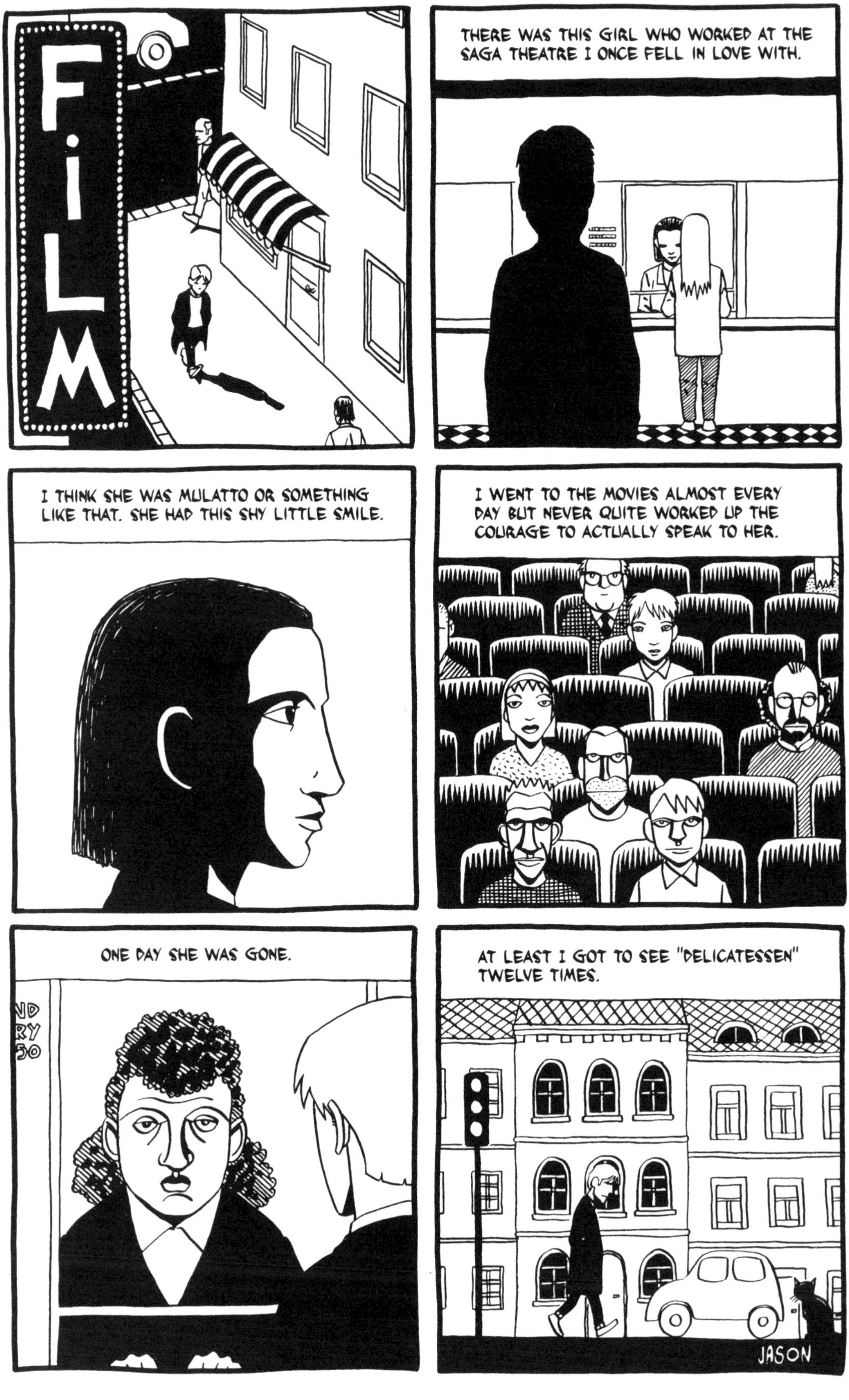
FILM
THERE WAS THIS GIRL WHO WORKED AT THE SAGA THEATRE I ONCE FELL IN LOVE WITH.
I THINK SHE WAS MULATTO OR SOMETHING LIKE THAT. SHE HAD THIS SHY LITTLE SMILE.
I WENT TO THE MOVIES ALMOST EVERY DAY BUT NEVER QUITE WORKED UP THE COURAGE TO ACTUALLY SPEAK TO HER.
ONE DAY SHE WAS GONE.
AT LEAST I GOT TO SEE "DELICATESSEN" TWELVE TIMES.
JASON

I'D MOVED TO OSLO TO GO TO SCHOOL.

NIGHT

MY LANDLORD WAS AN ALCOHOLIC. HE HAD A GIRLFRIEND HE OFTEN GOT INTO FIGHTS WITH. ONE NIGHT WAS PARTICULARLY BAD.

THEY ARGUED AND FOUGHT FOR A WHILE. THEN IT WOULD QUIET DOWN FOR MAYBE 20 MINUTES AND THEY'D START UP AGAIN.

THIS CYCLE REPEATED SEVERAL TIMES, BUT THEN SUDDENLY...

HEY, FELLA! AIN'T I RIGHT? TELL HER WHAT A FUCKING BITCH SHE IS!

GET OUT! I'M TRYING TO GET SOME SLEEP HERE!

UH... OKAY...

FINALLY THEY SETTLED DOWN AND THINGS GOT QUIET.

ANYWAY, YEARS LATER, ALL I FEEL IS A MILD ANNOYANCE THAT I DIDN'T THINK TO WRITE DOWN SOME OF THE STUFF THEY SCREAMED AT EACH OTHER.

I COULD HAVE USED IT IN A COMIC.

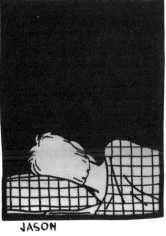

JASON

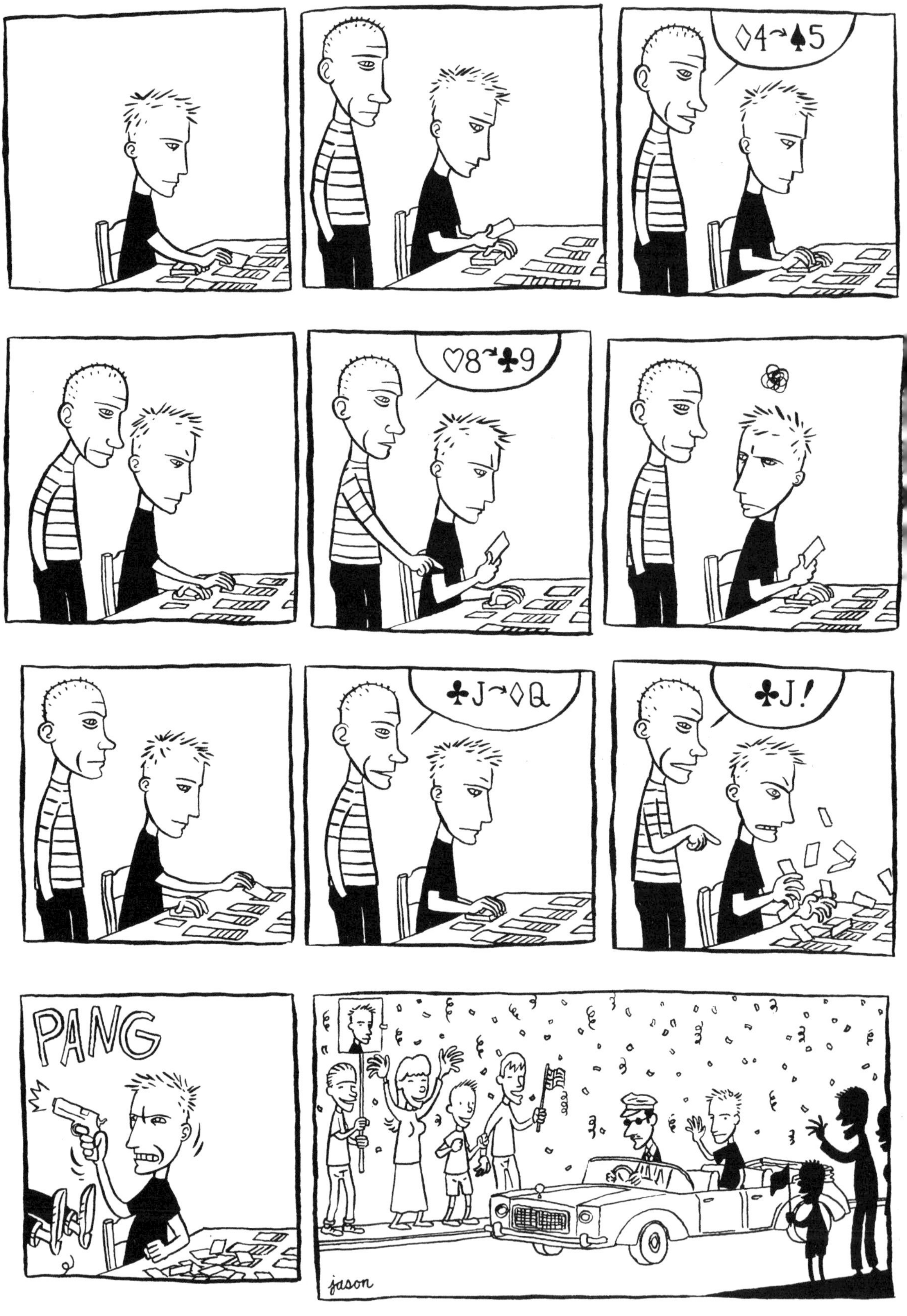

♢4 → ♠5
♡8 → ♣9
♣J → ♢Q
♣J!
PANG
jason

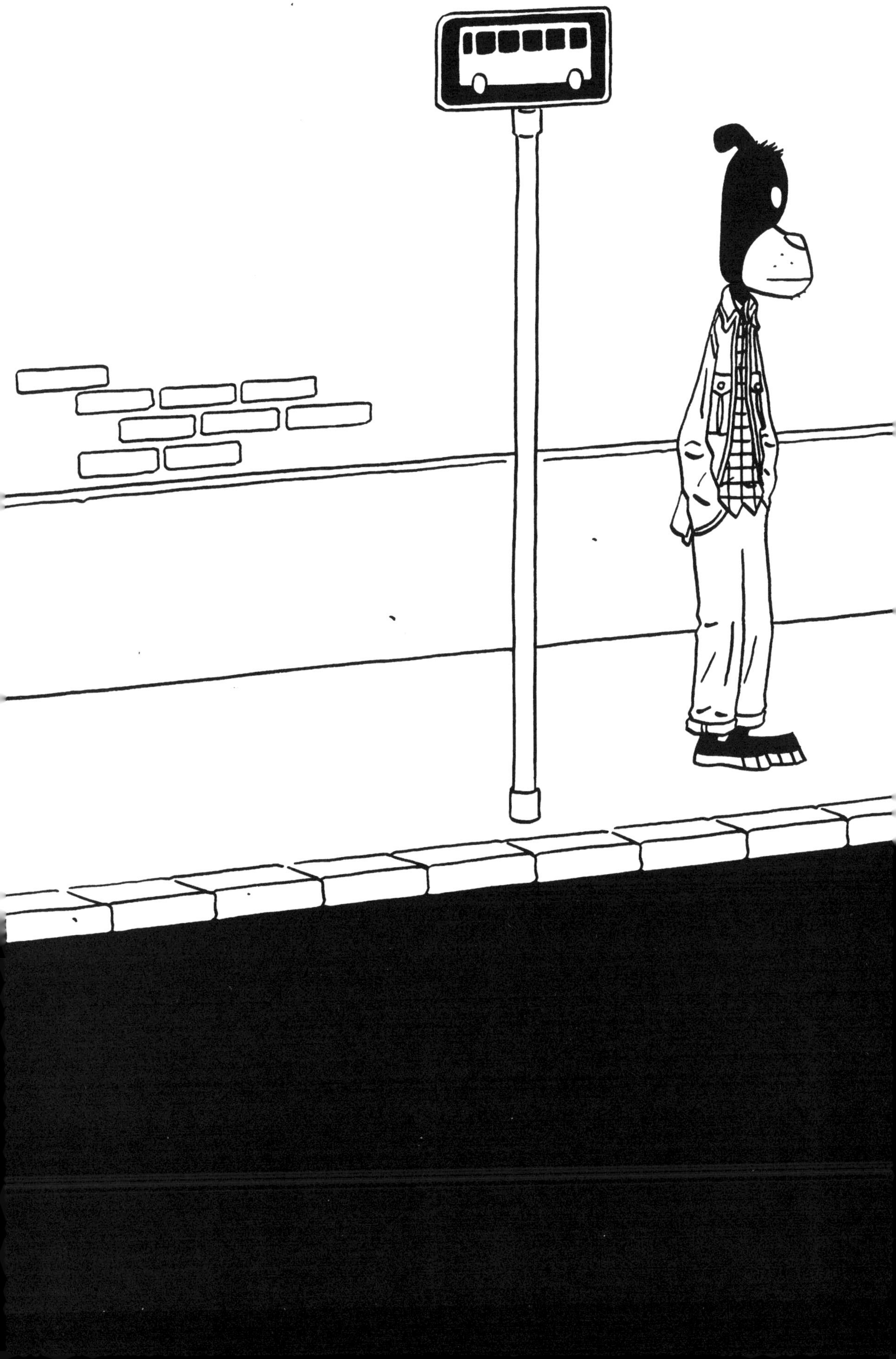

BUS

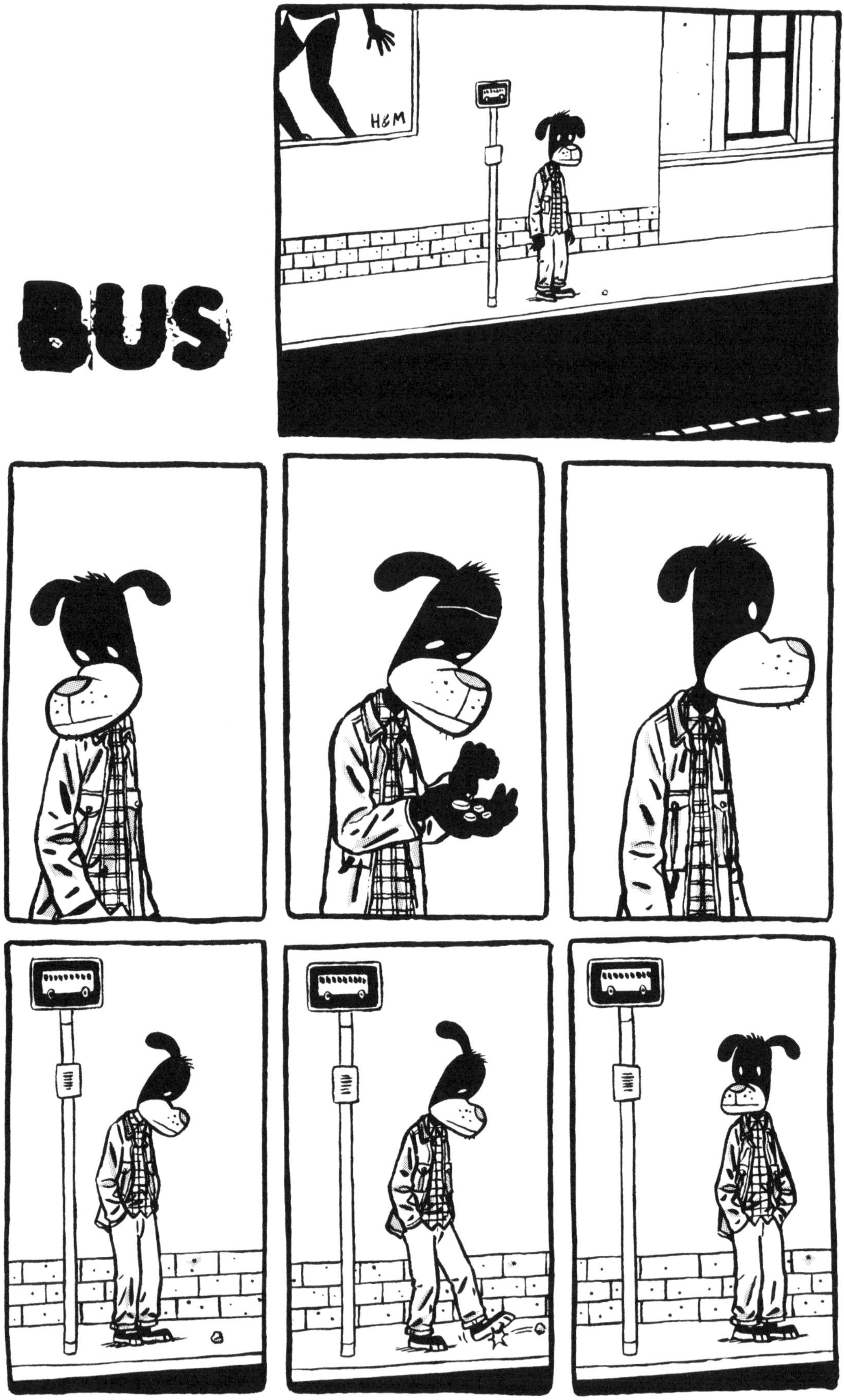
H&M

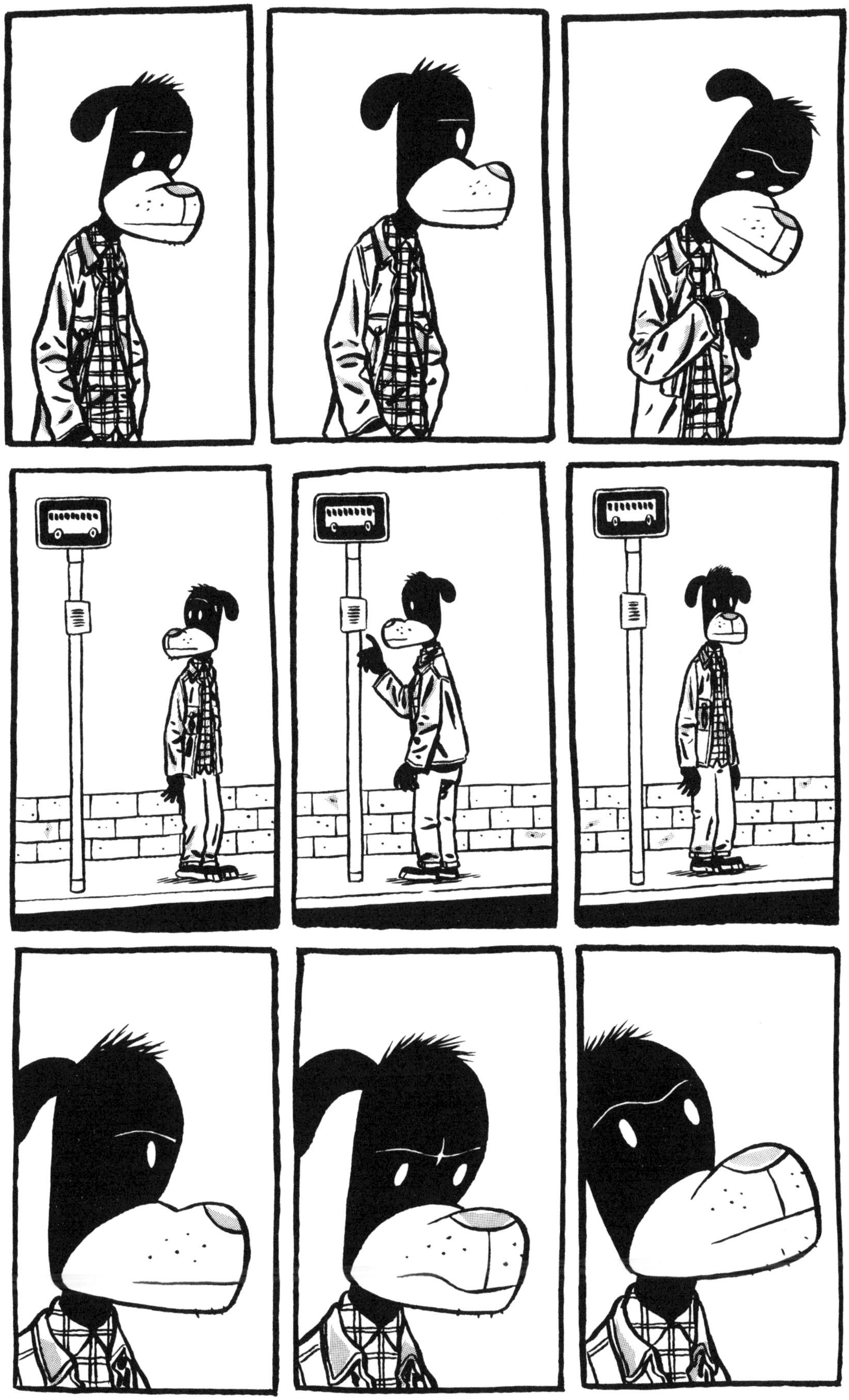

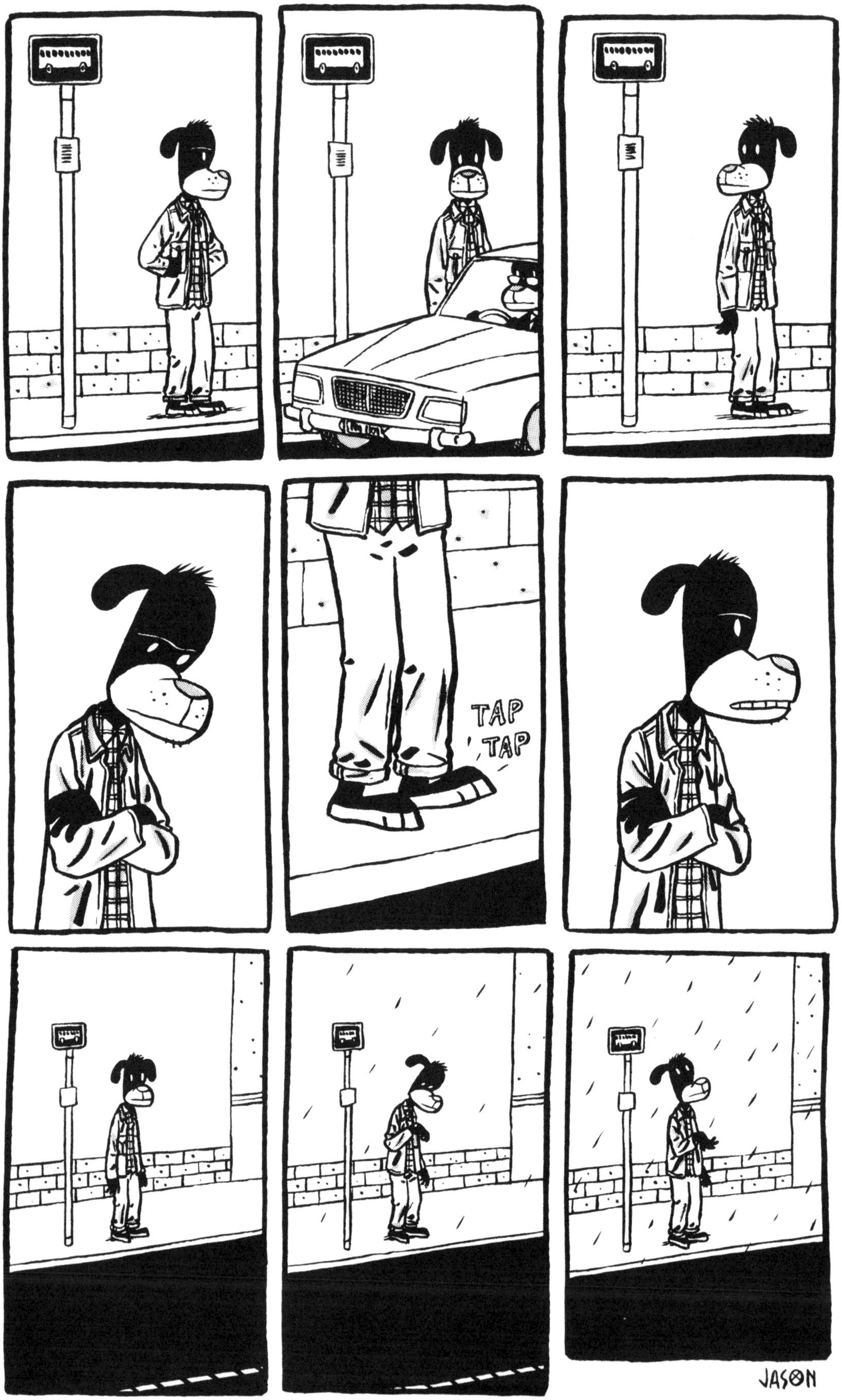
TAP
TAP
JASON

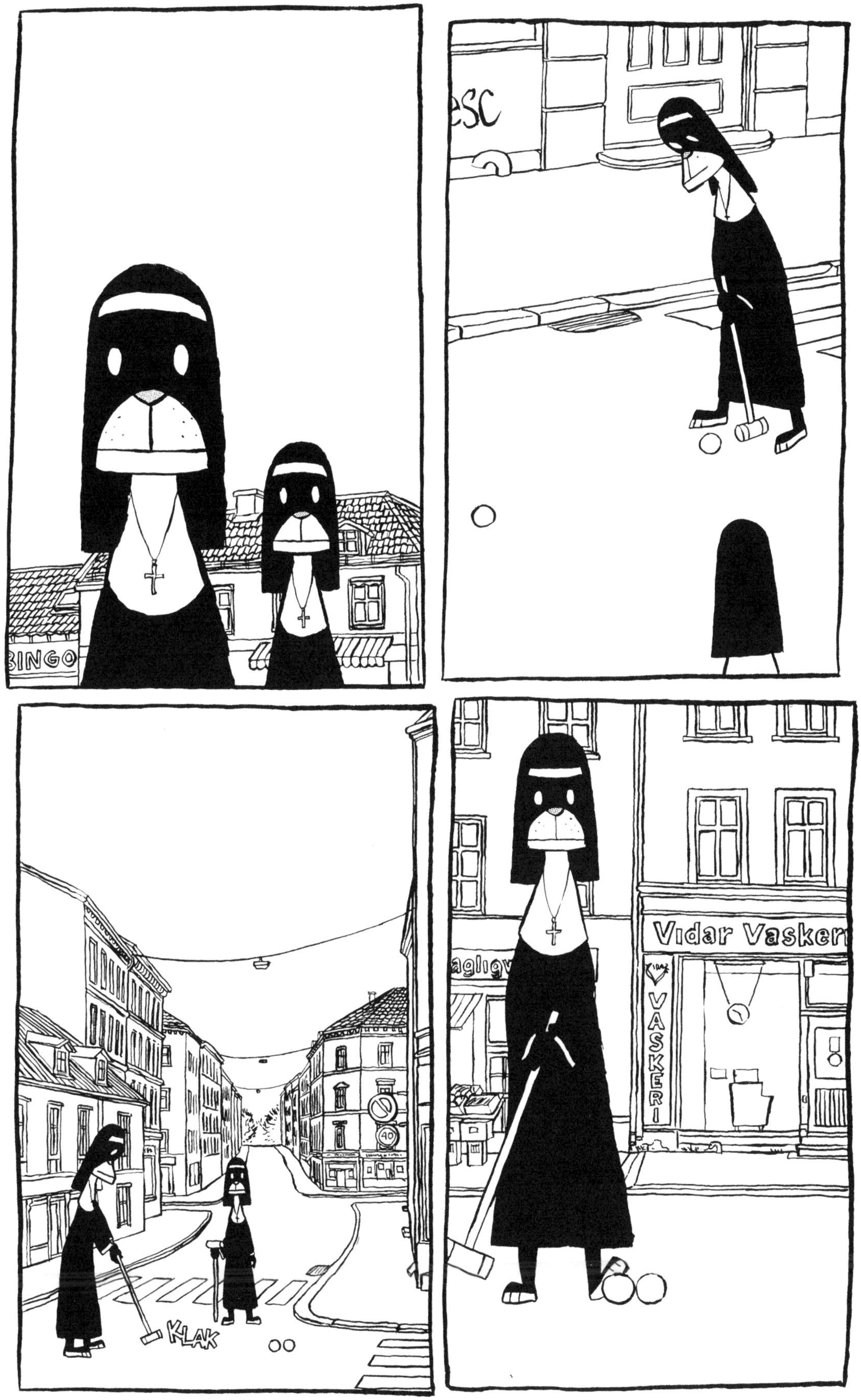
BINGO
esc
KLAK
40
Vidar Vasker
VASKERI

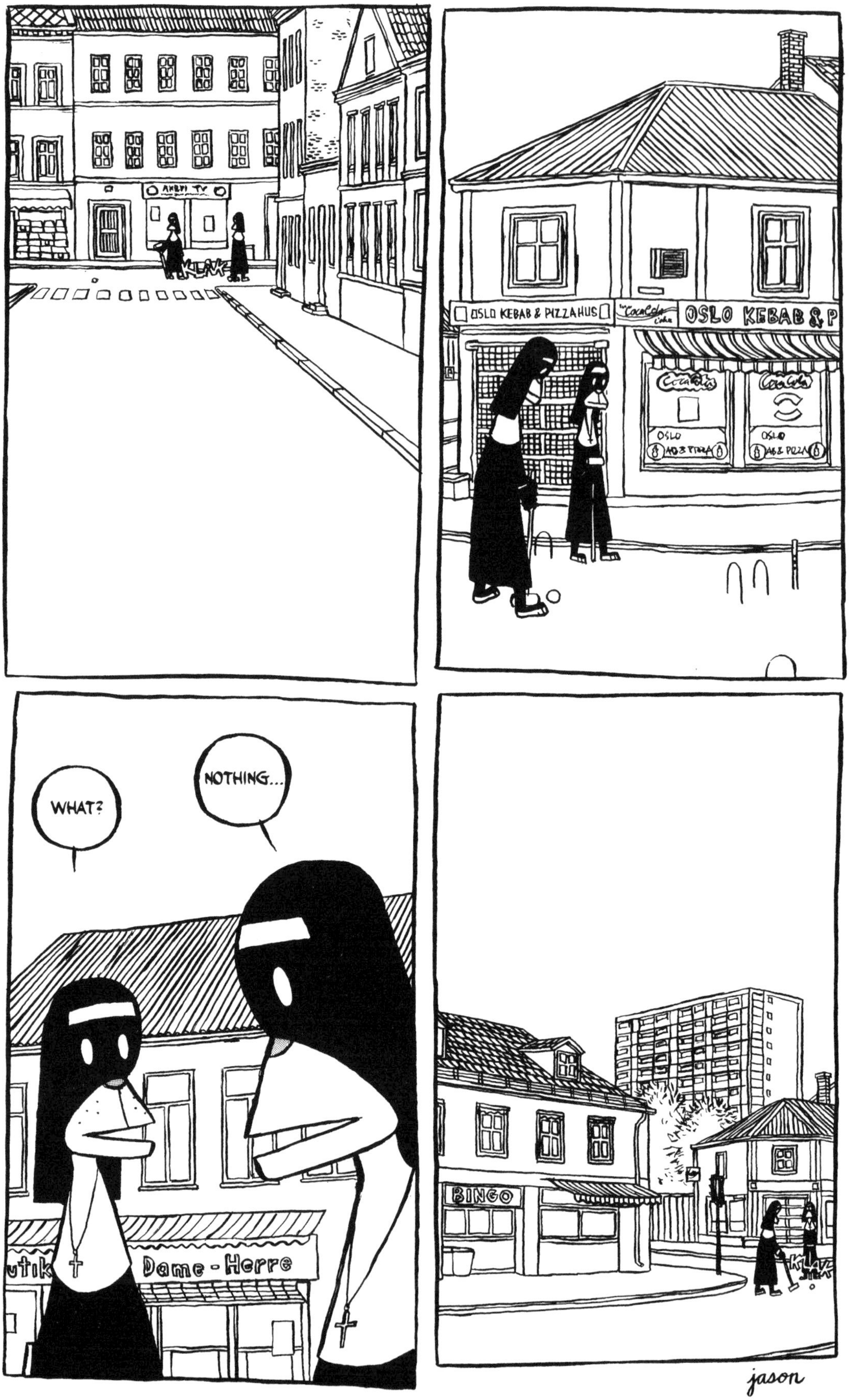
KLAK
OSLO KEBAB & PIZZAHUS
OSLO KEBAB & P
WHAT?
NOTHING...
Dame-Herre
BINGO
KLAK

jason

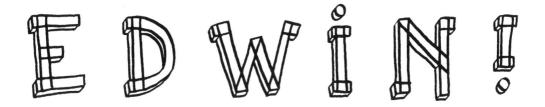

EDWIN!

THE HOUR WAS GETTING LATE. BOTH OF US WERE PRETTY SMASHED AT THIS POINT. (NOT THAT IT'S ANY KIND OF AN EXCUSE.)

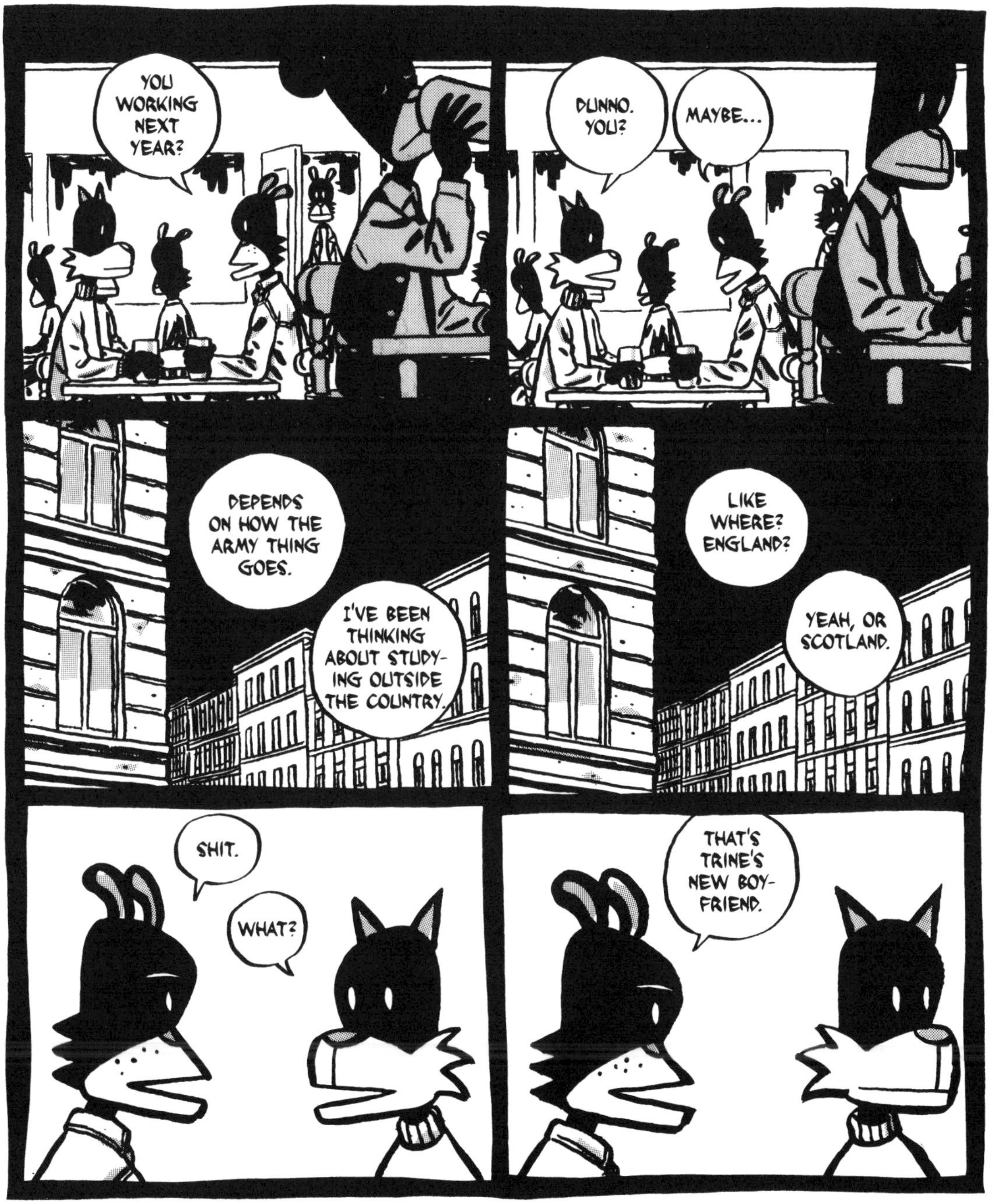
YOU WORKING NEXT YEAR?
DUNNO. YOU?
MAYBE...
DEPENDS ON HOW THE ARMY THING GOES.
I'VE BEEN THINKING ABOUT STUDYING OUTSIDE THE COUNTRY.
LIKE WHERE? ENGLAND?
YEAH, OR SCOTLAND.
SHIT.
WHAT?
THAT'S TRINE'S NEW BOYFRIEND.

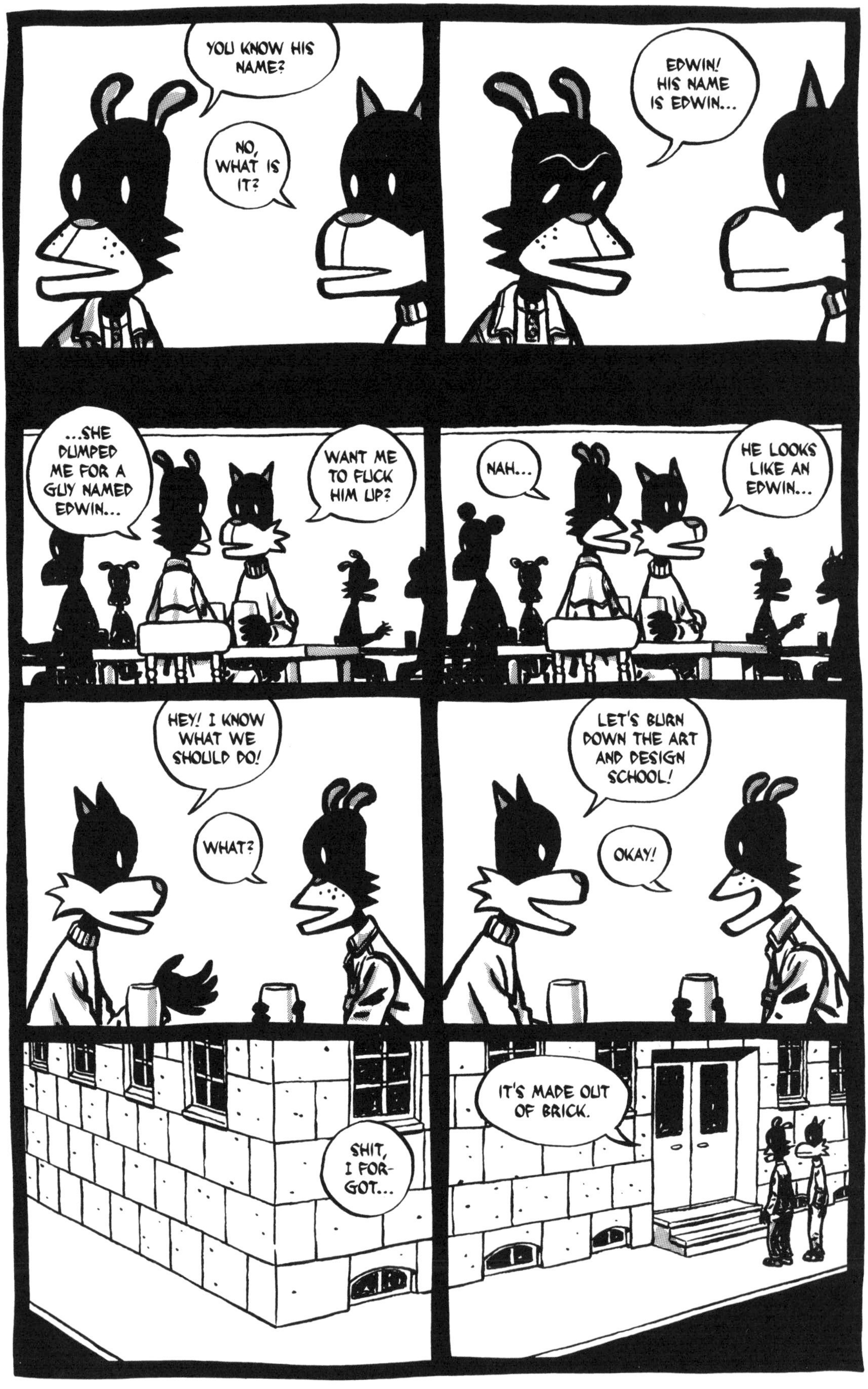
YOU KNOW HIS NAME?
NO, WHAT IS IT?
EDWIN! HIS NAME IS EDWIN...
...SHE DUMPED ME FOR A GUY NAMED EDWIN...
WANT ME TO FUCK HIM UP?
NAH...
HE LOOKS LIKE AN EDWIN...
HEY! I KNOW WHAT WE SHOULD DO!
WHAT?
LET'S BURN DOWN THE ART AND DESIGN SCHOOL!
OKAY!
SHIT, I FOR-GOT...
IT'S MADE OUT OF BRICK.

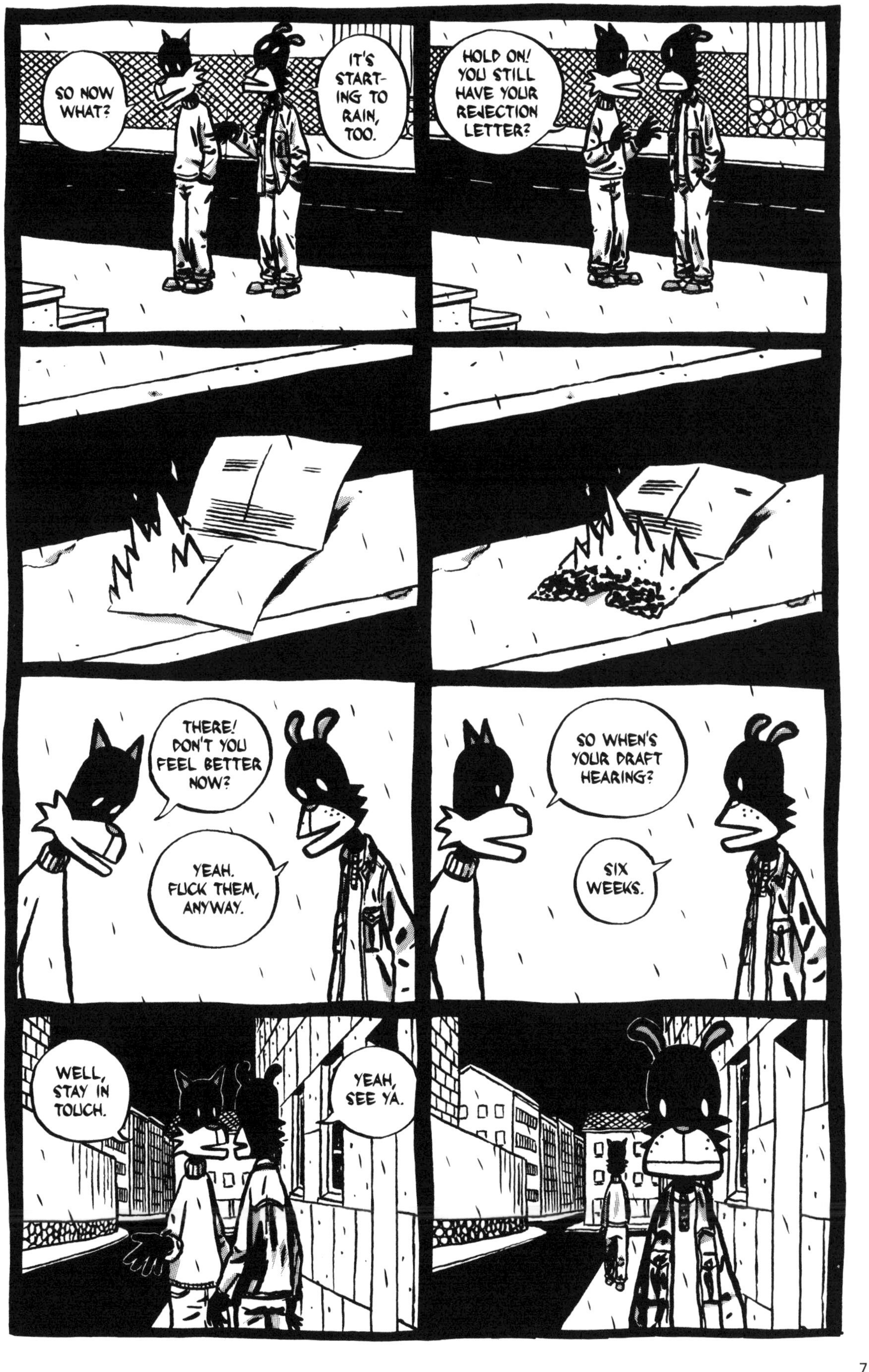
SO NOW WHAT?
IT'S START-ING TO RAIN, TOO.
HOLD ON! YOU STILL HAVE YOUR REJECTION LETTER?
THERE! DON'T YOU FEEL BETTER NOW?
YEAH. FUCK THEM, ANYWAY.
SO WHEN'S YOUR DRAFT HEARING?
SIX WEEKS.
WELL, STAY IN TOUCH.
YEAH, SEE YA.

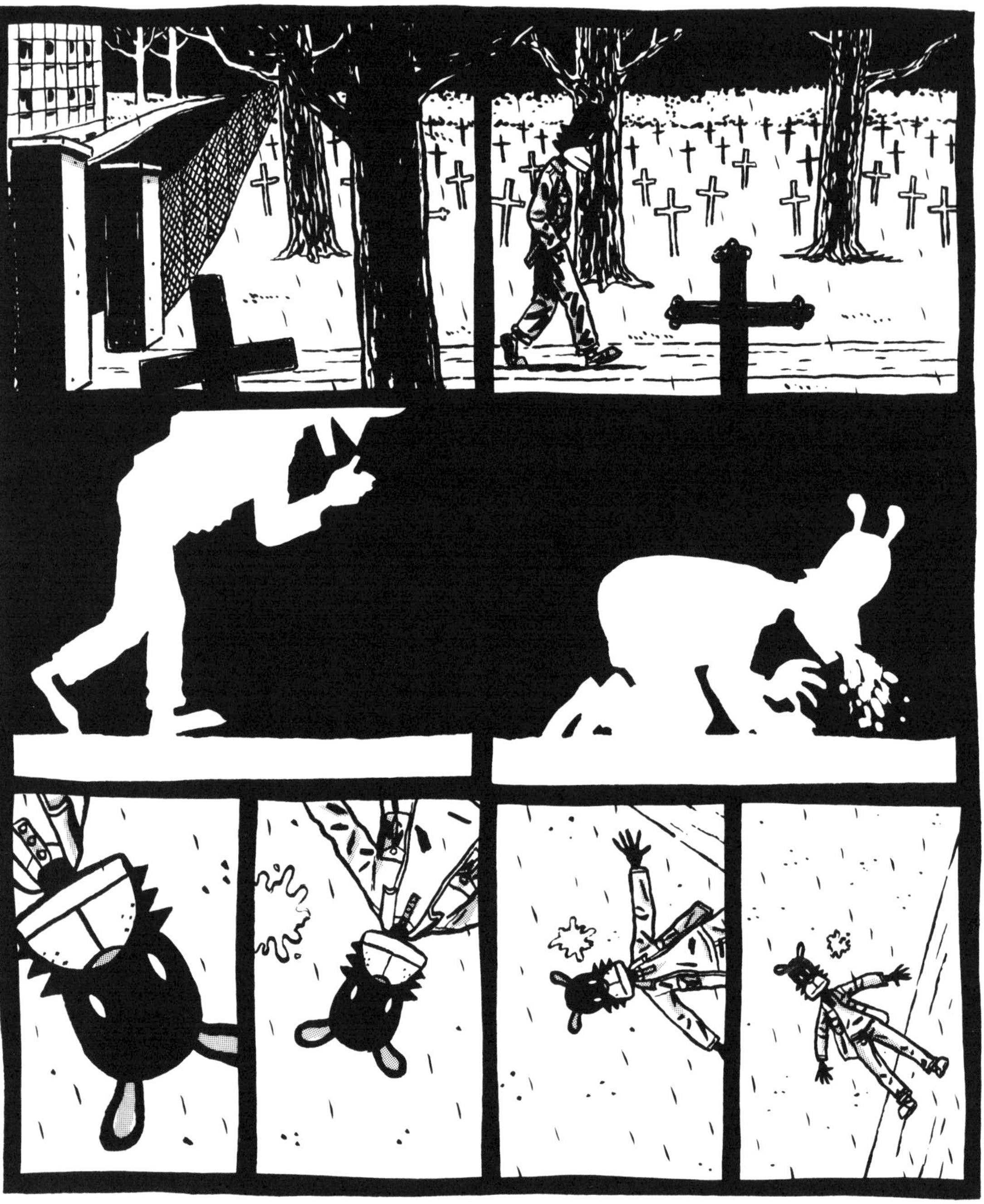

I REMAIN LYING IN THE WET GRASS AND LOOK UP INTO THE SKY. MY HEAD IS COMPLETELY CLEAR. FOR SOME REASON I'M CONVINCED THAT FROM THIS DAY ON EVERYTHING WILL BE FINE.

JASON

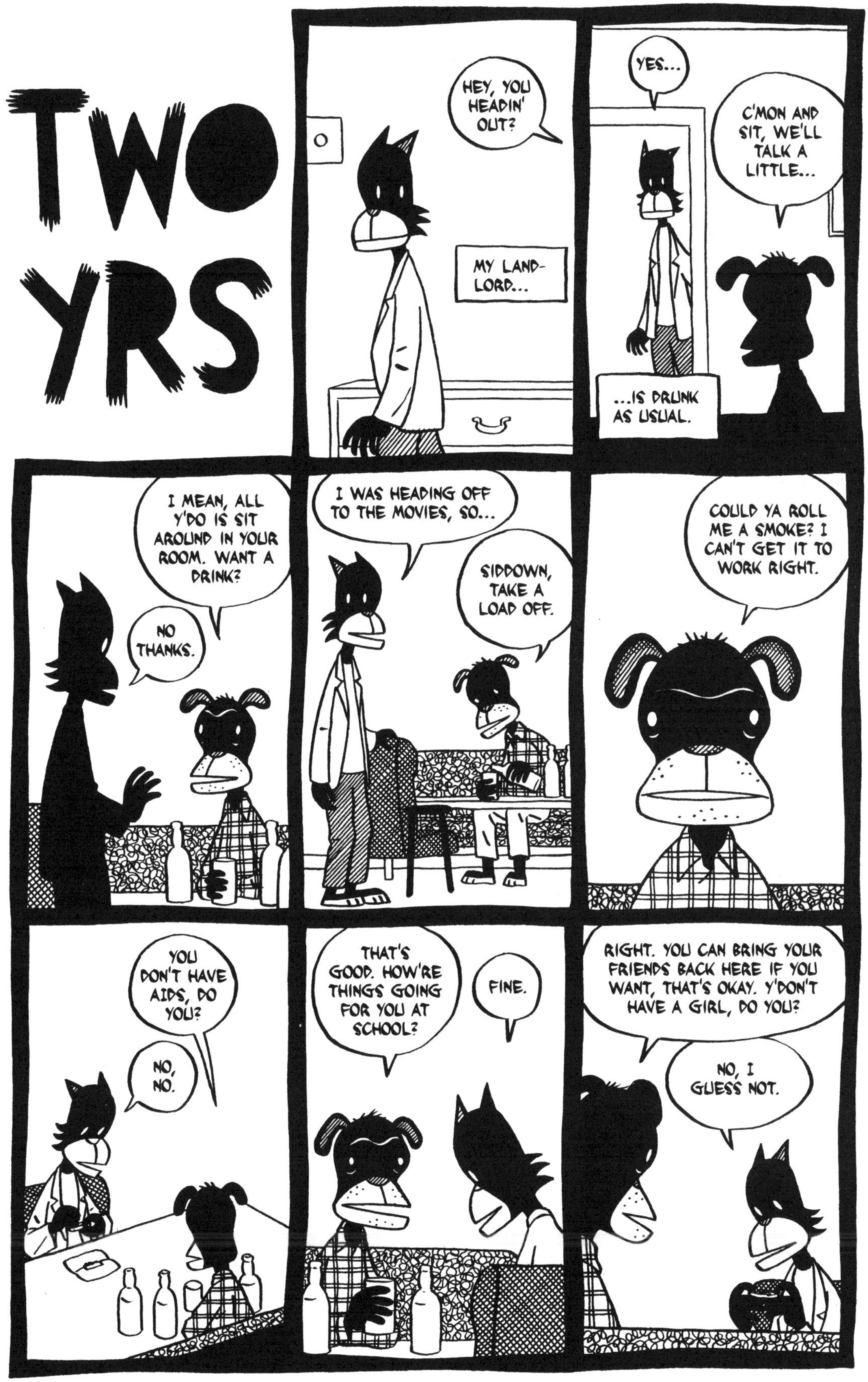
TWO YRS
HEY, YOU HEADIN' OUT?
MY LAND-LORD...
YES...
...IS DRUNK AS USUAL.
C'MON AND SIT, WE'LL TALK A LITTLE...
I MEAN, ALL Y'DO IS SIT AROUND IN YOUR ROOM. WANT A DRINK?
NO THANKS.
I WAS HEADING OFF TO THE MOVIES, SO...
SIDDOWN, TAKE A LOAD OFF.
COULD YA ROLL ME A SMOKE? I CAN'T GET IT TO WORK RIGHT.
YOU DON'T HAVE AIDS, DO YOU?
NO, NO.
THAT'S GOOD. HOW'RE THINGS GOING FOR YOU AT SCHOOL?
FINE.
RIGHT. YOU CAN BRING YOUR FRIENDS BACK HERE IF YOU WANT, THAT'S OKAY. Y'DON'T HAVE A GIRL, DO YOU?
NO, I GUESS NOT.

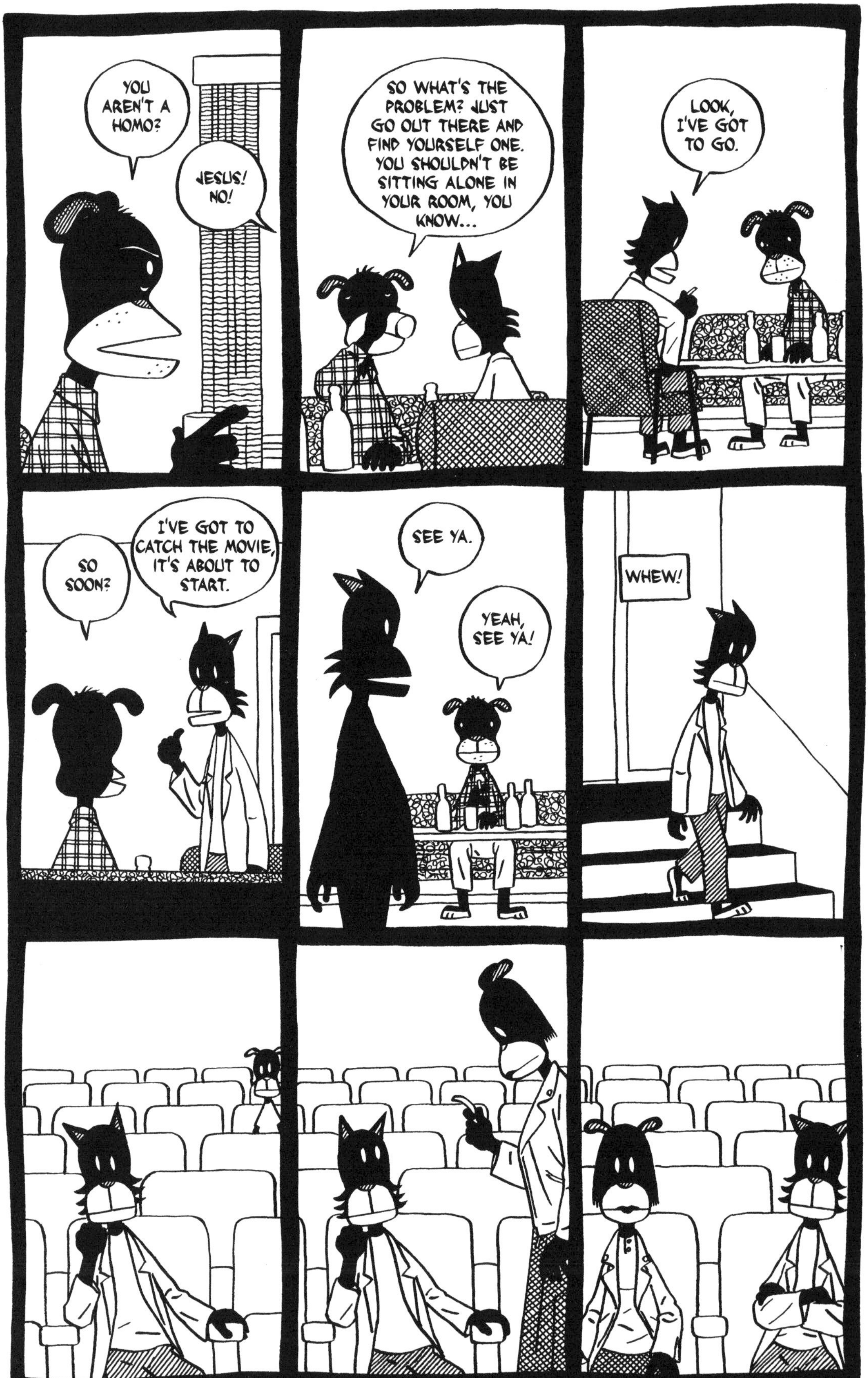
YOU AREN'T A HOMO?
JESUS! NO!
SO WHAT'S THE PROBLEM? JUST GO OUT THERE AND FIND YOURSELF ONE. YOU SHOULDN'T BE SITTING ALONE IN YOUR ROOM, YOU KNOW...
LOOK, I'VE GOT TO GO.
SO SOON?
I'VE GOT TO CATCH THE MOVIE, IT'S ABOUT TO START.
SEE YA.
YEAH, SEE YA!
WHEW!

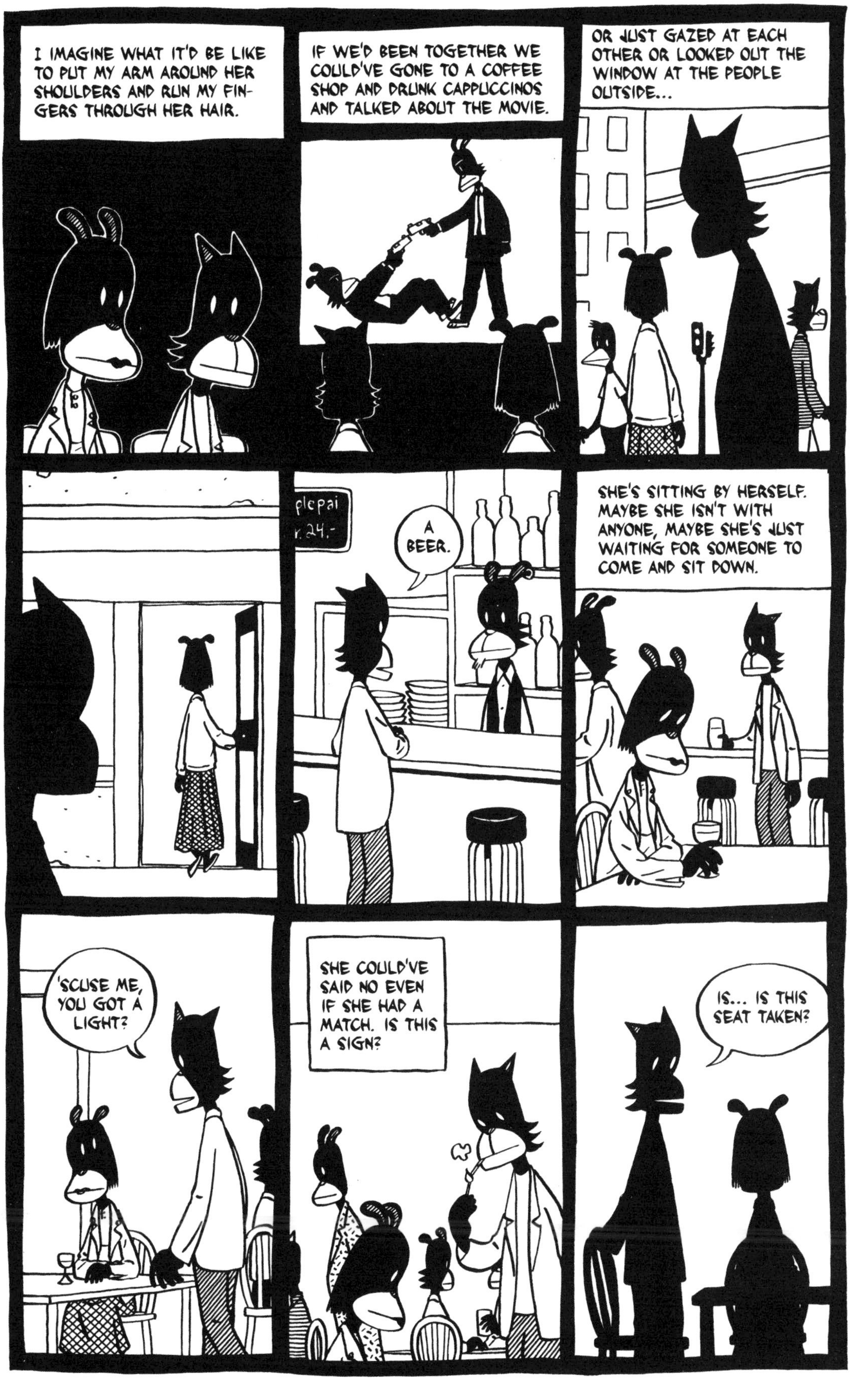
I IMAGINE WHAT IT'D BE LIKE TO PUT MY ARM AROUND HER SHOULDERS AND RUN MY FINGERS THROUGH HER HAIR.
IF WE'D BEEN TOGETHER WE COULD'VE GONE TO A COFFEE SHOP AND DRUNK CAPPUCCINOS AND TALKED ABOUT THE MOVIE.
OR JUST GAZED AT EACH OTHER OR LOOKED OUT THE WINDOW AT THE PEOPLE OUTSIDE...
plepai
r. 24.-
A BEER.
SHE'S SITTING BY HERSELF. MAYBE SHE ISN'T WITH ANYONE, MAYBE SHE'S JUST WAITING FOR SOMEONE TO COME AND SIT DOWN.
'SCUSE ME, YOU GOT A LIGHT?
SHE COULD'VE SAID NO EVEN IF SHE HAD A MATCH. IS THIS A SIGN?
IS... IS THIS SEAT TAKEN?

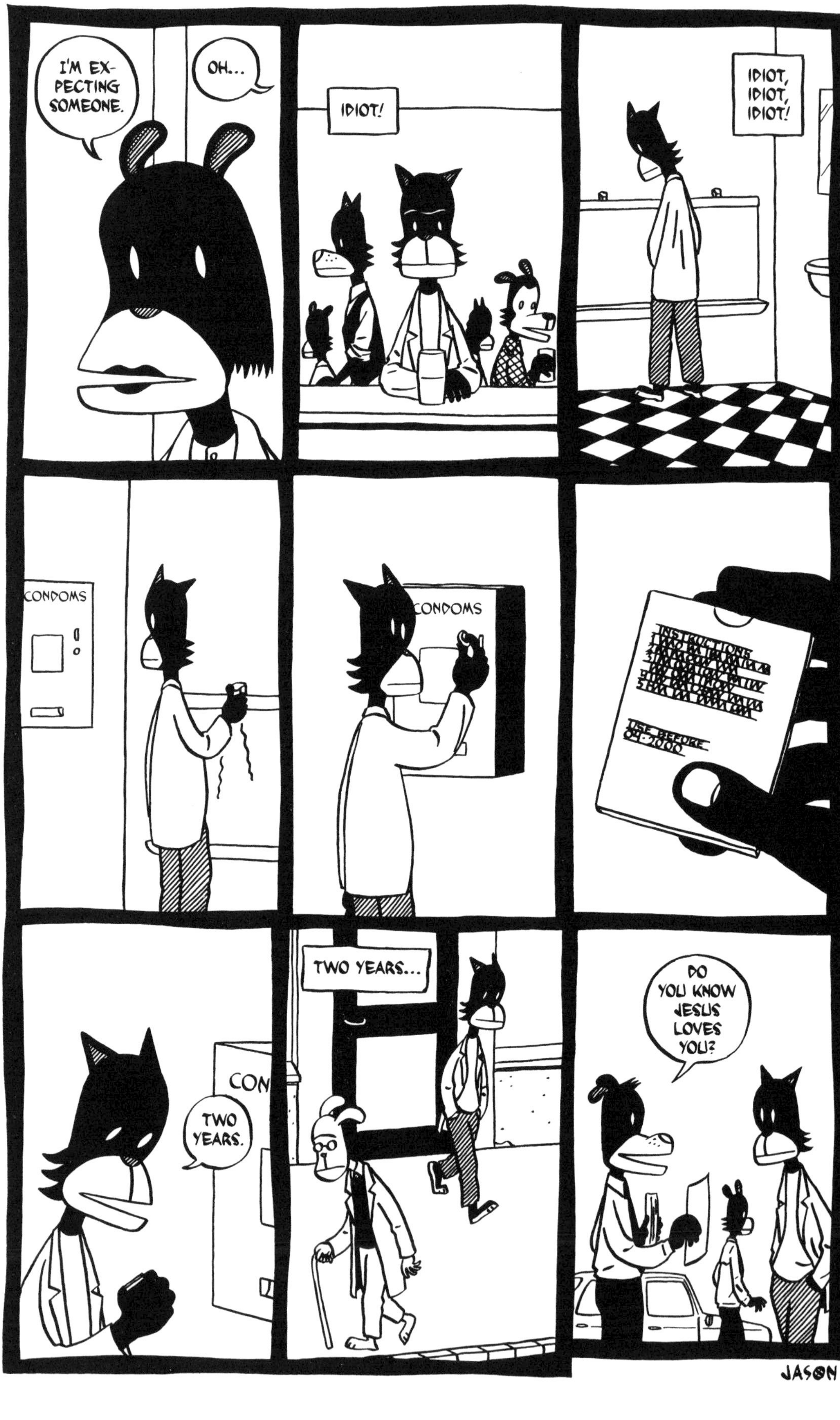
I'M EX-PECTING SOMEONE.
OH...
IDIOT!
IDIOT, IDIOT, IDIOT!
CONDOMS
CONDOMS
INSTRUCTIONS
USE BEFORE 04-2000
CON
TWO YEARS.
TWO YEARS...
DO YOU KNOW JESUS LOVES YOU?
JASON

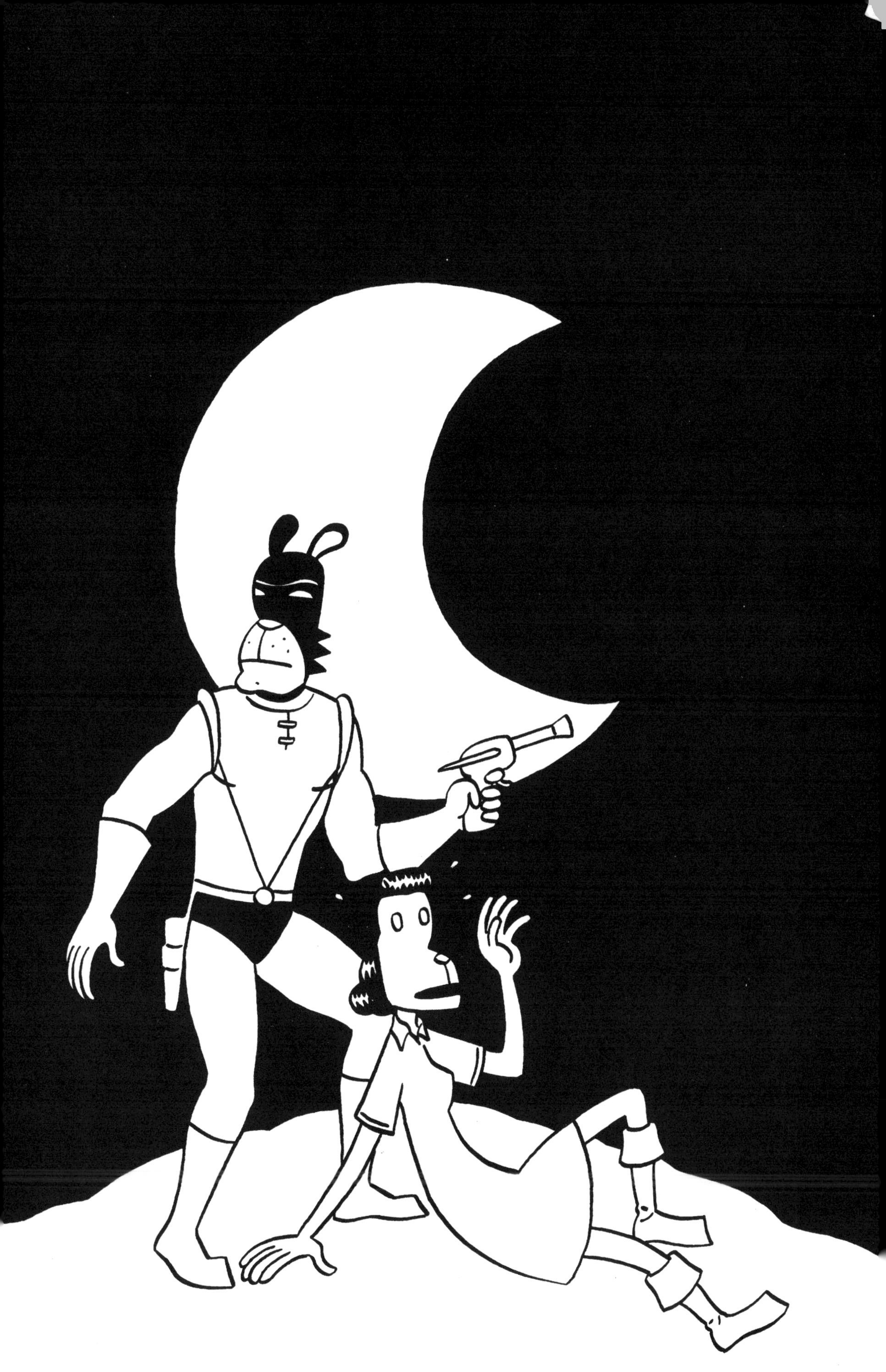

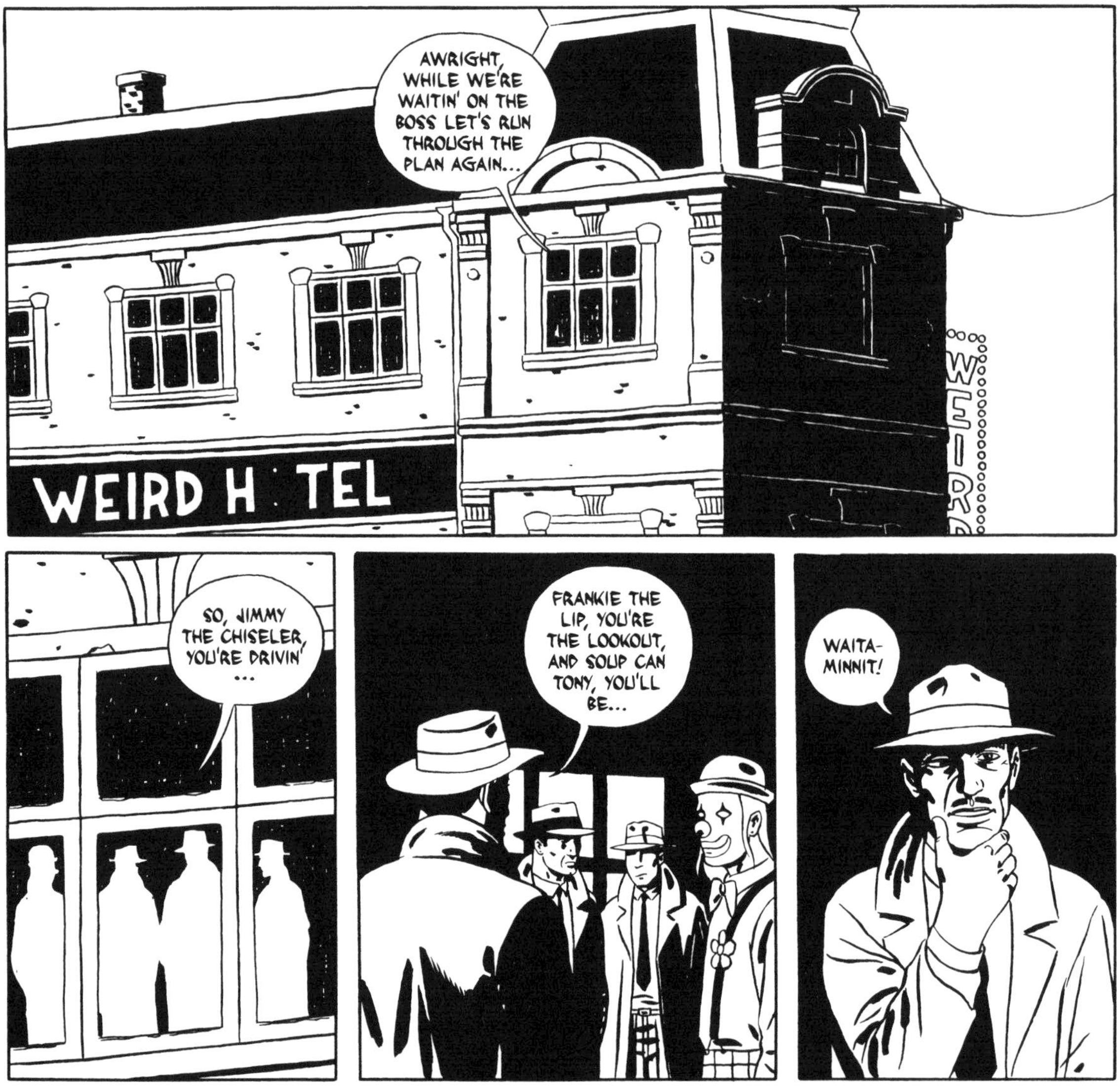

AWRIGHT, WHILE WE'RE WAITIN' ON THE BOSS LET'S RUN THROUGH THE PLAN AGAIN...
WEIRD H TEL
WEIRD
SO, JIMMY THE CHISELER, YOU'RE DRIVIN' ...
FRANKIE THE LIP, YOU'RE THE LOOKOUT, AND SOUP CAN TONY, YOU'LL BE...
WAITA-MINNIT!

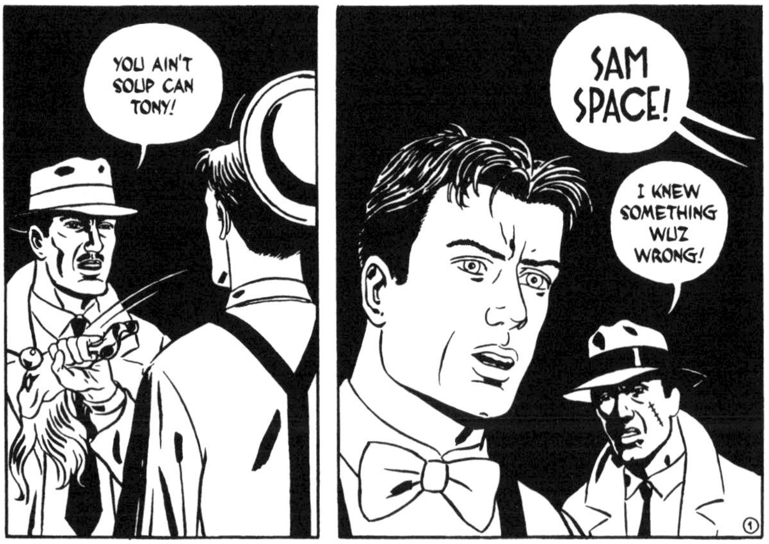

YOU AIN'T SOUP CAN TONY!
SAM SPACE!
I KNEW SOMETHING WUZ WRONG!
1

INVASION OF THE GIANT SNAILS

BY JASON

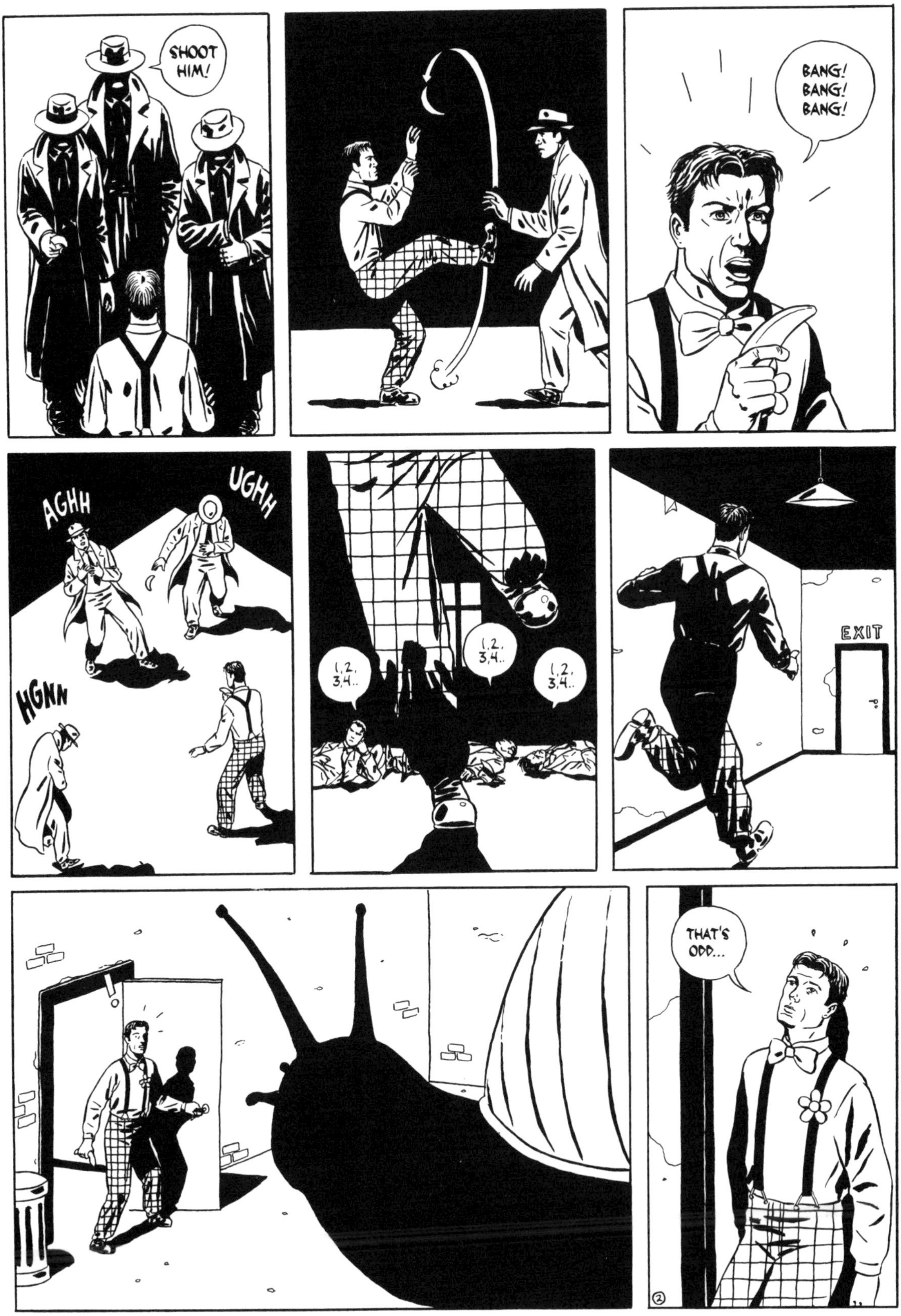
SHOOT HIM!
BANG! BANG! BANG!
AGHH
UGHH
HGNN
1,2, 3,4..
1,2, 3,4..
1,2, 3,4..
EXIT
THAT'S ODD...

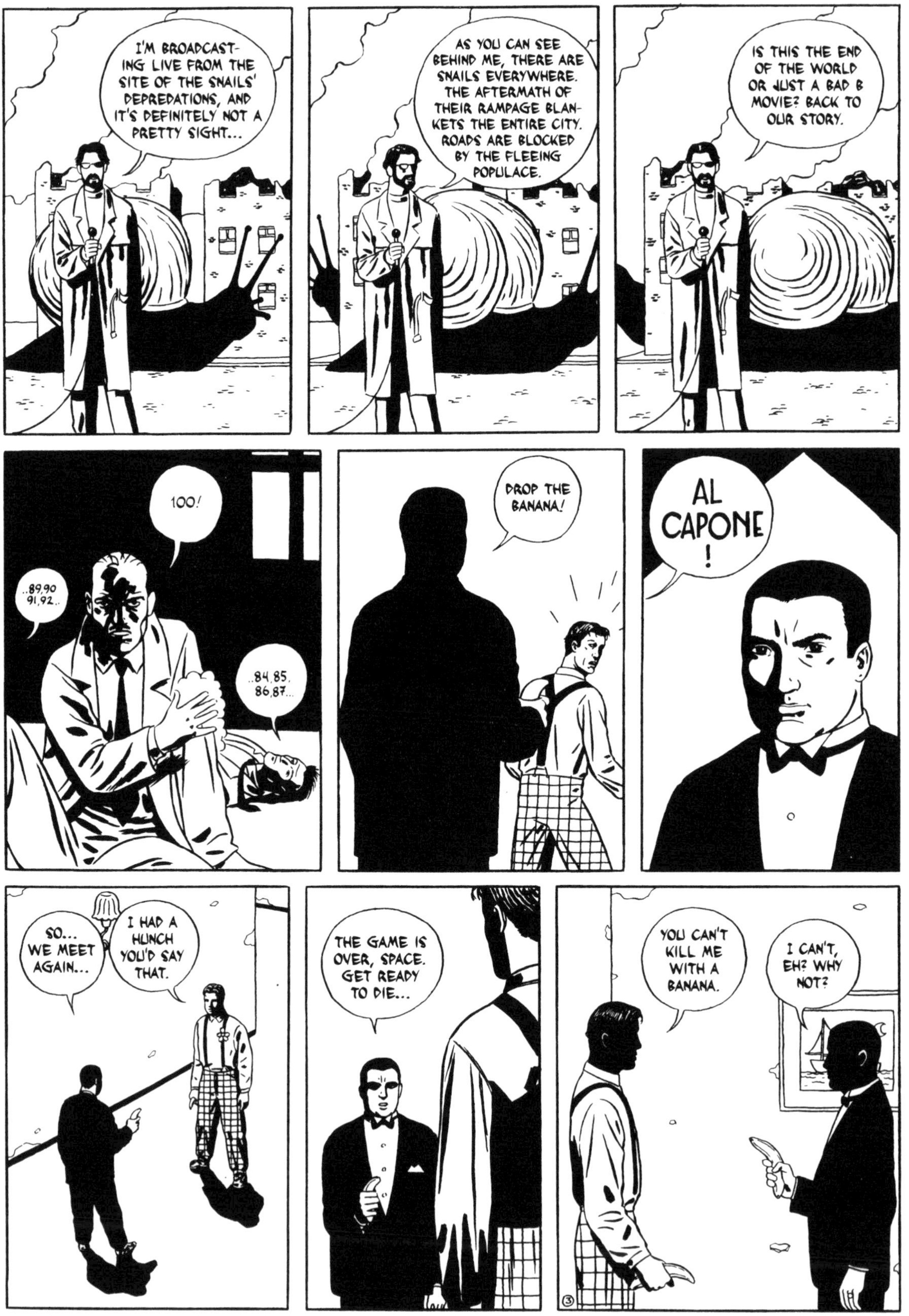
I'M BROADCASTING LIVE FROM THE SITE OF THE SNAILS' DEPREDATIONS, AND IT'S DEFINITELY NOT A PRETTY SIGHT...
AS YOU CAN SEE BEHIND ME, THERE ARE SNAILS EVERYWHERE. THE AFTERMATH OF THEIR RAMPAGE BLANKETS THE ENTIRE CITY. ROADS ARE BLOCKED BY THE FLEEING POPULACE.
IS THIS THE END OF THE WORLD OR JUST A BAD B MOVIE? BACK TO OUR STORY.
..89,90 91,92..
100!
..84,85, 86,87...
DROP THE BANANA!
AL CAPONE !
SO... WE MEET AGAIN...
I HAD A HUNCH YOU'D SAY THAT.
THE GAME IS OVER, SPACE. GET READY TO DIE...
YOU CAN'T KILL ME WITH A BANANA.
I CAN'T, EH? WHY NOT?
3

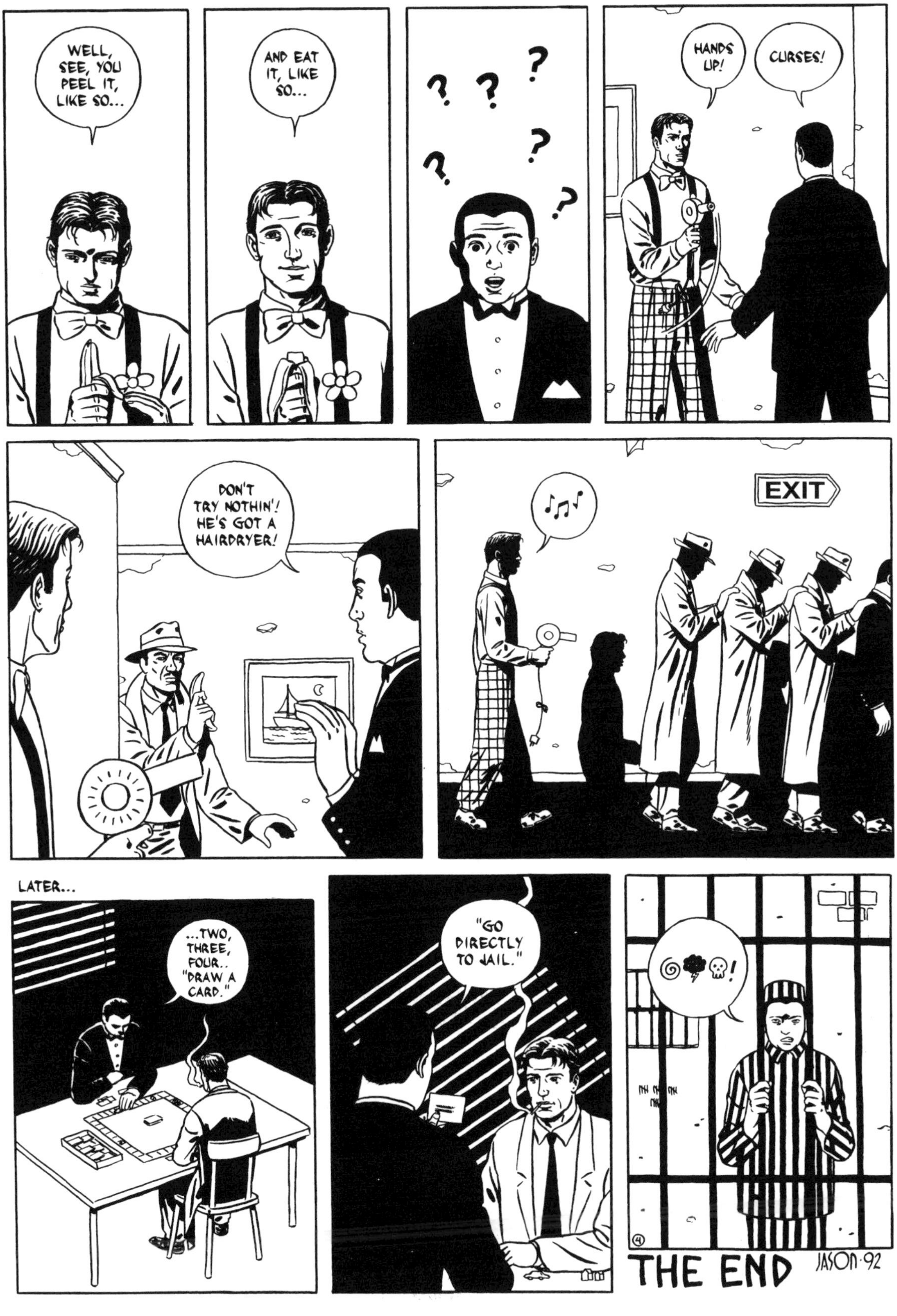

WELL, SEE, YOU PEEL IT, LIKE SO...
AND EAT IT, LIKE SO...
? ? ? ? ? ?
HANDS UP!
CURSES!
DON'T TRY NOTHIN'! HE'S GOT A HAIRDRYER!
EXIT
LATER...
...TWO, THREE, FOUR.. "DRAW A CARD."
"GO DIRECTLY TO JAIL."
THE END
JASON·92

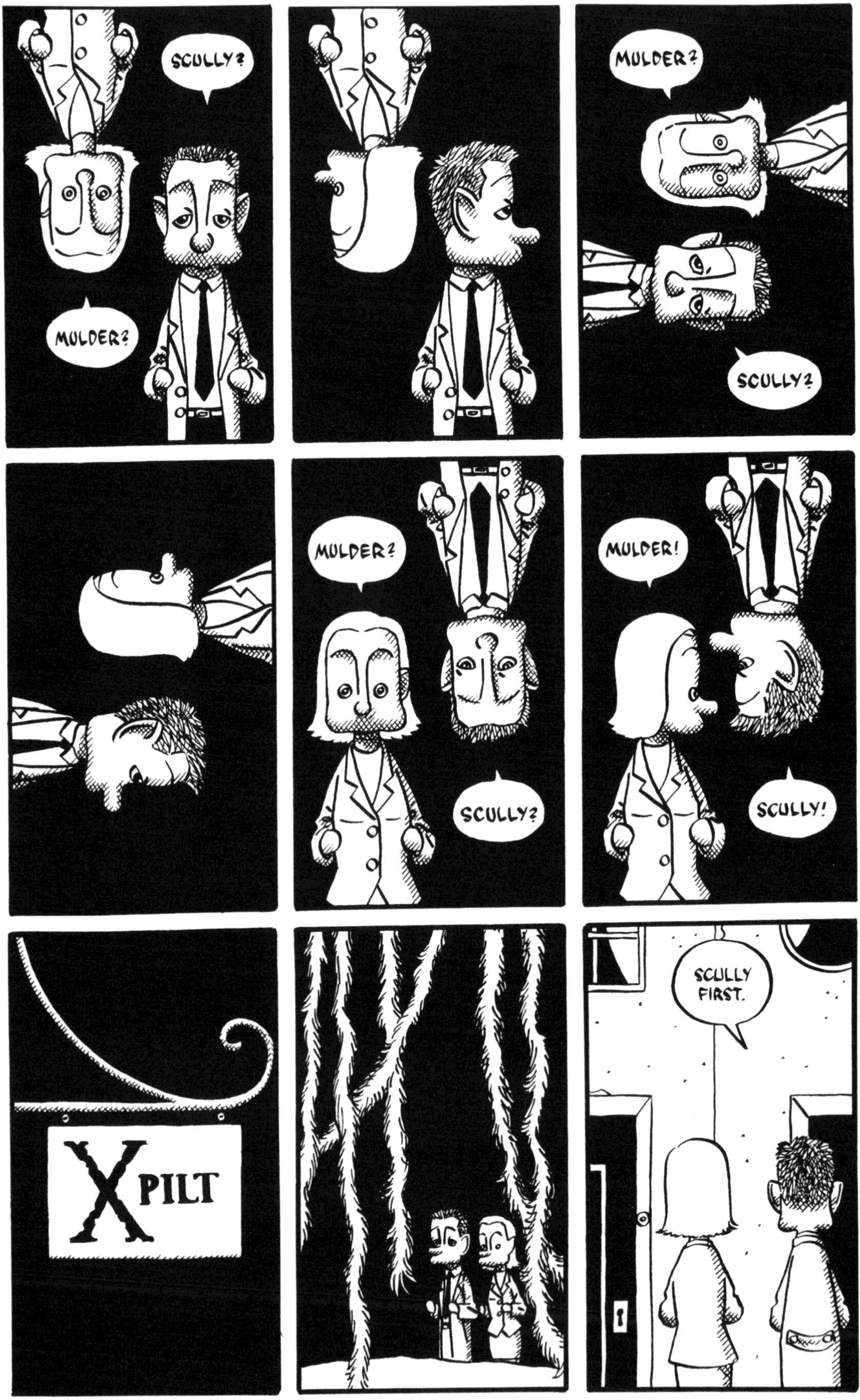
SCULLY?
MULDER?
MULDER?
SCULLY?
MULDER?
SCULLY?
MULDER!
SCULLY!
XPILT
SCULLY FIRST.

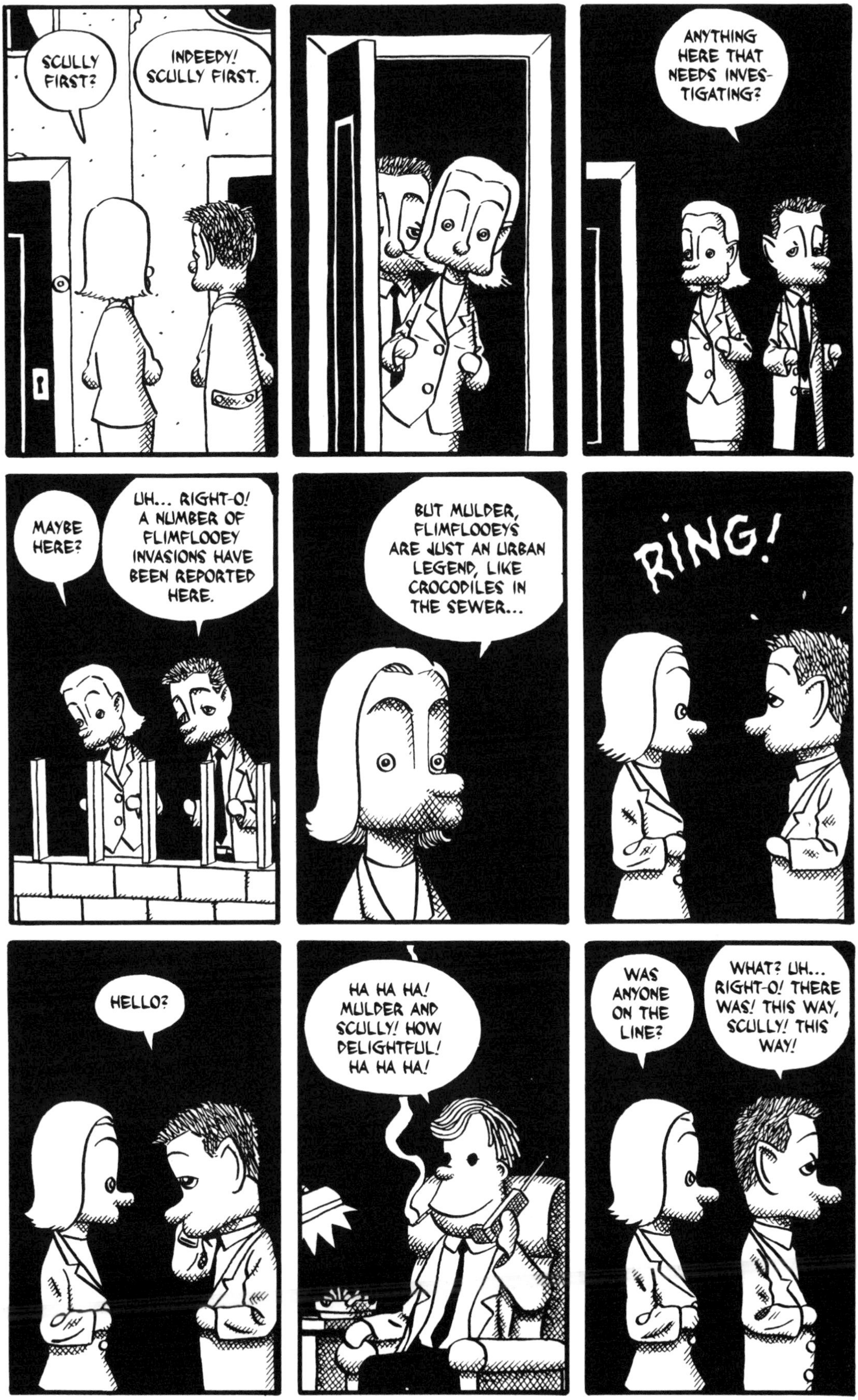
SCULLY FIRST?
INDEEDY! SCULLY FIRST.
ANYTHING HERE THAT NEEDS INVES-TIGATING?
MAYBE HERE?
UH... RIGHT-O! A NUMBER OF FLIMFLOOEY INVASIONS HAVE BEEN REPORTED HERE.
BUT MULDER, FLIMFLOOEYS ARE JUST AN URBAN LEGEND, LIKE CROCODILES IN THE SEWER...
RING!
HELLO?
HA HA HA! MULDER AND SCULLY! HOW DELIGHTFUL! HA HA HA!
WAS ANYONE ON THE LINE?
WHAT? UH... RIGHT-O! THERE WAS! THIS WAY, SCULLY! THIS WAY!

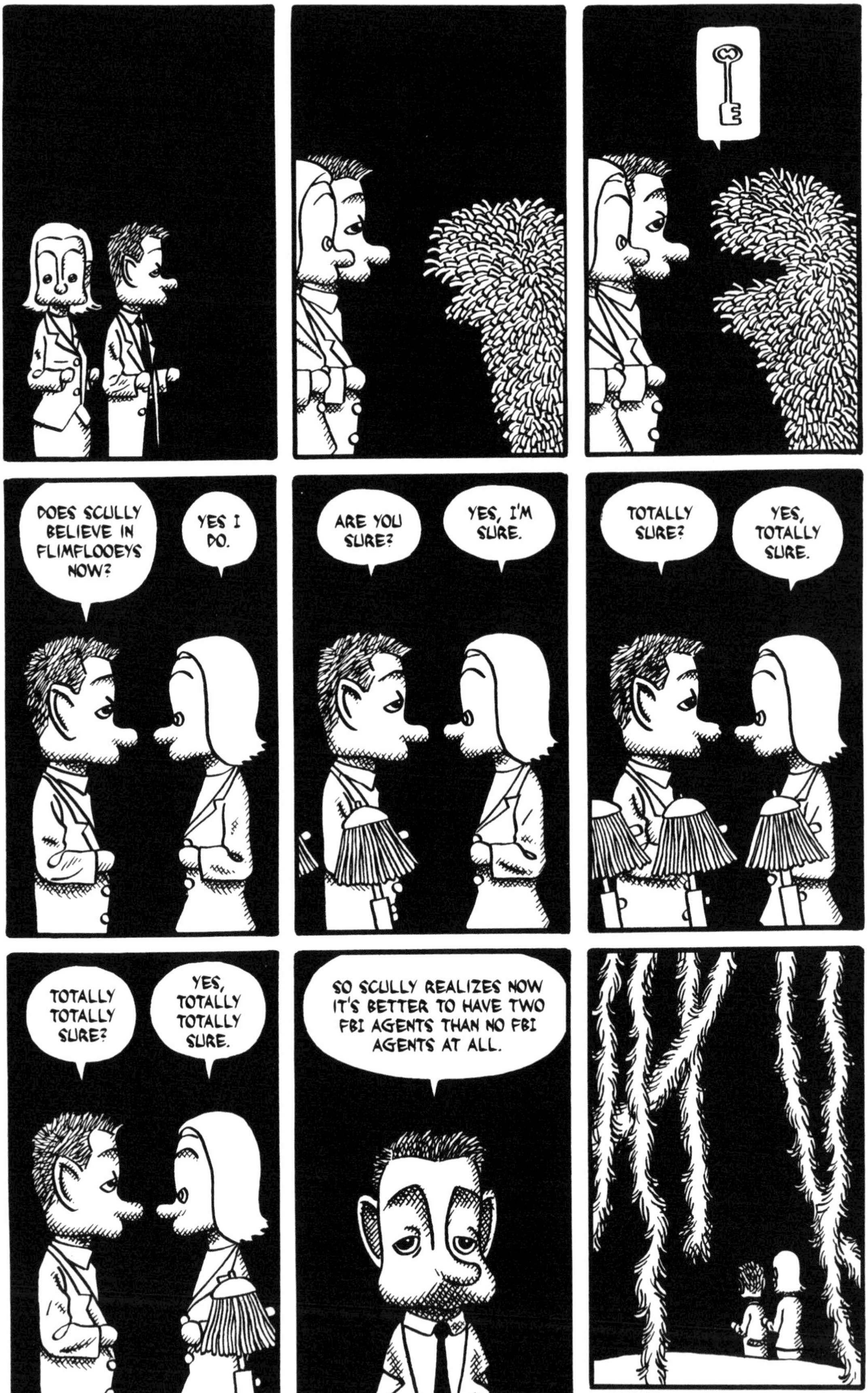
DOES SCULLY BELIEVE IN FLIMFLOOEYS NOW?
YES I DO.
ARE YOU SURE?
YES, I'M SURE.
TOTALLY SURE?
YES, TOTALLY SURE.
TOTALLY TOTALLY SURE?
YES, TOTALLY TOTALLY SURE.
SO SCULLY REALIZES NOW IT'S BETTER TO HAVE TWO FBI AGENTS THAN NO FBI AGENTS AT ALL.
JASON

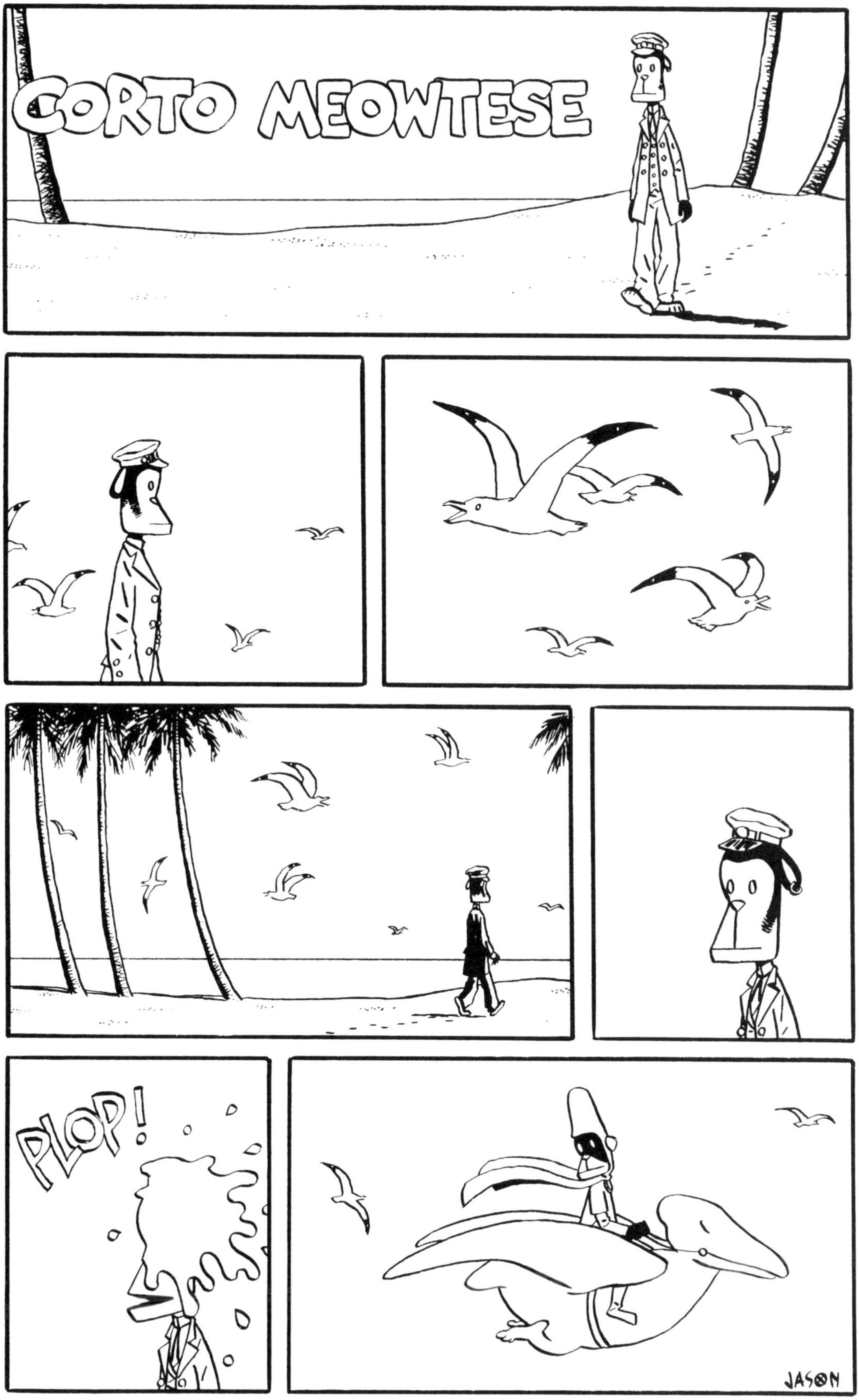
CORTO MEOWTESE
PLOP!
JASON

SPACECAT
BY JASON
IN A LABORATORY ON THE PLANET NEPTUNE PRINCESS AIEL IS HELD CAPTIVE BY THE EVIL DR. X.
MARRY ME SO I CAN BE KING. OR ELSE I WILL MELT YOU INTO A STINKING PILE OF SLIME!
A SPACESHIP APPROACHES.
FOR THE LAST TIME... DO AS I COMMAND, OR SUF-FER AN AGONIZING DEATH!
NEVER!
A SOUND BEHIND DR. X CAUSES HIM TO SPIN AROUND.
CURSES! SPACECAT!

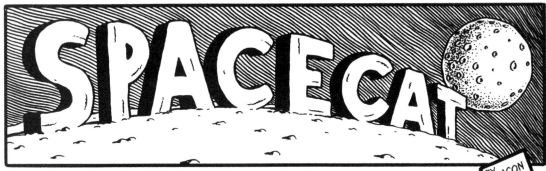

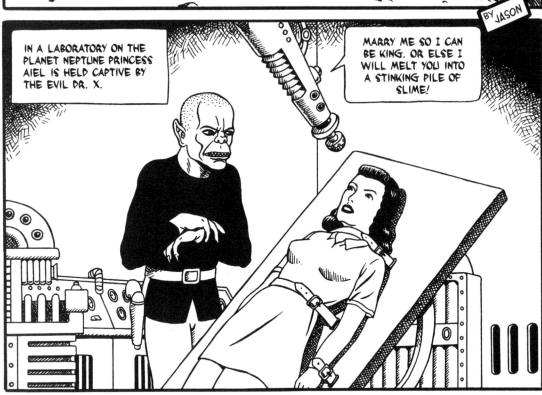

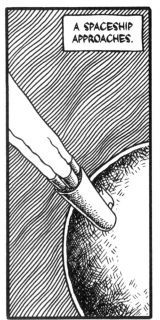

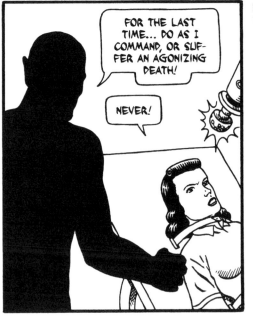

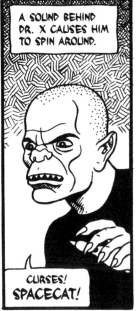

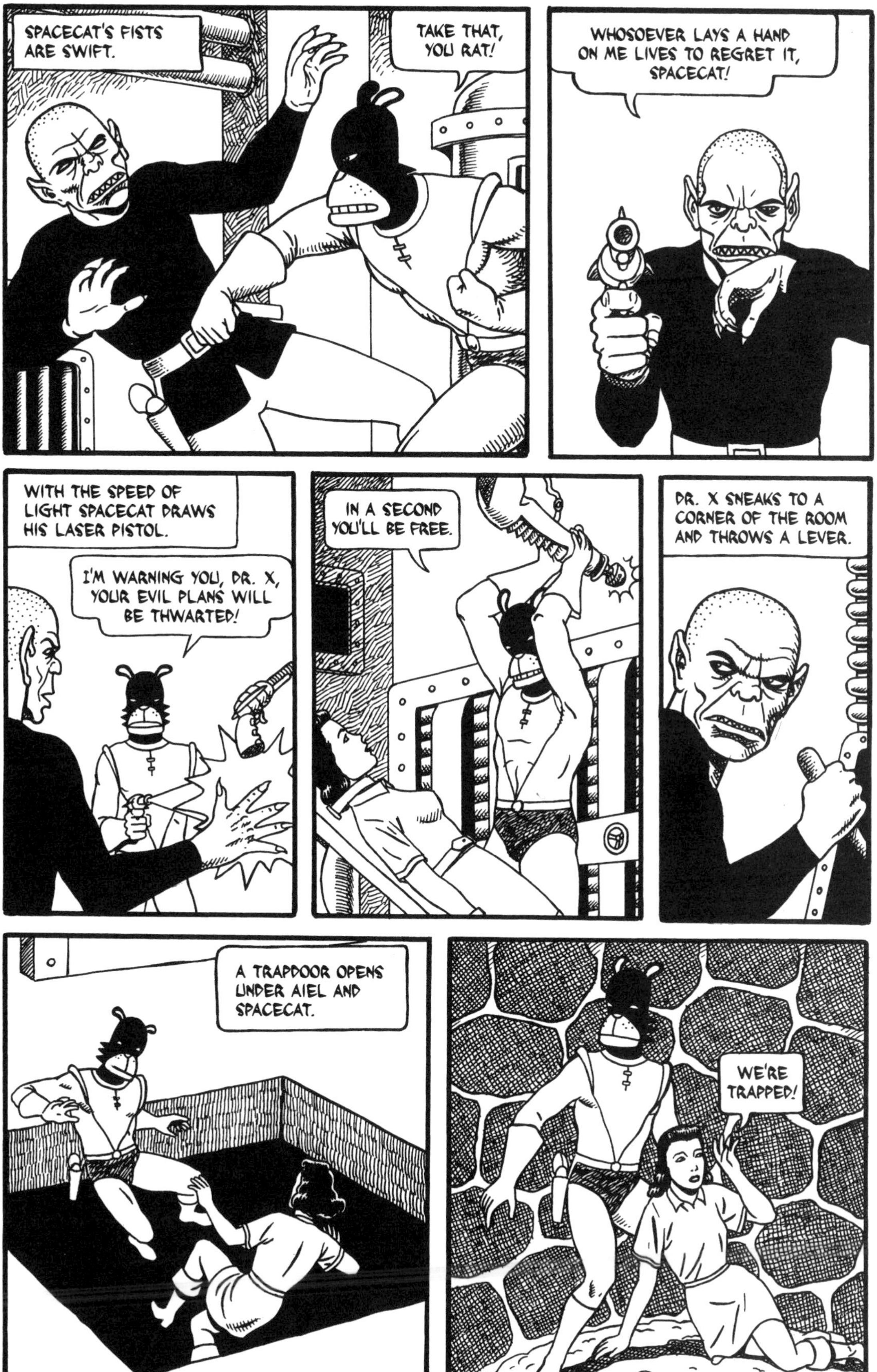
SPACECAT'S FISTS ARE SWIFT.
TAKE THAT, YOU RAT!
WHOSOEVER LAYS A HAND ON ME LIVES TO REGRET IT, SPACECAT!
WITH THE SPEED OF LIGHT SPACECAT DRAWS HIS LASER PISTOL.
I'M WARNING YOU, DR. X, YOUR EVIL PLANS WILL BE THWARTED!
IN A SECOND YOU'LL BE FREE.
DR. X SNEAKS TO A CORNER OF THE ROOM AND THROWS A LEVER.
A TRAPDOOR OPENS UNDER AIEL AND SPACECAT.
WE'RE TRAPPED!

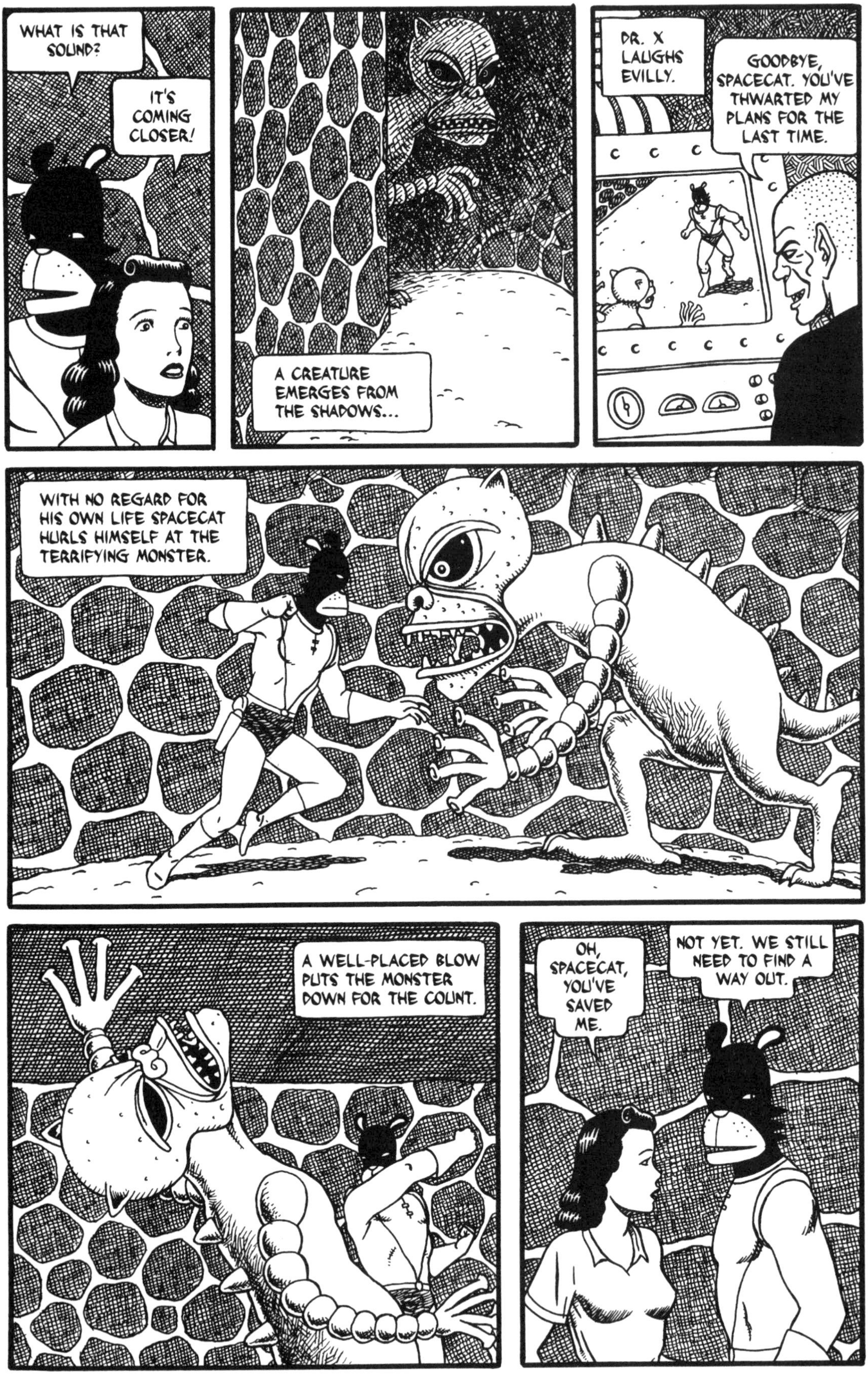
WHAT IS THAT SOUND?
IT'S COMING CLOSER!
A CREATURE EMERGES FROM THE SHADOWS...
DR. X LAUGHS EVILLY.
GOODBYE, SPACECAT. YOU'VE THWARTED MY PLANS FOR THE LAST TIME.
WITH NO REGARD FOR HIS OWN LIFE SPACECAT HURLS HIMSELF AT THE TERRIFYING MONSTER.
A WELL-PLACED BLOW PUTS THE MONSTER DOWN FOR THE COUNT.
OH, SPACECAT, YOU'VE SAVED ME.
NOT YET. WE STILL NEED TO FIND A WAY OUT.

WITH THE HELP OF SPACECAT'S ANTI-GRAVITY BELT THEY FLY TO SAFETY.

HOLD IT RIGHT THERE, DR. X!

SPACECAT! YOU AGAIN!

THIS TIME YOU WILL NOT ESCAPE!

HIS NECK IS BROKEN... NOW YOUR PLANET IS FINALLY SAFE FROM DR. X'S DEVIOUS INTRIGUES.

THANK YOU SO MUCH, SPACE-CAT. WILL I SEE YOU AGAIN?

THE STARS ARE MY HOME, AIEL. BUT ONE DAY I SHALL VISIT YOU AGAIN.

OH, SPACECAT. THOSE WORDS ARE MUSIC TO MY EARS.

I WILL COUNT THE HOURS...

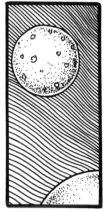

READ MORE IN THE NEXT THRILLING EPISODE OF
SPACECAT

PAPA

JASON

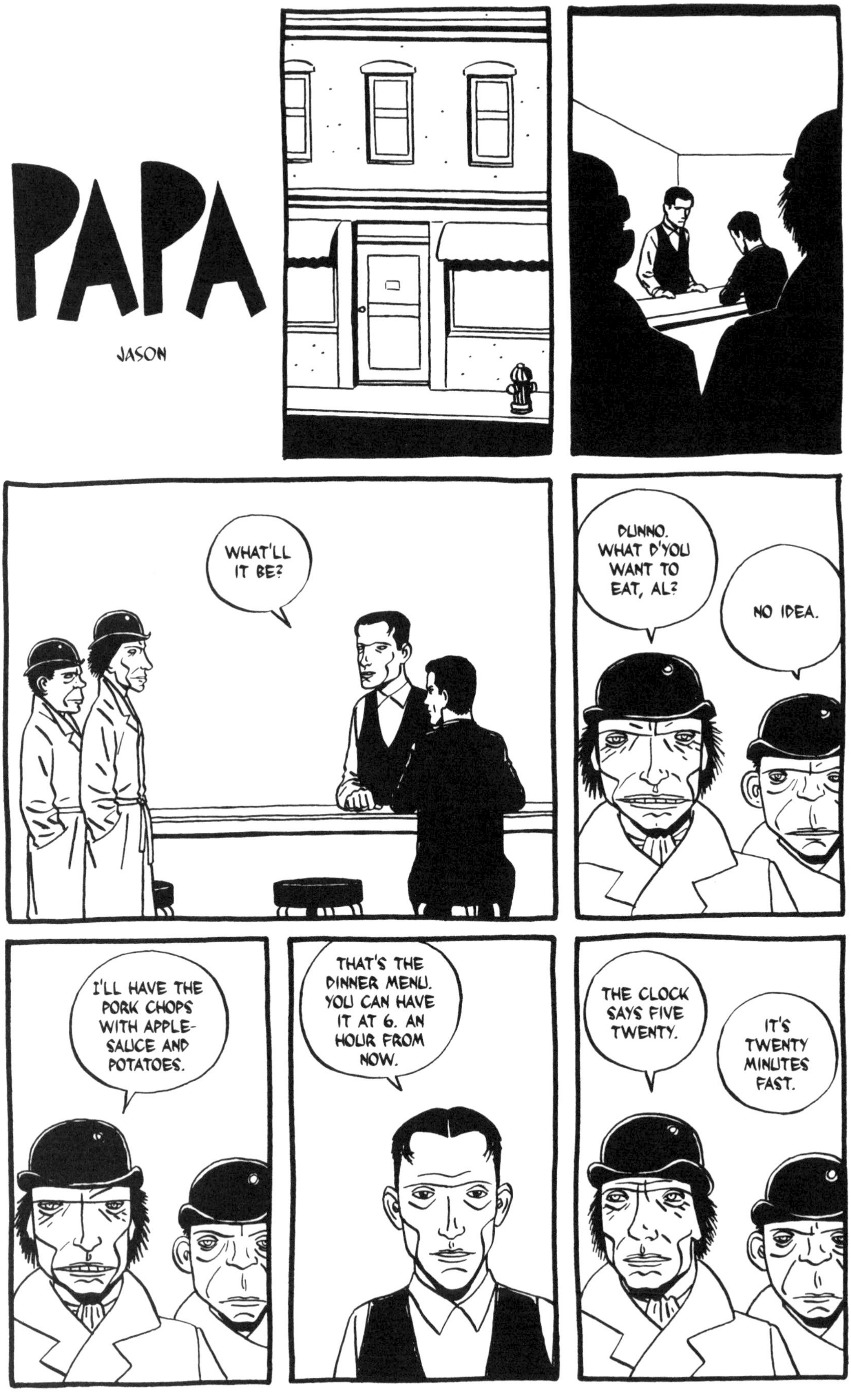
WHAT'LL IT BE?
DUNNO. WHAT D'YOU WANT TO EAT, AL?
NO IDEA.
I'LL HAVE THE PORK CHOPS WITH APPLE-SAUCE AND POTATOES.
THAT'S THE DINNER MENU. YOU CAN HAVE IT AT 6. AN HOUR FROM NOW.
THE CLOCK SAYS FIVE TWENTY.
IT'S TWENTY MINUTES FAST.

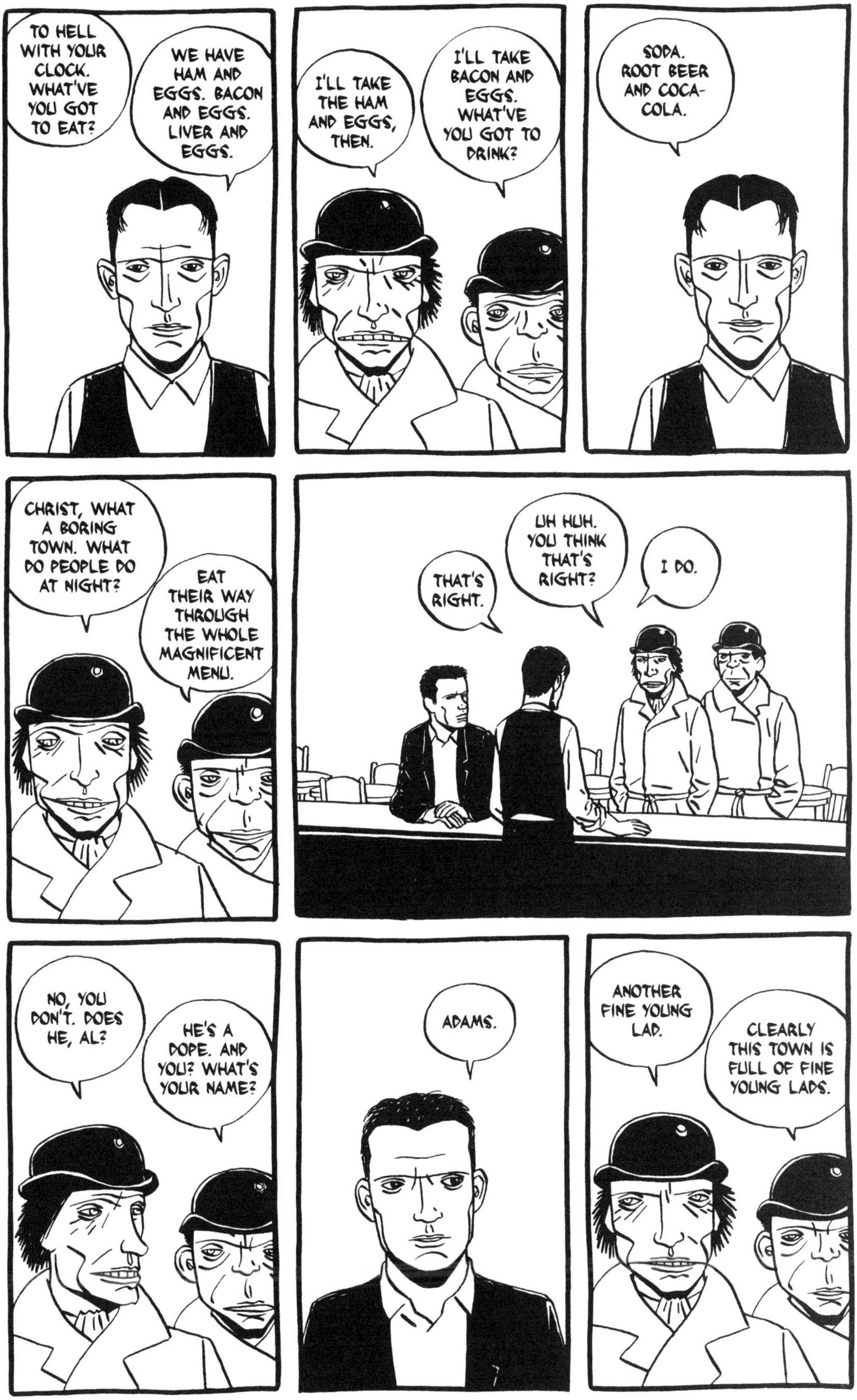
TO HELL WITH YOUR CLOCK. WHAT'VE YOU GOT TO EAT?
WE HAVE HAM AND EGGS. BACON AND EGGS. LIVER AND EGGS.
I'LL TAKE THE HAM AND EGGS, THEN.
I'LL TAKE BACON AND EGGS. WHAT'VE YOU GOT TO DRINK?
SODA. ROOT BEER AND COCA-COLA.
CHRIST, WHAT A BORING TOWN. WHAT DO PEOPLE DO AT NIGHT?
EAT THEIR WAY THROUGH THE WHOLE MAGNIFICENT MENU.
THAT'S RIGHT.
UH HUH. YOU THINK THAT'S RIGHT?
I DO.
NO, YOU DON'T. DOES HE, AL?
HE'S A DOPE. AND YOU? WHAT'S YOUR NAME?
ADAMS.
ANOTHER FINE YOUNG LAD.
CLEARLY THIS TOWN IS FULL OF FINE YOUNG LADS.

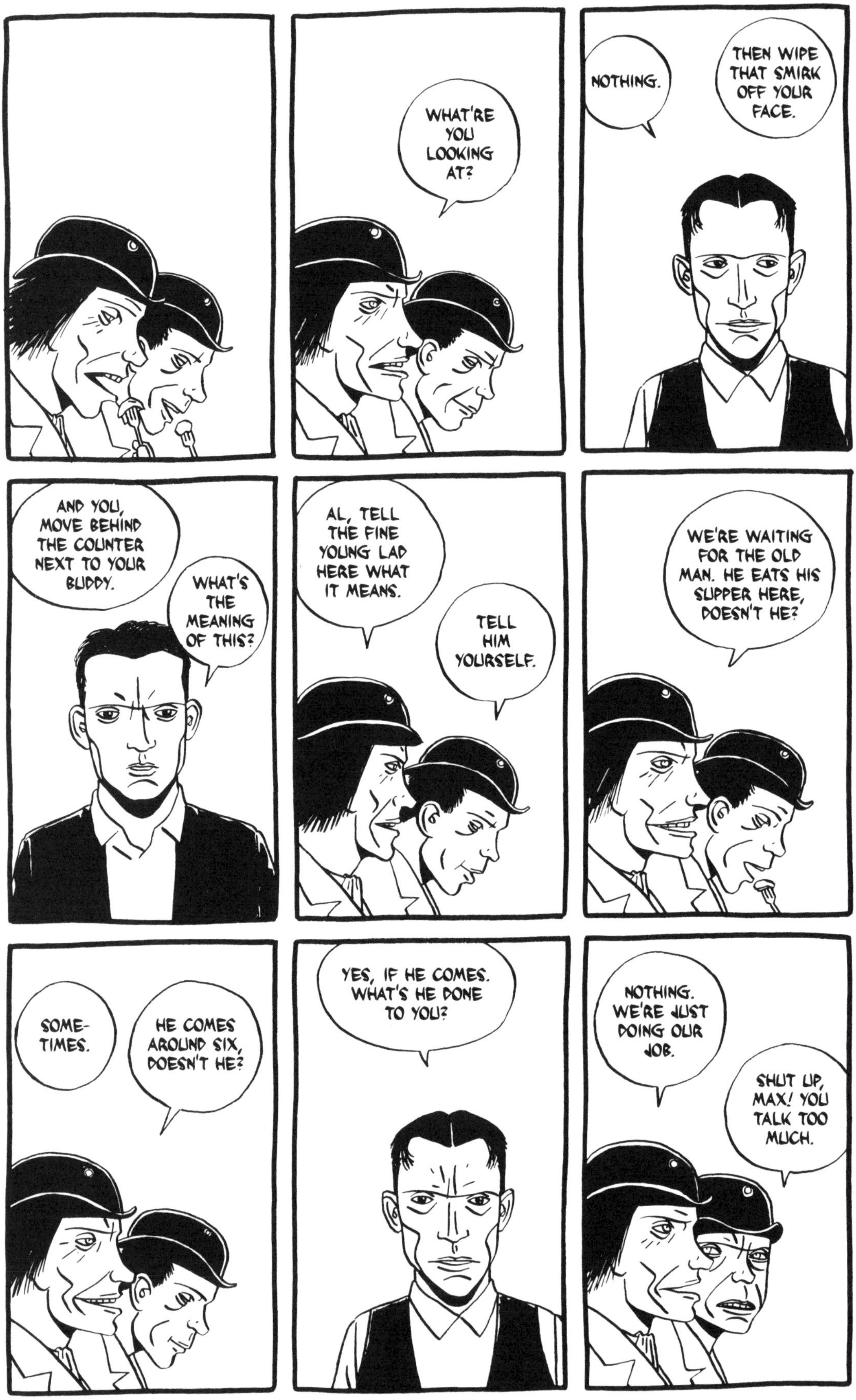
WHAT'RE YOU LOOKING AT?
NOTHING.
THEN WIPE THAT SMIRK OFF YOUR FACE.
AND YOU, MOVE BEHIND THE COUNTER NEXT TO YOUR BUDDY.
WHAT'S THE MEANING OF THIS?
AL, TELL THE FINE YOUNG LAD HERE WHAT IT MEANS.
TELL HIM YOURSELF.
WE'RE WAITING FOR THE OLD MAN. HE EATS HIS SUPPER HERE, DOESN'T HE?
SOME-TIMES.
HE COMES AROUND SIX, DOESN'T HE?
YES, IF HE COMES. WHAT'S HE DONE TO YOU?
NOTHING. WE'RE JUST DOING OUR JOB.
SHUT UP, MAX! YOU TALK TOO MUCH.

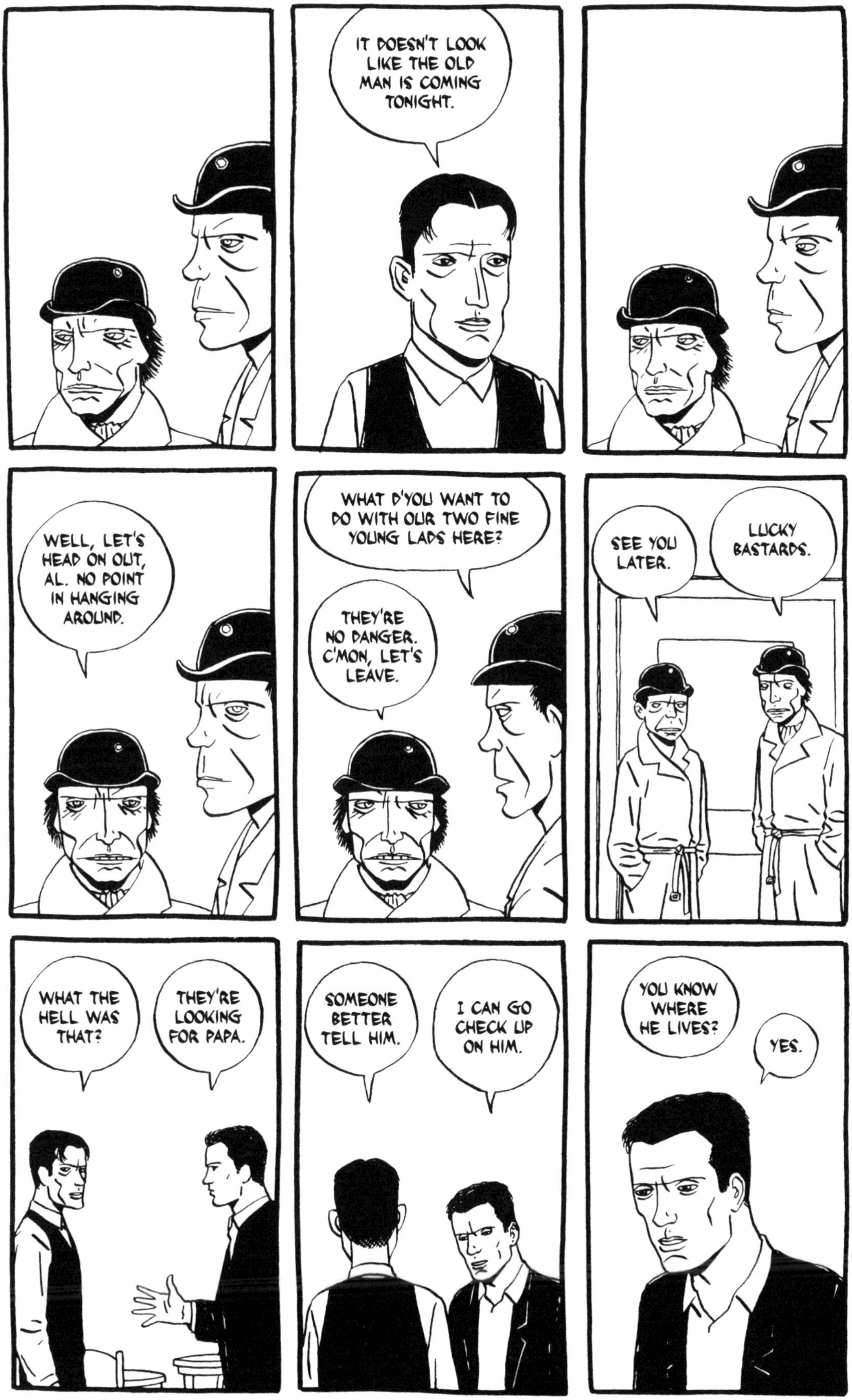
IT DOESN'T LOOK LIKE THE OLD MAN IS COMING TONIGHT.
WELL, LET'S HEAD ON OUT, AL. NO POINT IN HANGING AROUND.
WHAT D'YOU WANT TO DO WITH OUR TWO FINE YOUNG LADS HERE?
THEY'RE NO DANGER. C'MON, LET'S LEAVE.
SEE YOU LATER.
LUCKY BASTARDS.
WHAT THE HELL WAS THAT?
THEY'RE LOOKING FOR PAPA.
SOMEONE BETTER TELL HIM.
I CAN GO CHECK UP ON HIM.
YOU KNOW WHERE HE LIVES?
YES.

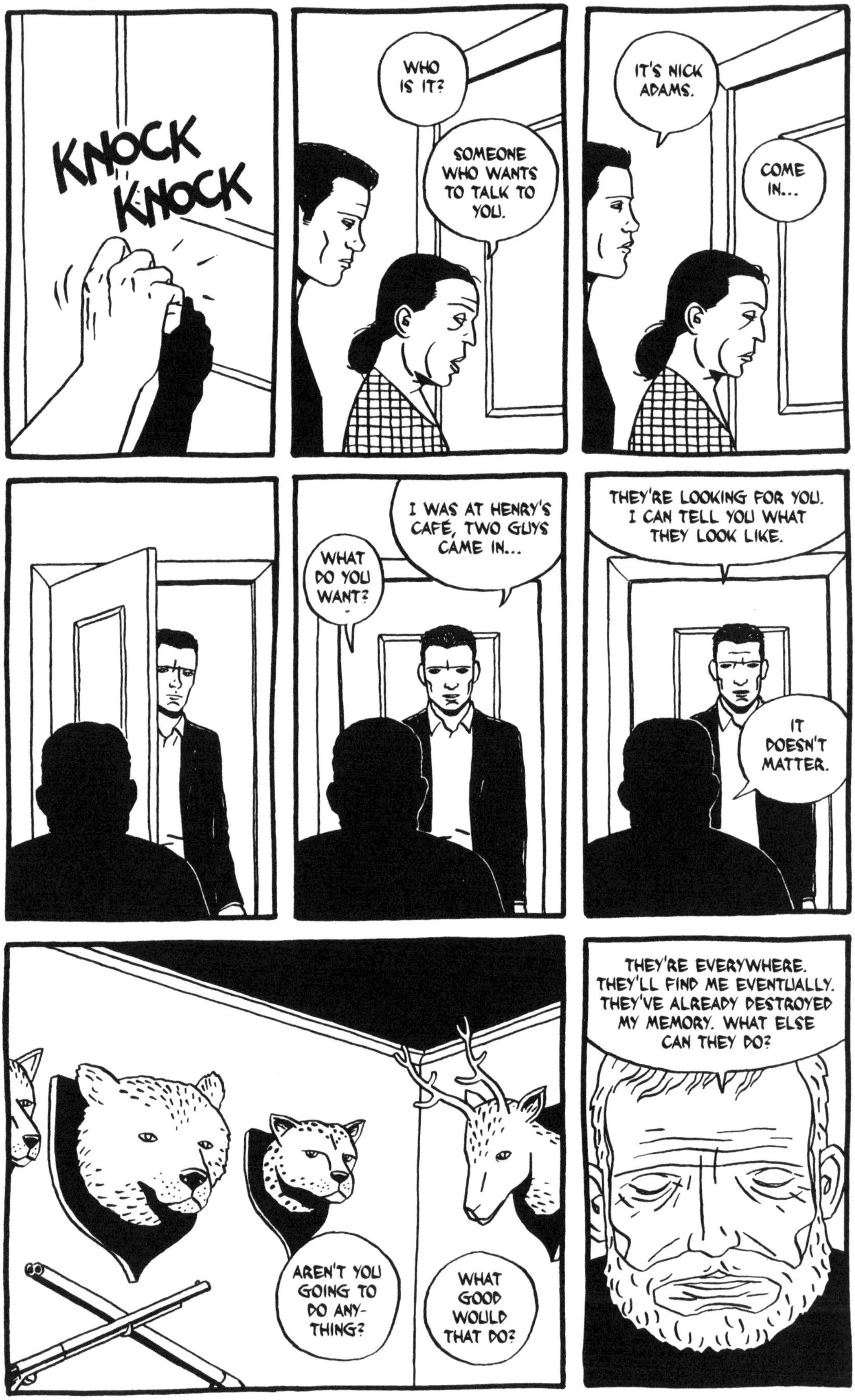
KNOCK KNOCK
WHO IS IT?
SOMEONE WHO WANTS TO TALK TO YOU.
IT'S NICK ADAMS.
COME IN...
WHAT DO YOU WANT?
I WAS AT HENRY'S CAFÉ, TWO GUYS CAME IN...
THEY'RE LOOKING FOR YOU. I CAN TELL YOU WHAT THEY LOOK LIKE.
IT DOESN'T MATTER.
AREN'T YOU GOING TO DO ANY-THING?
WHAT GOOD WOULD THAT DO?
THEY'RE EVERYWHERE. THEY'LL FIND ME EVENTUALLY. THEY'VE ALREADY DESTROYED MY MEMORY. WHAT ELSE CAN THEY DO?

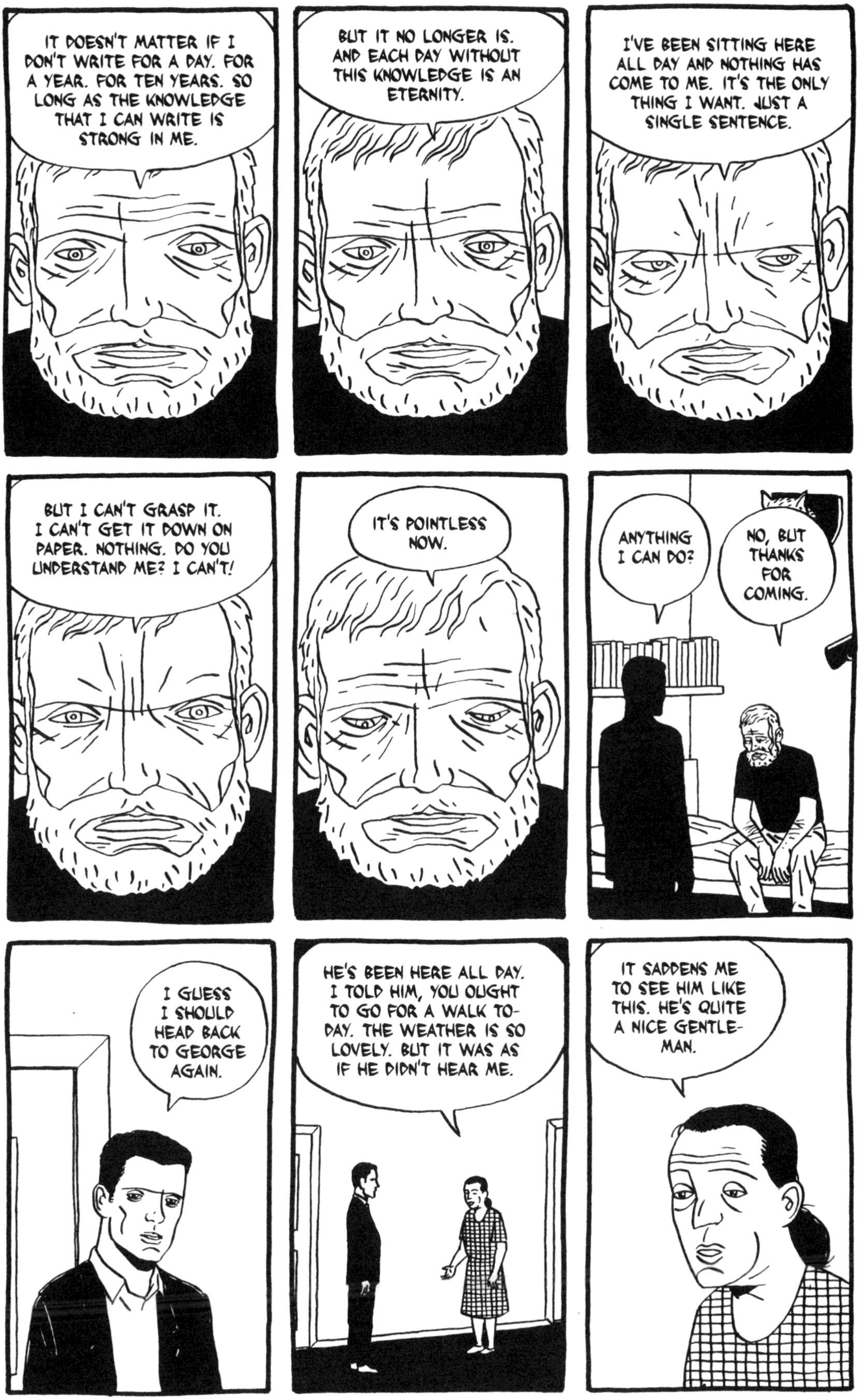
IT DOESN'T MATTER IF I DON'T WRITE FOR A DAY. FOR A YEAR. FOR TEN YEARS. SO LONG AS THE KNOWLEDGE THAT I CAN WRITE IS STRONG IN ME.
BUT IT NO LONGER IS. AND EACH DAY WITHOUT THIS KNOWLEDGE IS AN ETERNITY.
I'VE BEEN SITTING HERE ALL DAY AND NOTHING HAS COME TO ME. IT'S THE ONLY THING I WANT. JUST A SINGLE SENTENCE.
BUT I CAN'T GRASP IT. I CAN'T GET IT DOWN ON PAPER. NOTHING. DO YOU UNDERSTAND ME? I CAN'T!
IT'S POINTLESS NOW.
ANYTHING I CAN DO?
NO, BUT THANKS FOR COMING.
I GUESS I SHOULD HEAD BACK TO GEORGE AGAIN.
HE'S BEEN HERE ALL DAY. I TOLD HIM, YOU OUGHT TO GO FOR A WALK TO-DAY. THE WEATHER IS SO LOVELY. BUT IT WAS AS IF HE DIDN'T HEAR ME.
IT SADDENS ME TO SEE HIM LIKE THIS. HE'S QUITE A NICE GENTLE-MAN.

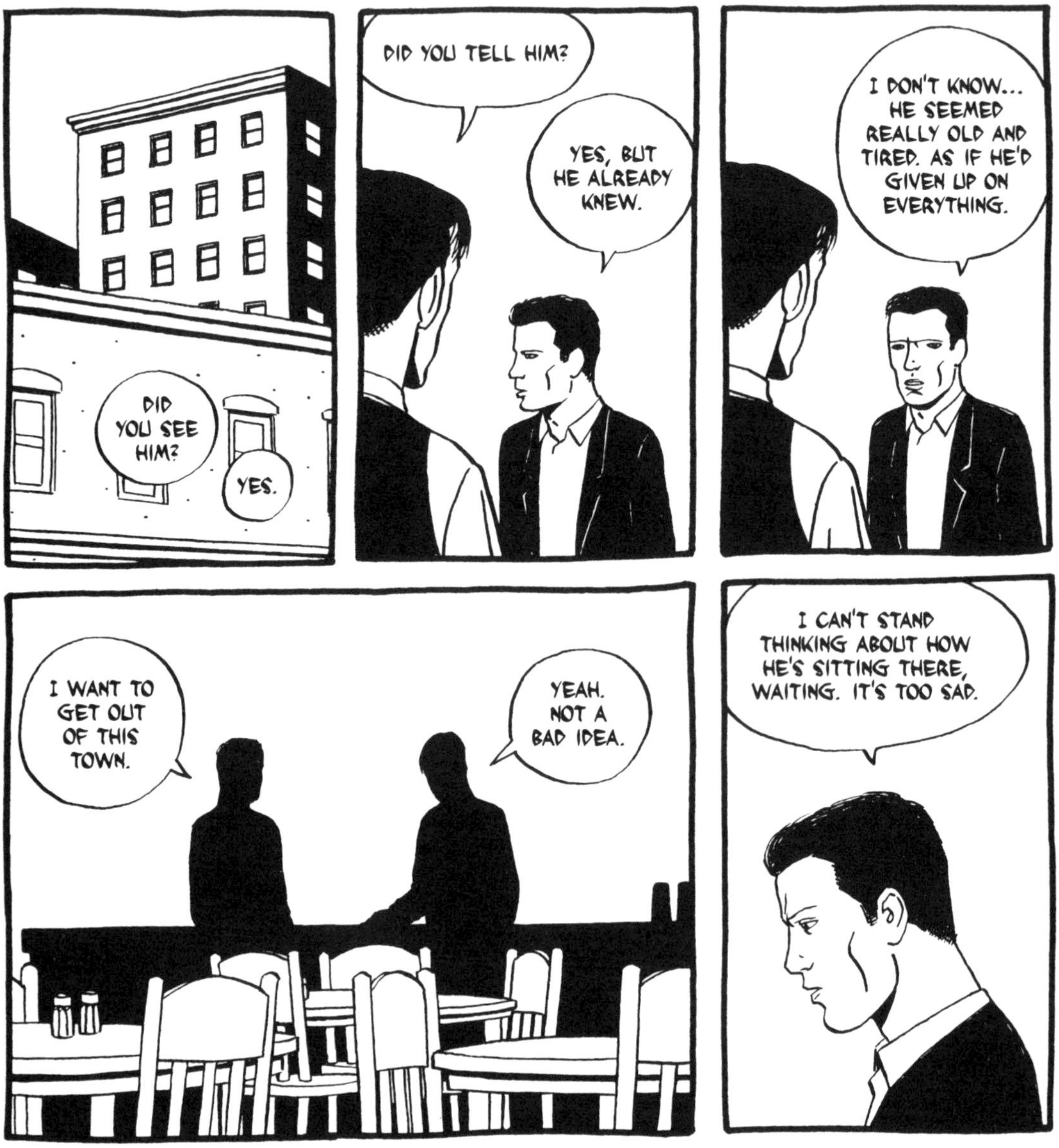
DID YOU SEE HIM?
YES.
DID YOU TELL HIM?
YES, BUT HE ALREADY KNEW.
I DON'T KNOW... HE SEEMED REALLY OLD AND TIRED. AS IF HE'D GIVEN UP ON EVERYTHING.
I WANT TO GET OUT OF THIS TOWN.
YEAH. NOT A BAD IDEA.
I CAN'T STAND THINKING ABOUT HOW HE'S SITTING THERE, WAITING. IT'S TOO SAD.

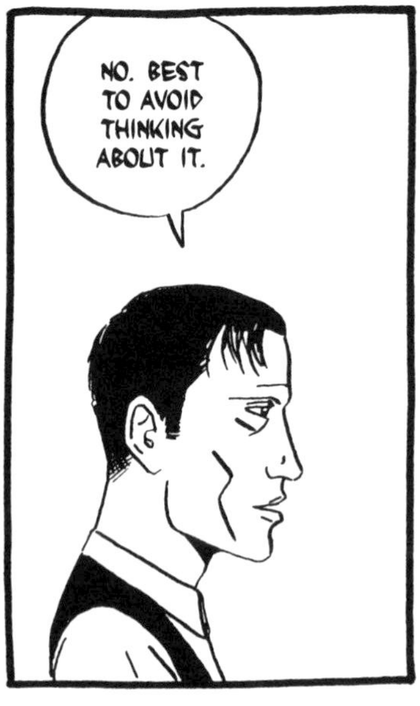
NO. BEST TO AVOID THINKING ABOUT IT.

THE LAST FEW YEARS OF HIS LIFE HEMINGWAY SUFFERED FROM PARANOIA. HE WAS CONVINCED THAT HE WAS BEING WATCHED, AND THAT AGENTS WERE GOING TO ARREST HIM AND LOCK HIM UP IN JAIL.

A PROGRAM OF ELECTROSHOCK THERAPY HAD NO POSITIVE EFFECT.

ERNEST HEMINGWAY COMMITTED SUICIDE IN 1961.

SOURCE:
"PAPA HEMINGWAY"
A.E. HOTCHNER

JASON

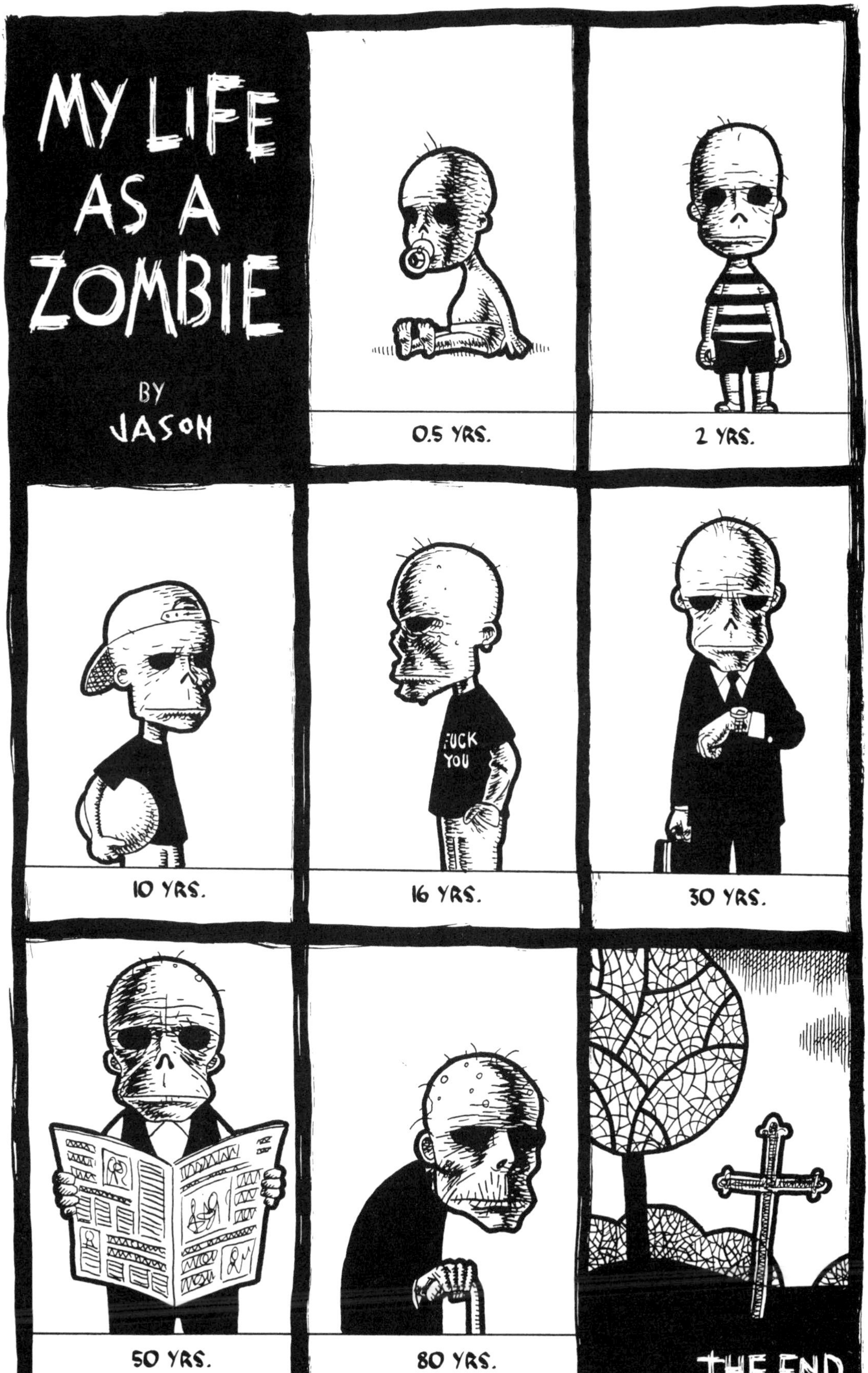
MY LIFE AS A ZOMBIE
BY JASON
0.5 YRS.
2 YRS.
10 YRS.
FUCK YOU
16 YRS.
30 YRS.
50 YRS.
80 YRS.
THE END

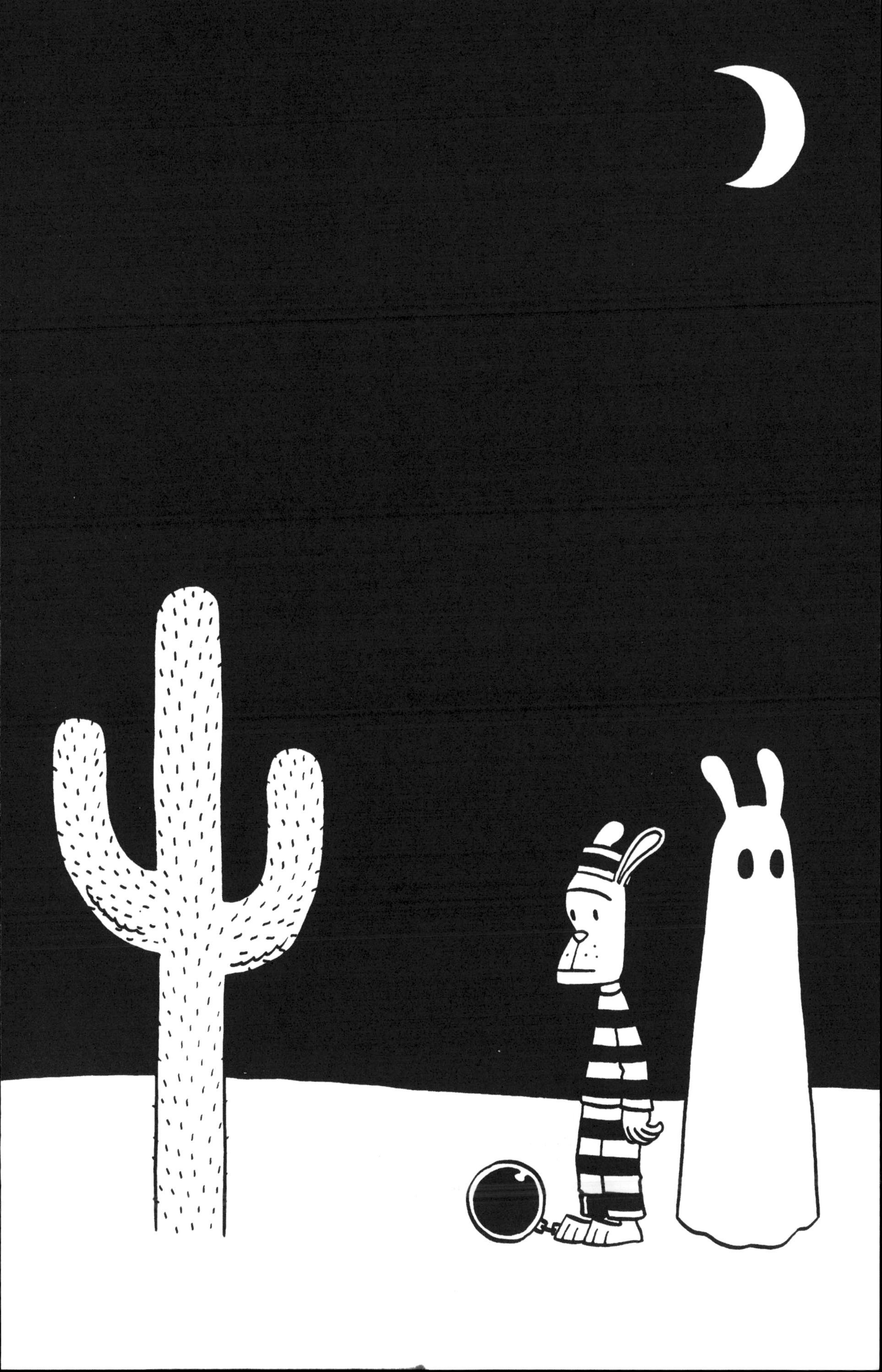

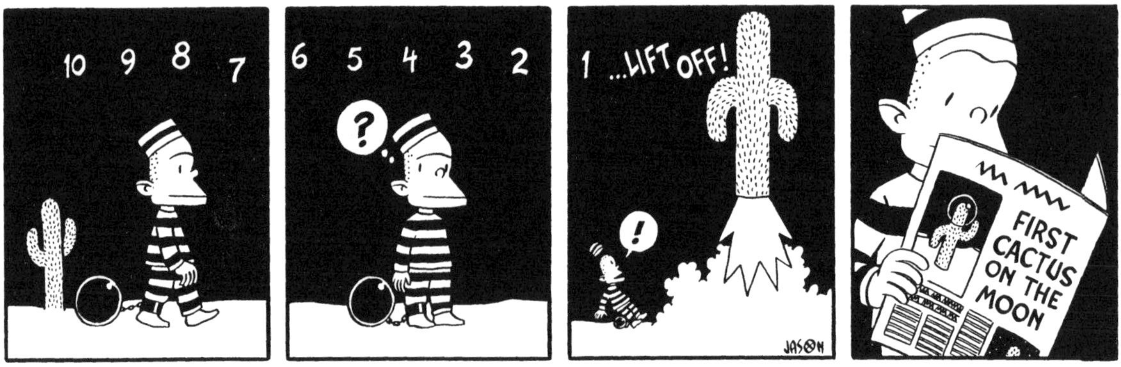
10 9 8 7
6 5 4 3 2
?
1 ...LIFT OFF!
!
FIRST CACTUS ON THE MOON
JASON

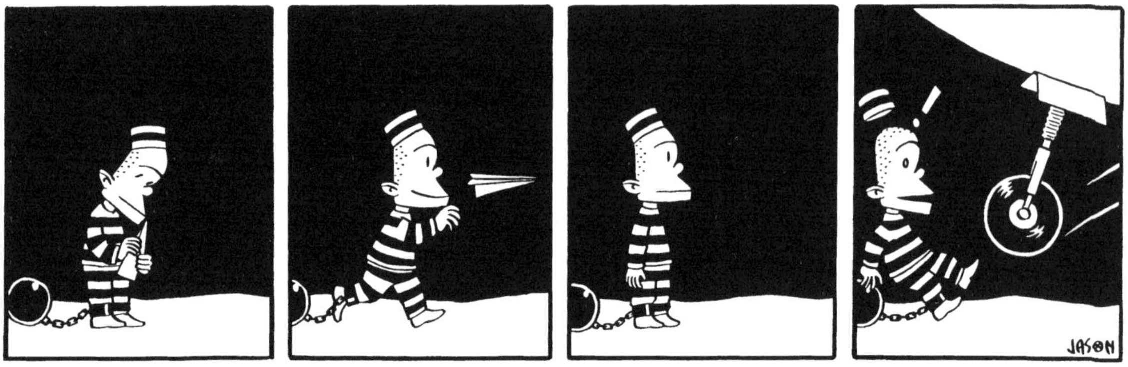
!
JASON

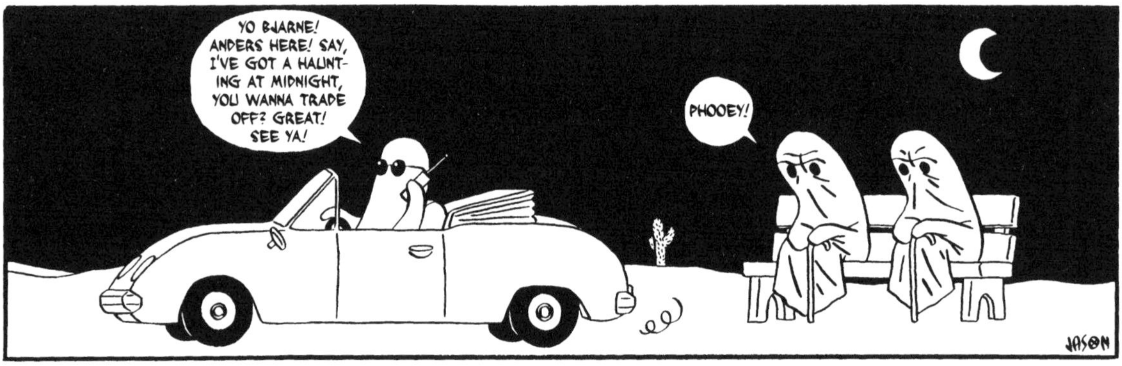
YO BJARNE! ANDERS HERE! SAY, I'VE GOT A HAUNTING AT MIDNIGHT, YOU WANNA TRADE OFF? GREAT! SEE YA!
PHOOEY!
JASON

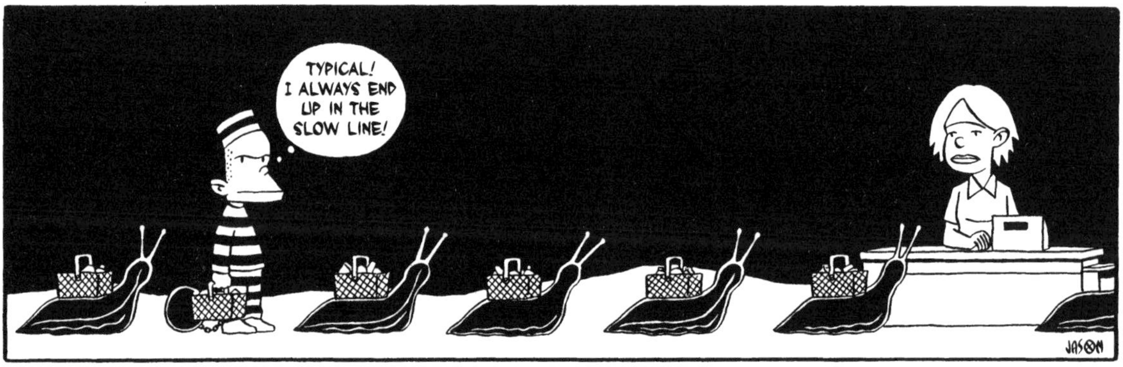
TYPICAL! I ALWAYS END UP IN THE SLOW LINE!
JASON

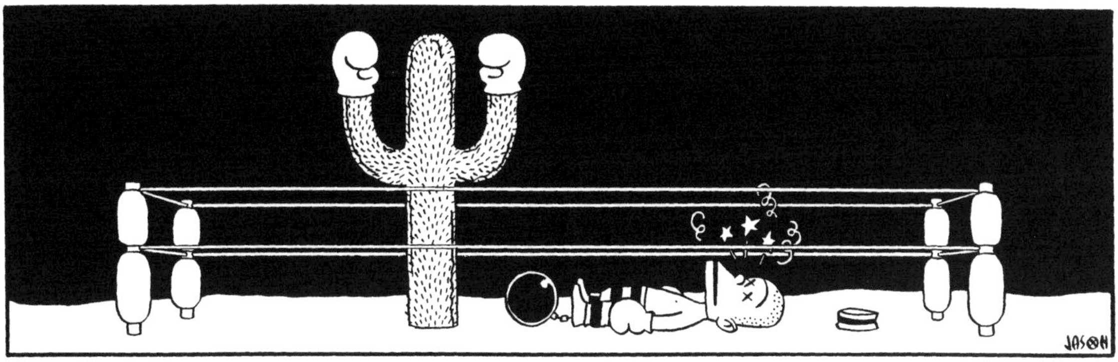
JASON

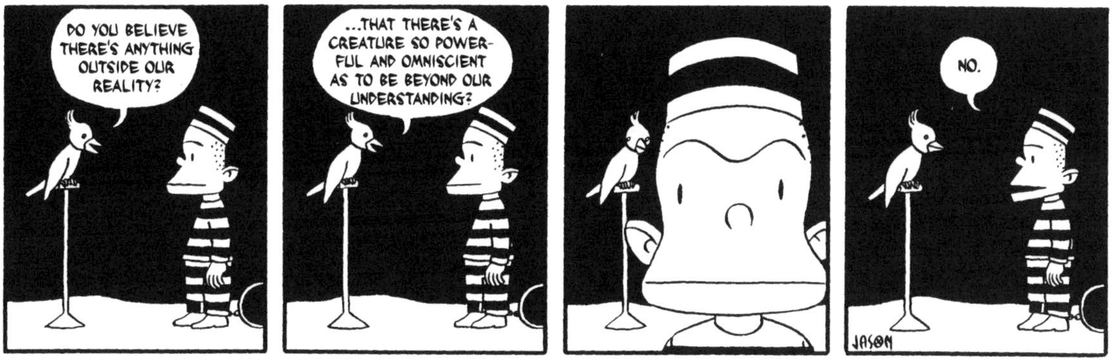
DO YOU BELIEVE THERE'S ANYTHING OUTSIDE OUR REALITY?
...THAT THERE'S A CREATURE SO POWER-FUL AND OMNISCIENT AS TO BE BEYOND OUR UNDERSTANDING?
NO.
JASON

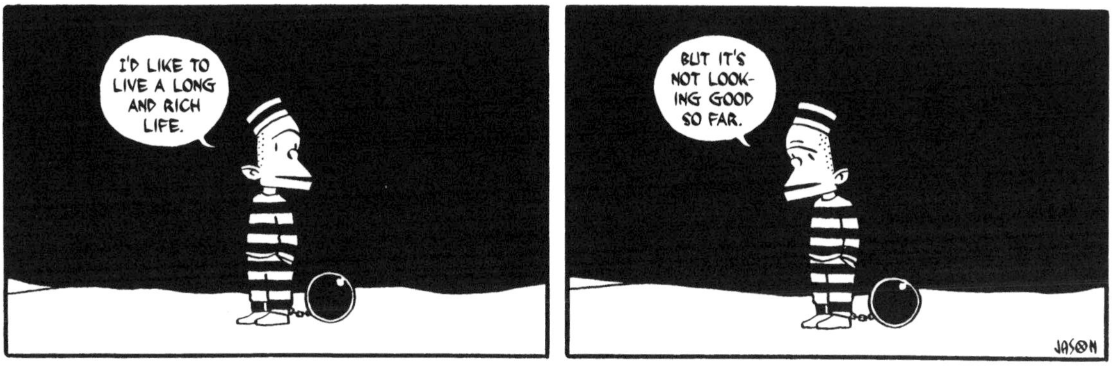
I'D LIKE TO LIVE A LONG AND RICH LIFE.
BUT IT'S NOT LOOK-ING GOOD SO FAR.
JASON

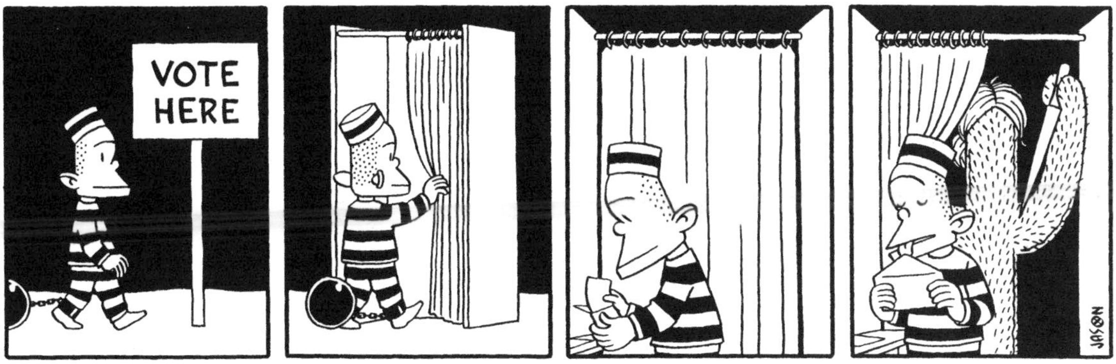
VOTE HERE
JASON

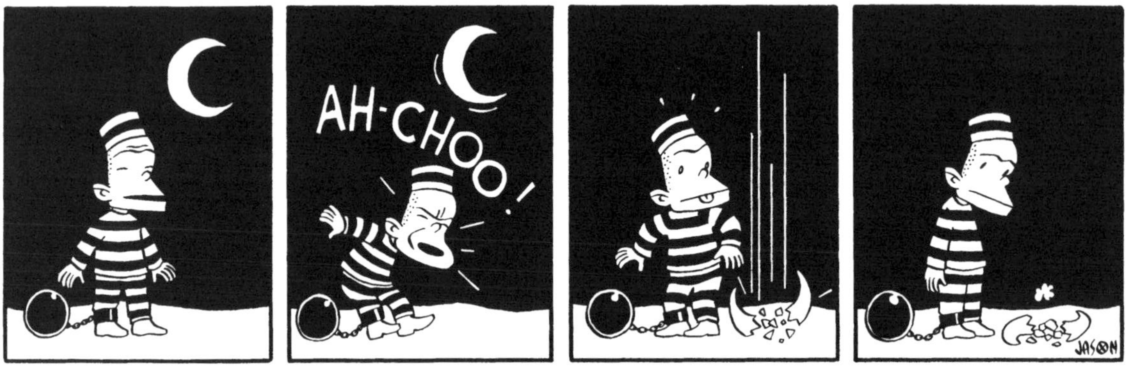
AH-CHOO!
JASON

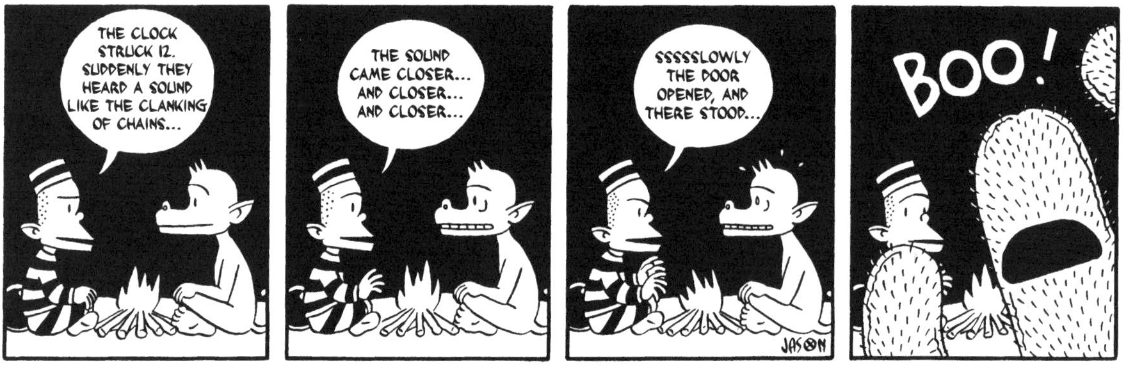
THE CLOCK STRUCK 12. SUDDENLY THEY HEARD A SOUND LIKE THE CLANKING OF CHAINS...
THE SOUND CAME CLOSER... AND CLOSER... AND CLOSER...
SSSSSLOWLY THE DOOR OPENED, AND THERE STOOD...
JASON
BOO!

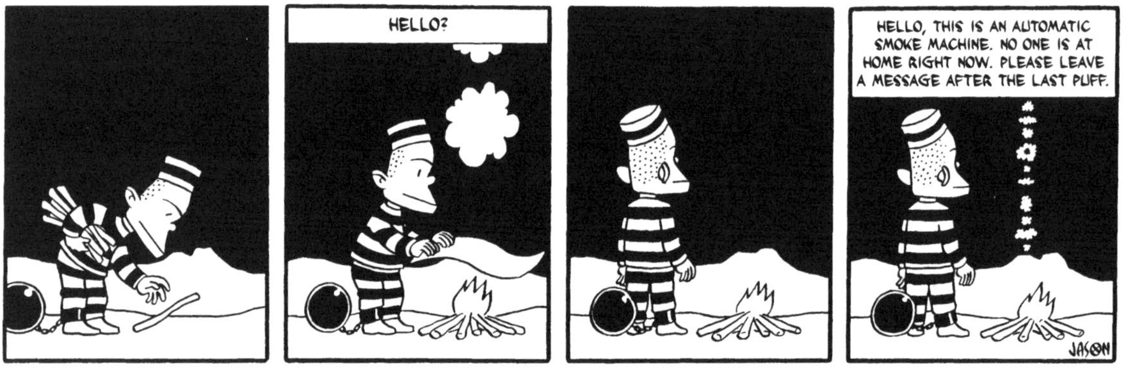
HELLO?
HELLO, THIS IS AN AUTOMATIC SMOKE MACHINE. NO ONE IS AT HOME RIGHT NOW. PLEASE LEAVE A MESSAGE AFTER THE LAST PUFF.
JASON

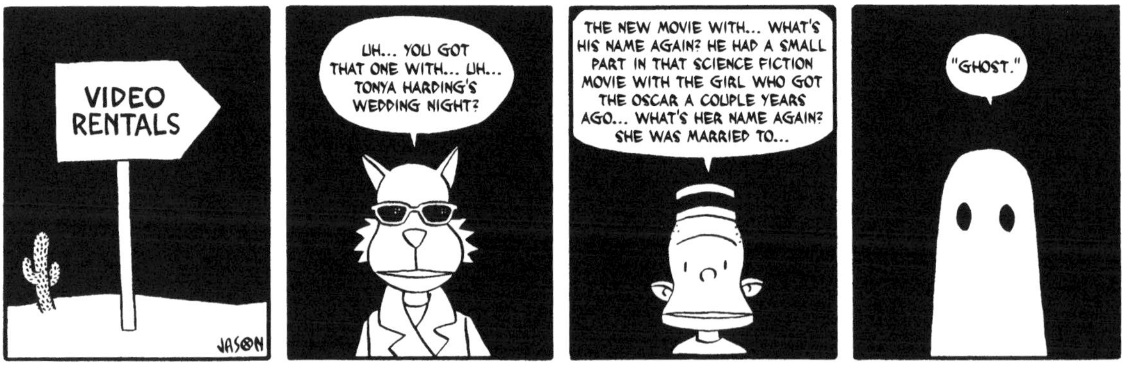
VIDEO RENTALS
JASON
UH... YOU GOT THAT ONE WITH... UH... TONYA HARDING'S WEDDING NIGHT?
THE NEW MOVIE WITH... WHAT'S HIS NAME AGAIN? HE HAD A SMALL PART IN THAT SCIENCE FICTION MOVIE WITH THE GIRL WHO GOT THE OSCAR A COUPLE YEARS AGO... WHAT'S HER NAME AGAIN? SHE WAS MARRIED TO...
"GHOST."

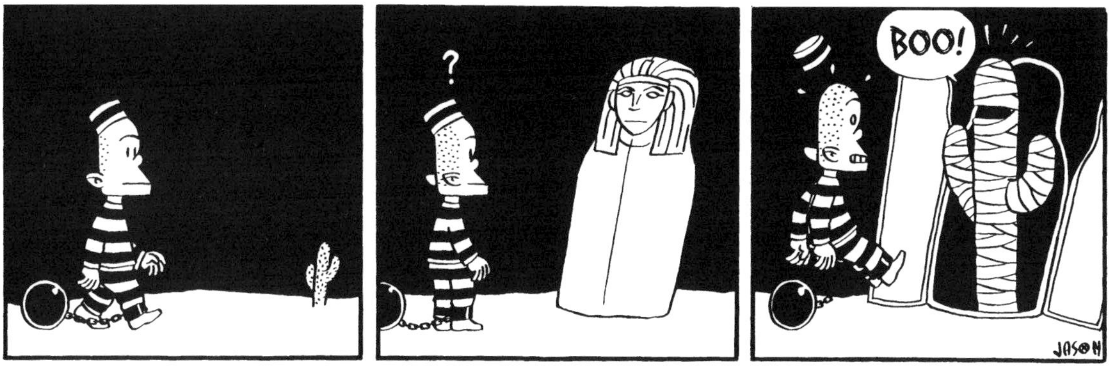
?
BOO!
JASON

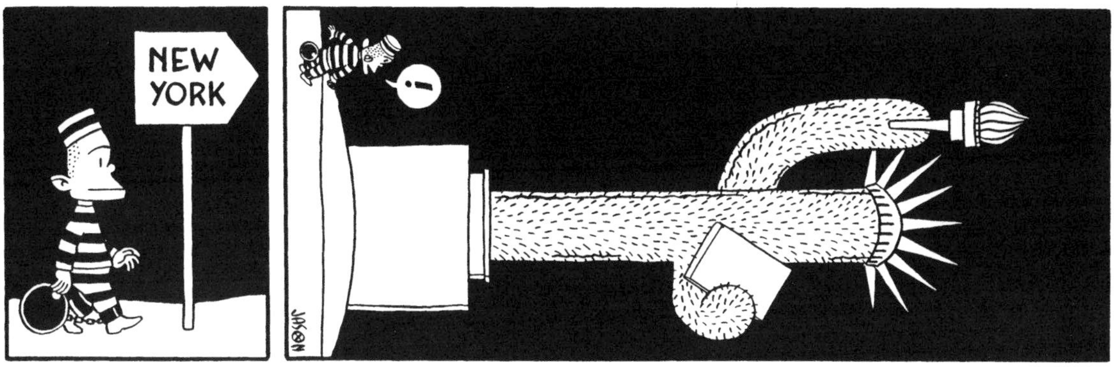
NEW YORK
JASON

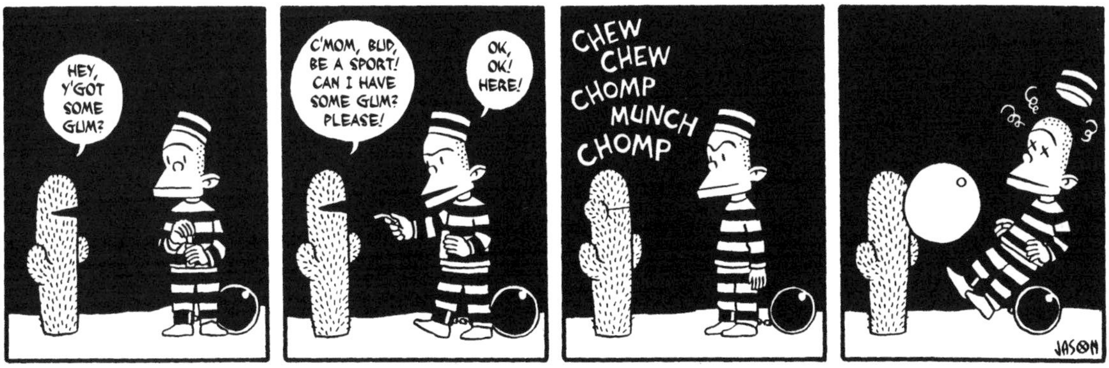
HEY, Y'GOT SOME GUM?
C'MOM, BUD, BE A SPORT! CAN I HAVE SOME GUM? PLEASE!
OK, OK! HERE!
CHEW CHEW CHOMP MUNCH CHOMP
JASON

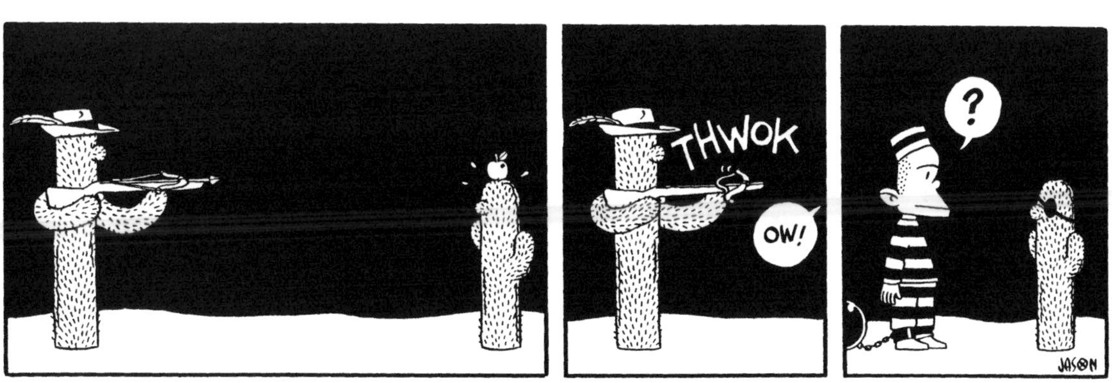
THWOK
OW!
?
JASON

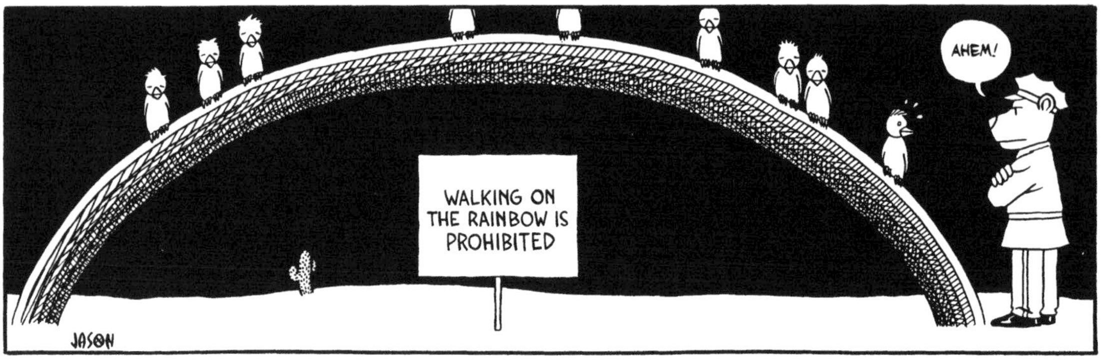
WALKING ON
THE RAINBOW IS
PROHIBITED
AHEM!
JASON

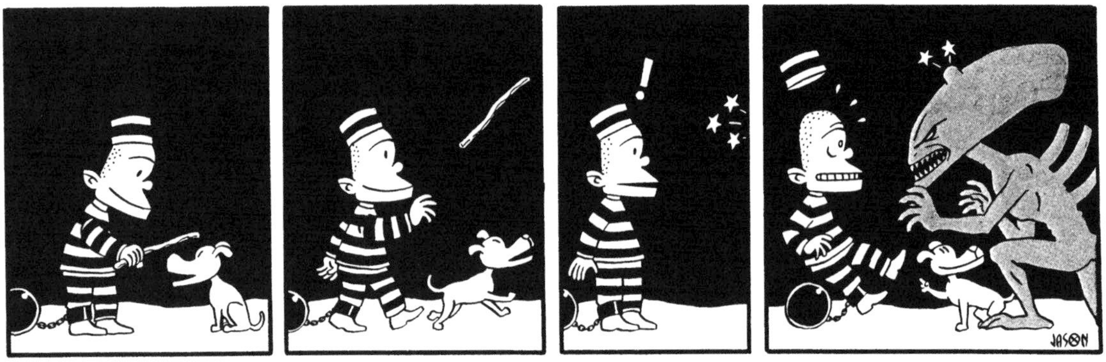
JASON

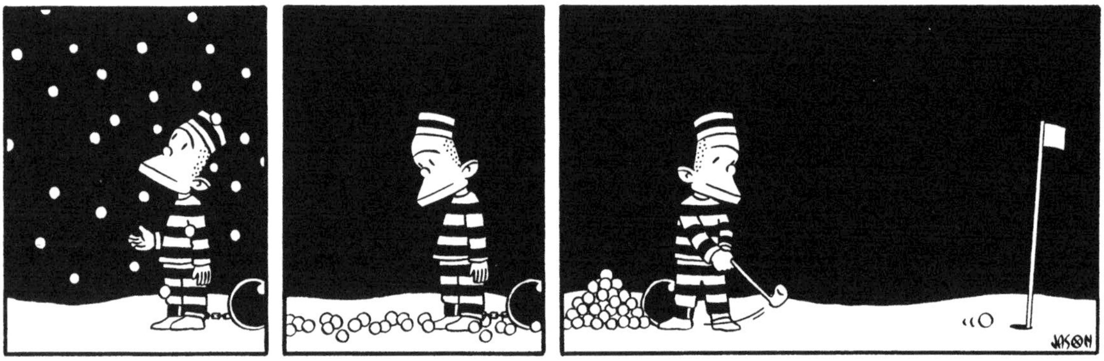
JASON

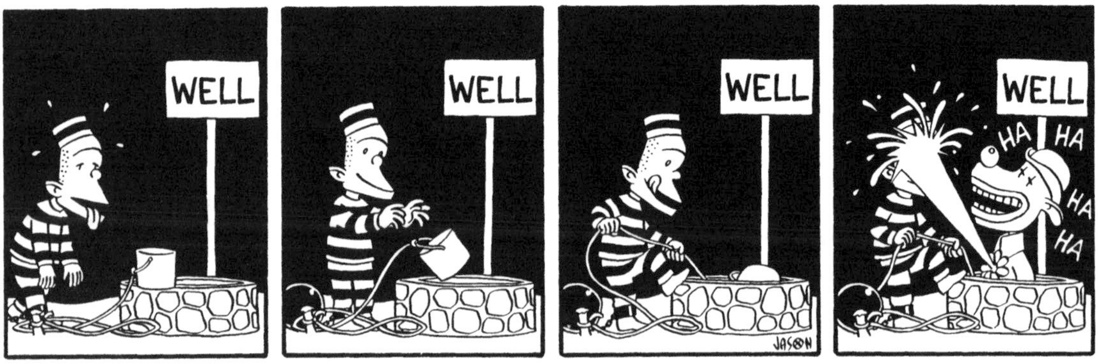
WELL
WELL
WELL
JASON
WELL
HA
HA
HA
HA

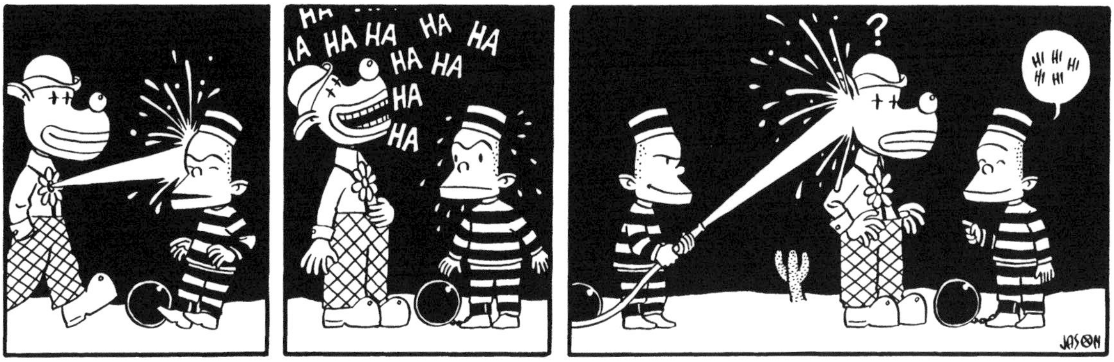
HA HA HA HA HA HA HA HA HA HA
?
HI HI HI HI HI
JASON

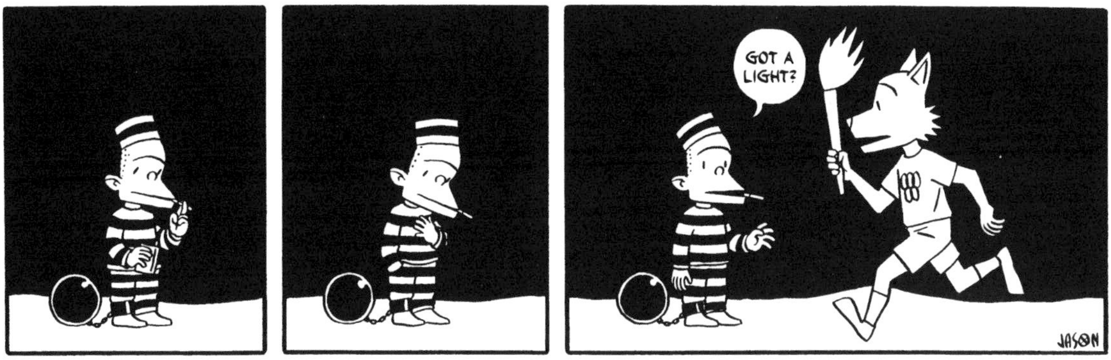
GOT A LIGHT?
JASON

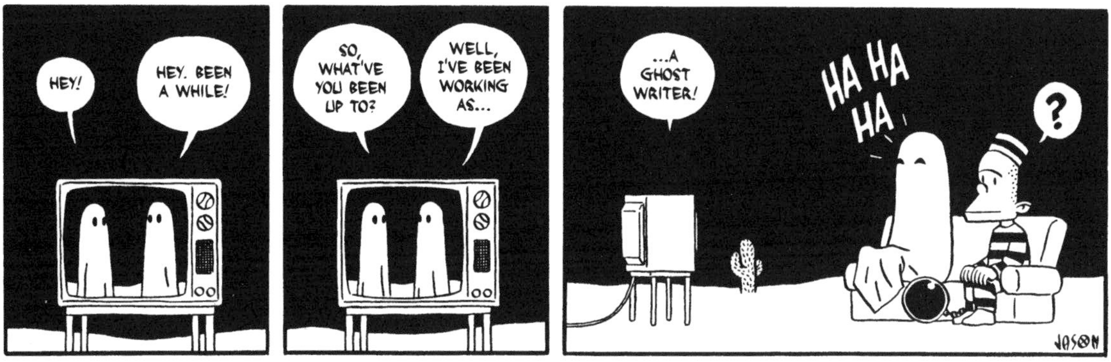
HEY!
HEY. BEEN A WHILE!
SO, WHAT'VE YOU BEEN UP TO?
WELL, I'VE BEEN WORKING AS...
...A GHOST WRITER!
HA HA HA
?
JASON

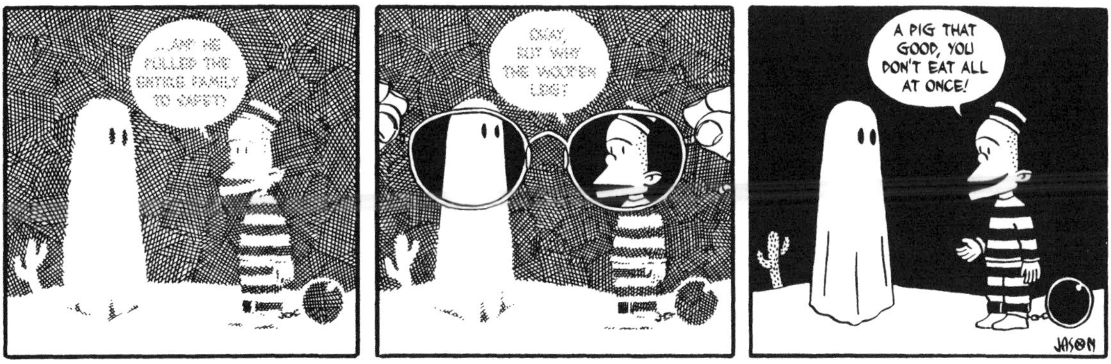
A PIG THAT GOOD, YOU DON'T EAT ALL AT ONCE!
JASON

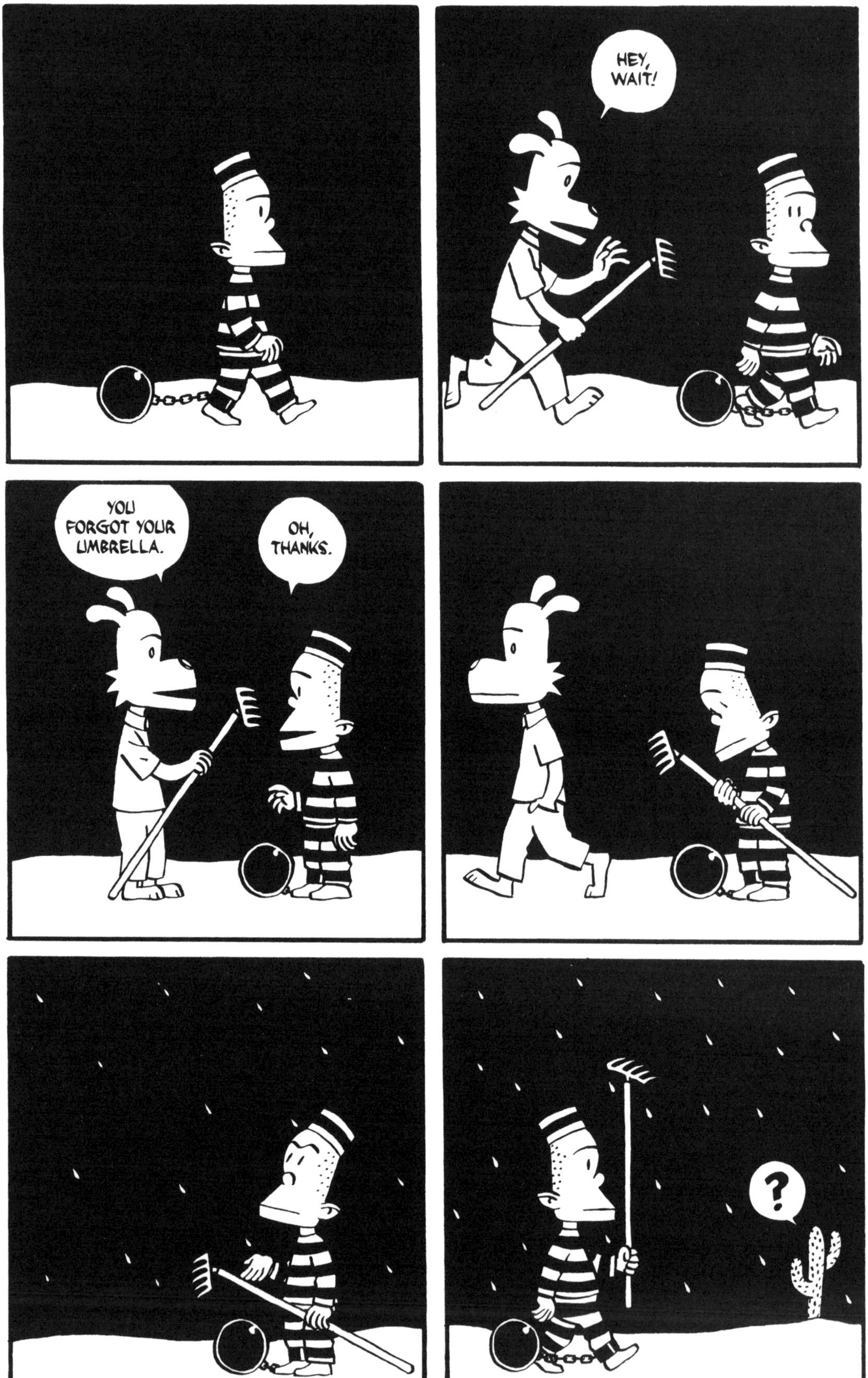
HEY, WAIT!
YOU FORGOT YOUR UMBRELLA.
OH, THANKS.
?
JASON

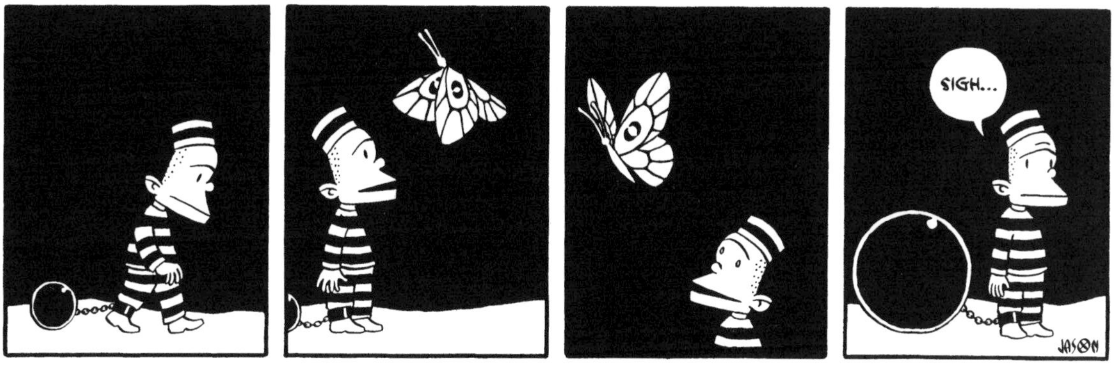
SIGH...

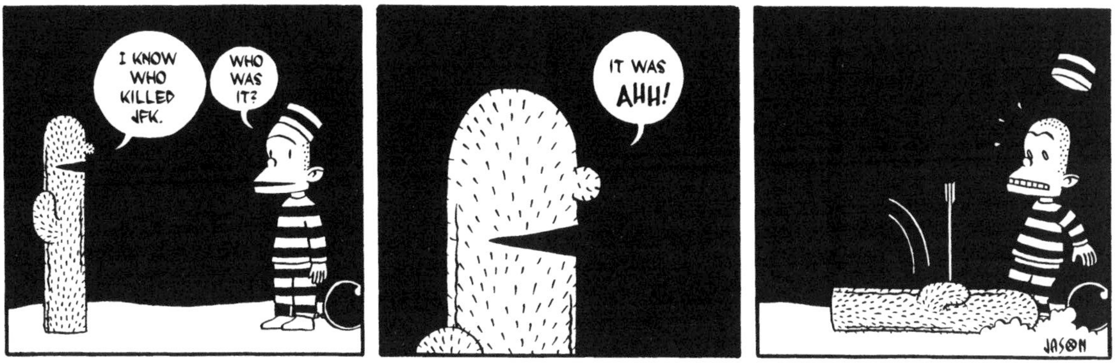
I KNOW WHO KILLED JFK.
WHO WAS IT?
IT WAS AHH!

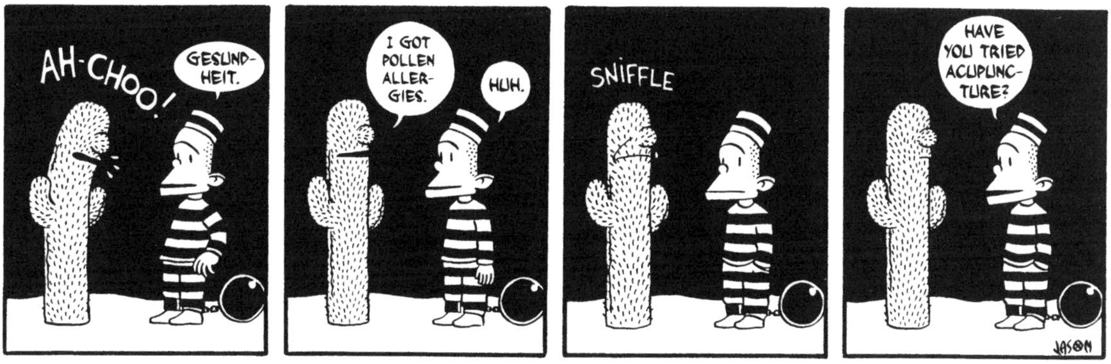
AH-CHOO!
GESUND-HEIT.
I GOT POLLEN ALLER-GIES.
HUH.
SNIFFLE
HAVE YOU TRIED ACUPUNC-TURE?

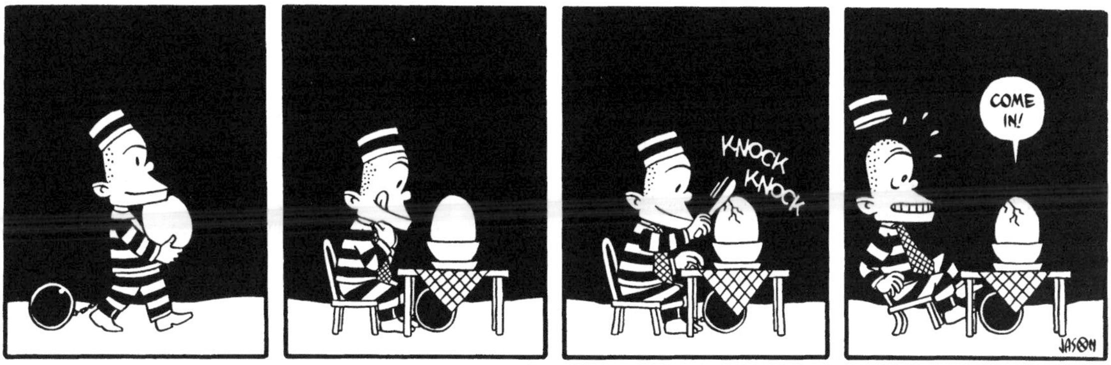
KNOCK KNOCK
COME IN!

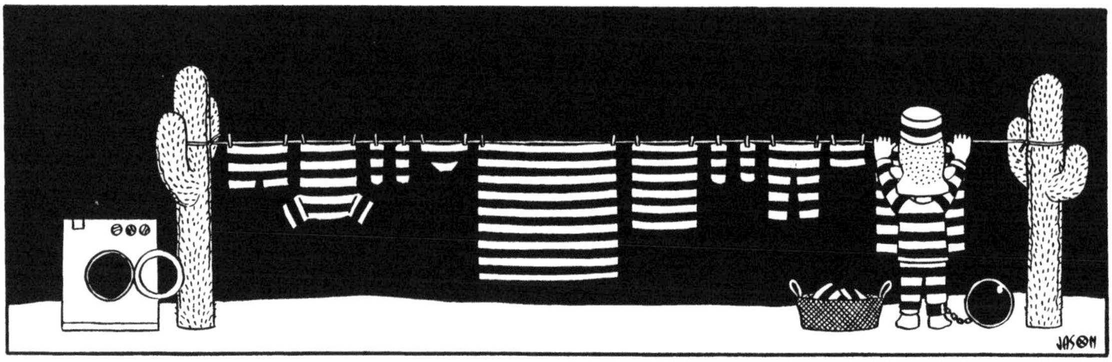
JASON

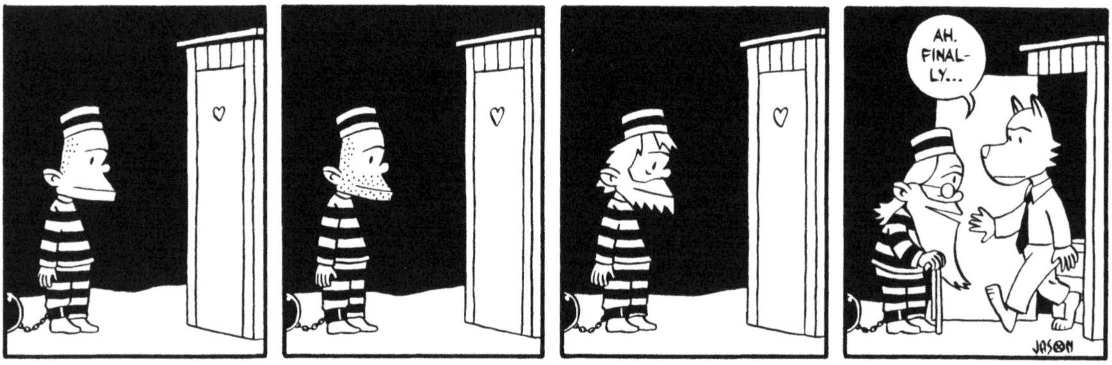
AH. FINAL-LY...
JASON

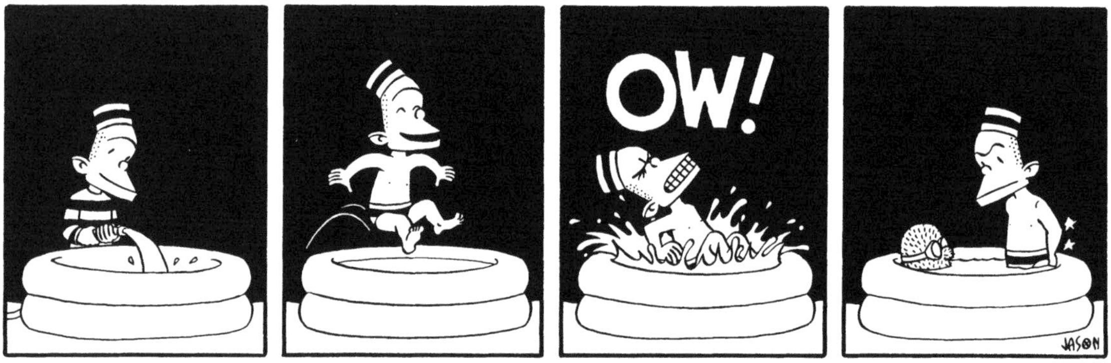
OW!
JASON

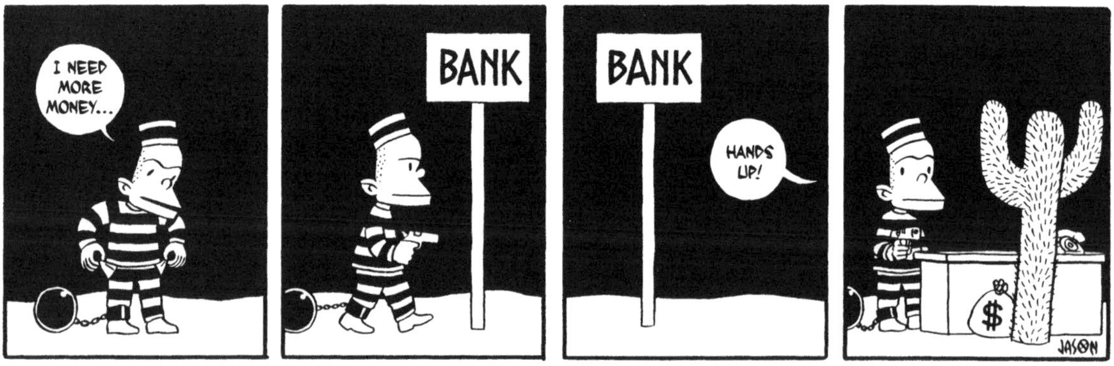
I NEED MORE MONEY...
BANK
BANK
HANDS UP!
$
JASON

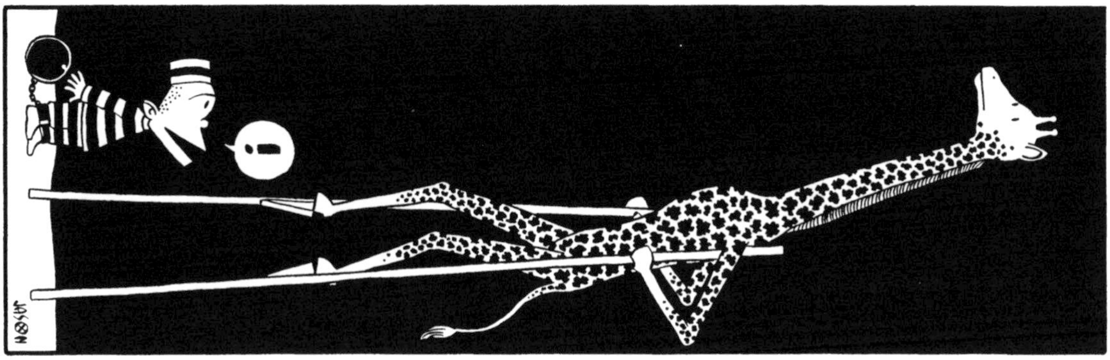
JASON

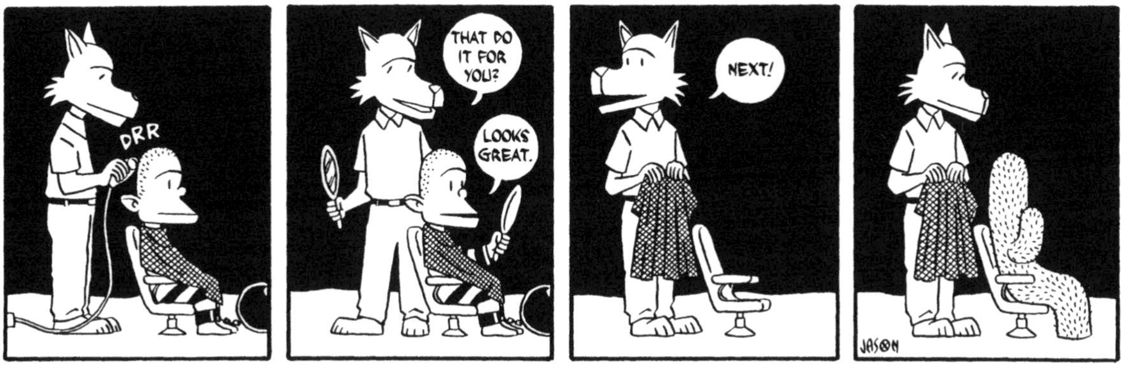
DRR
THAT DO IT FOR YOU?
LOOKS GREAT.
NEXT!
JASON

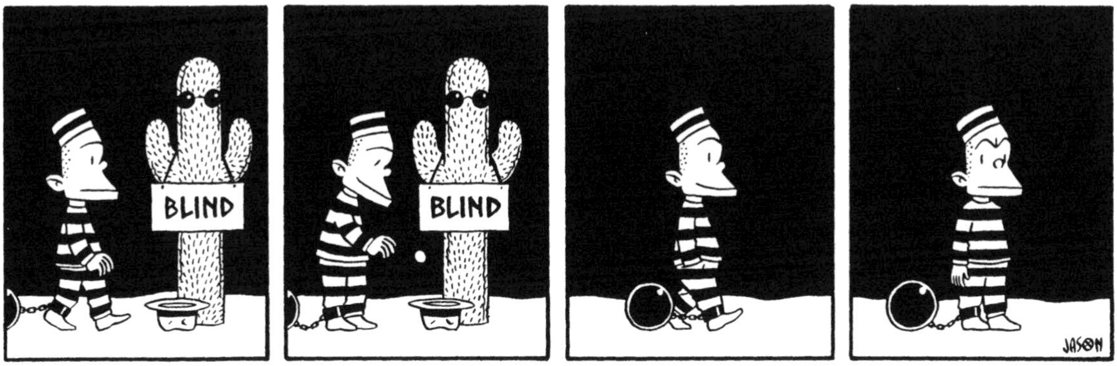
BLIND
BLIND
JASON

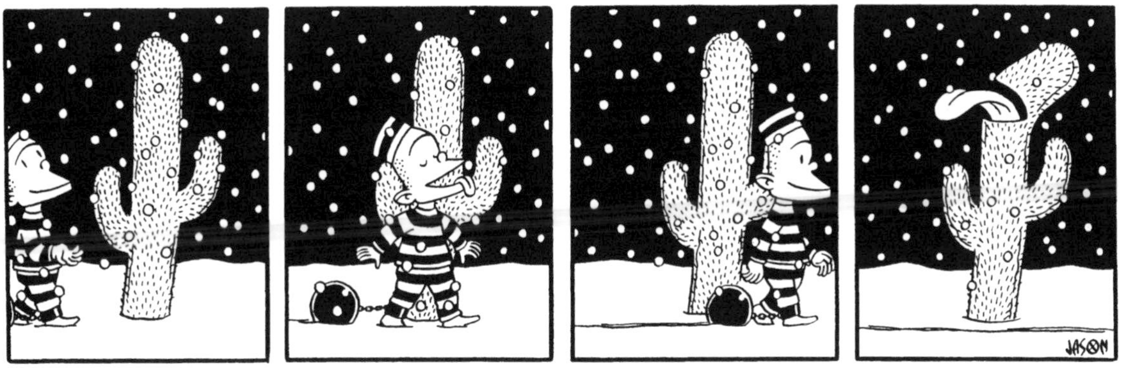
JASON

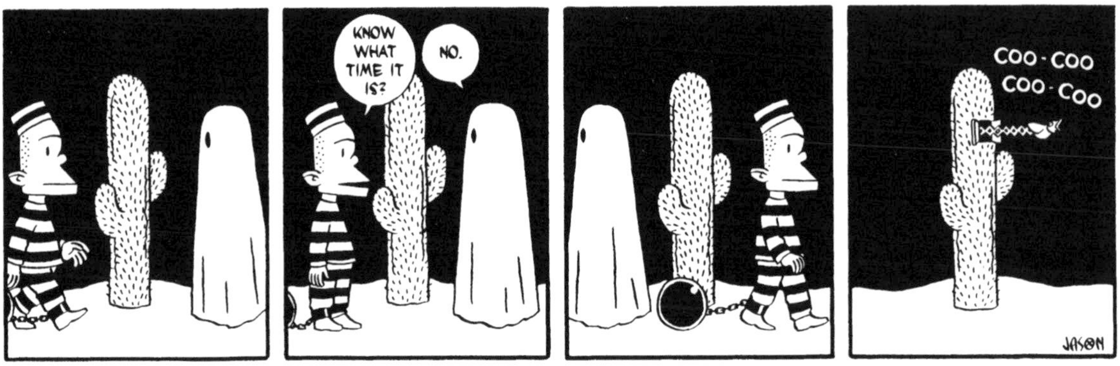
KNOW WHAT TIME IT IS?
NO.
COO-COO
COO-COO
JASON

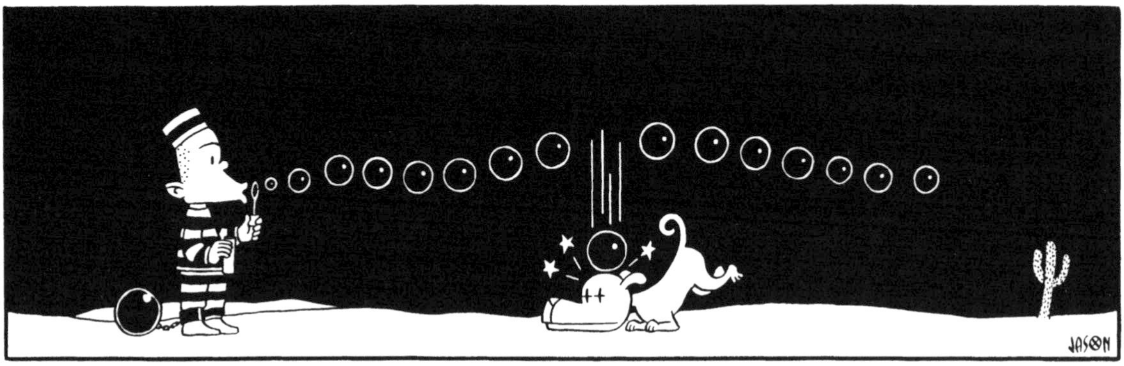
JASON

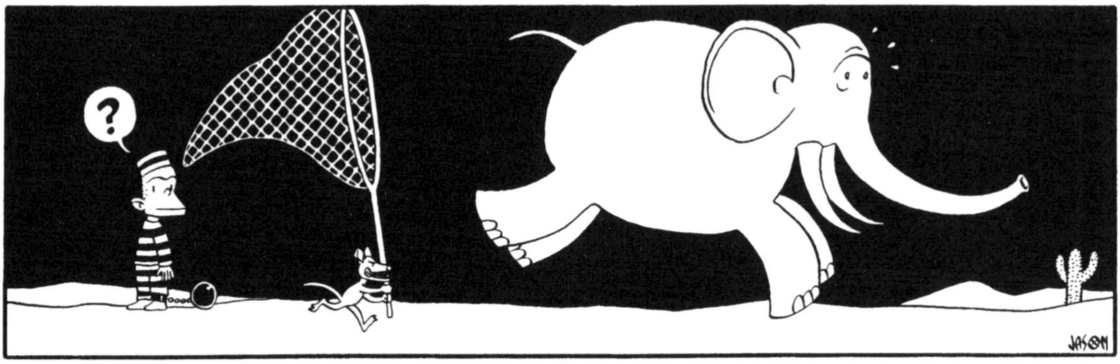
?
JASON

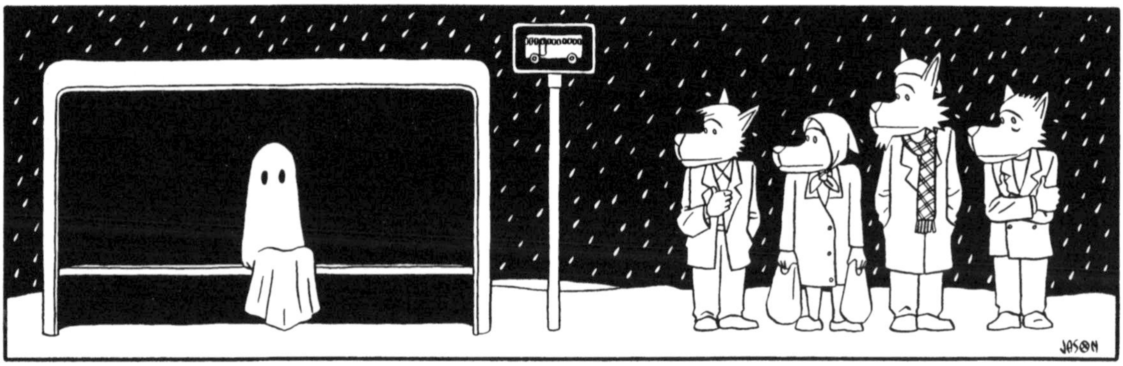
JASON

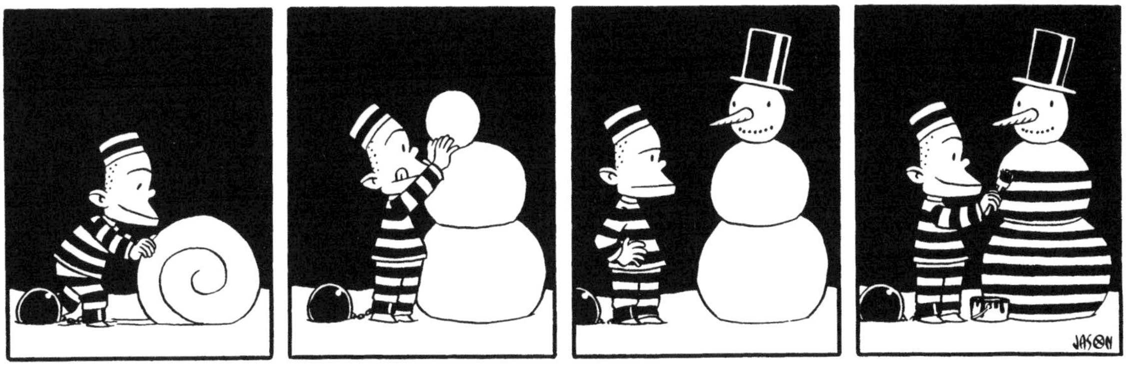
JASON

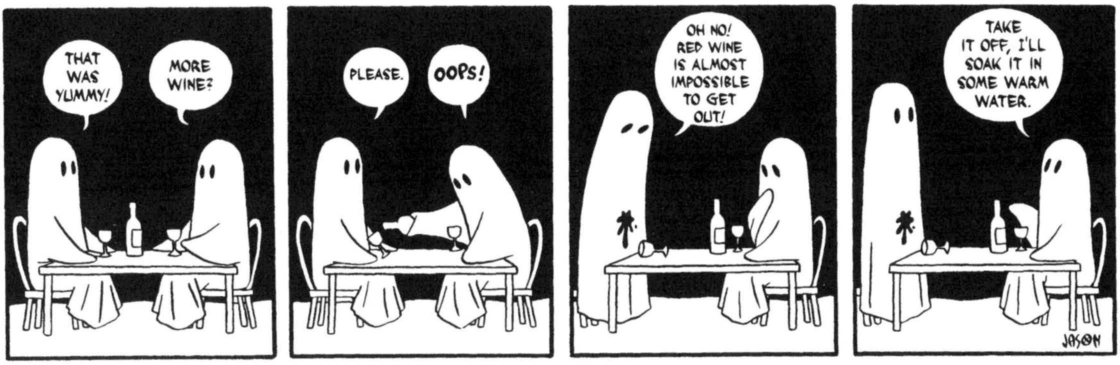
THAT WAS YUMMY!
MORE WINE?
PLEASE.
OOPS!
OH NO! RED WINE IS ALMOST IMPOSSIBLE TO GET OUT!
TAKE IT OFF, I'LL SOAK IT IN SOME WARM WATER.
JASON

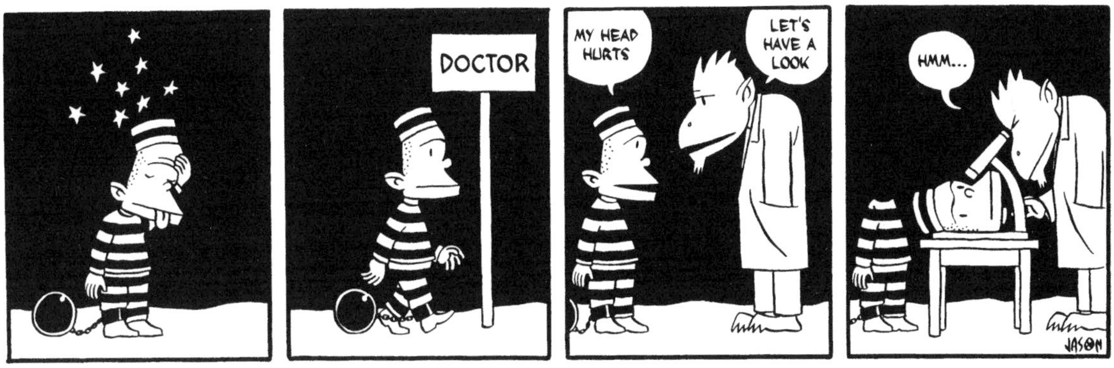
DOCTOR
MY HEAD HURTS
LET'S HAVE A LOOK
HMM...
JASON

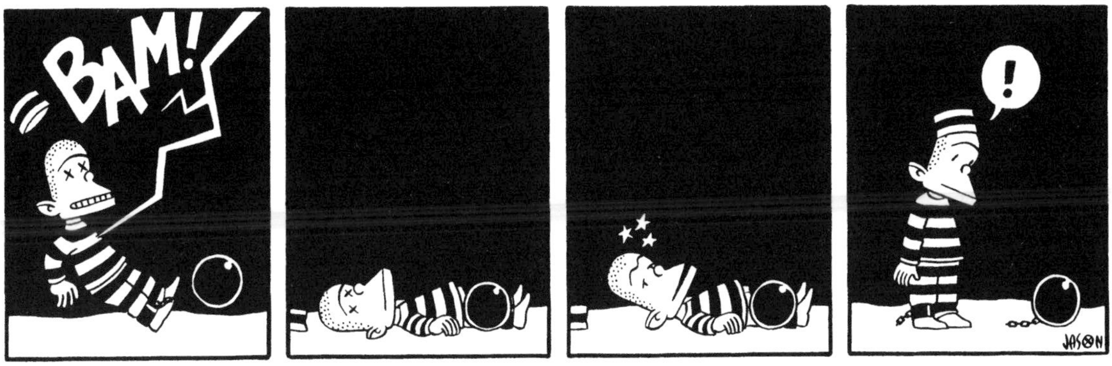
BAM!
!
JASON

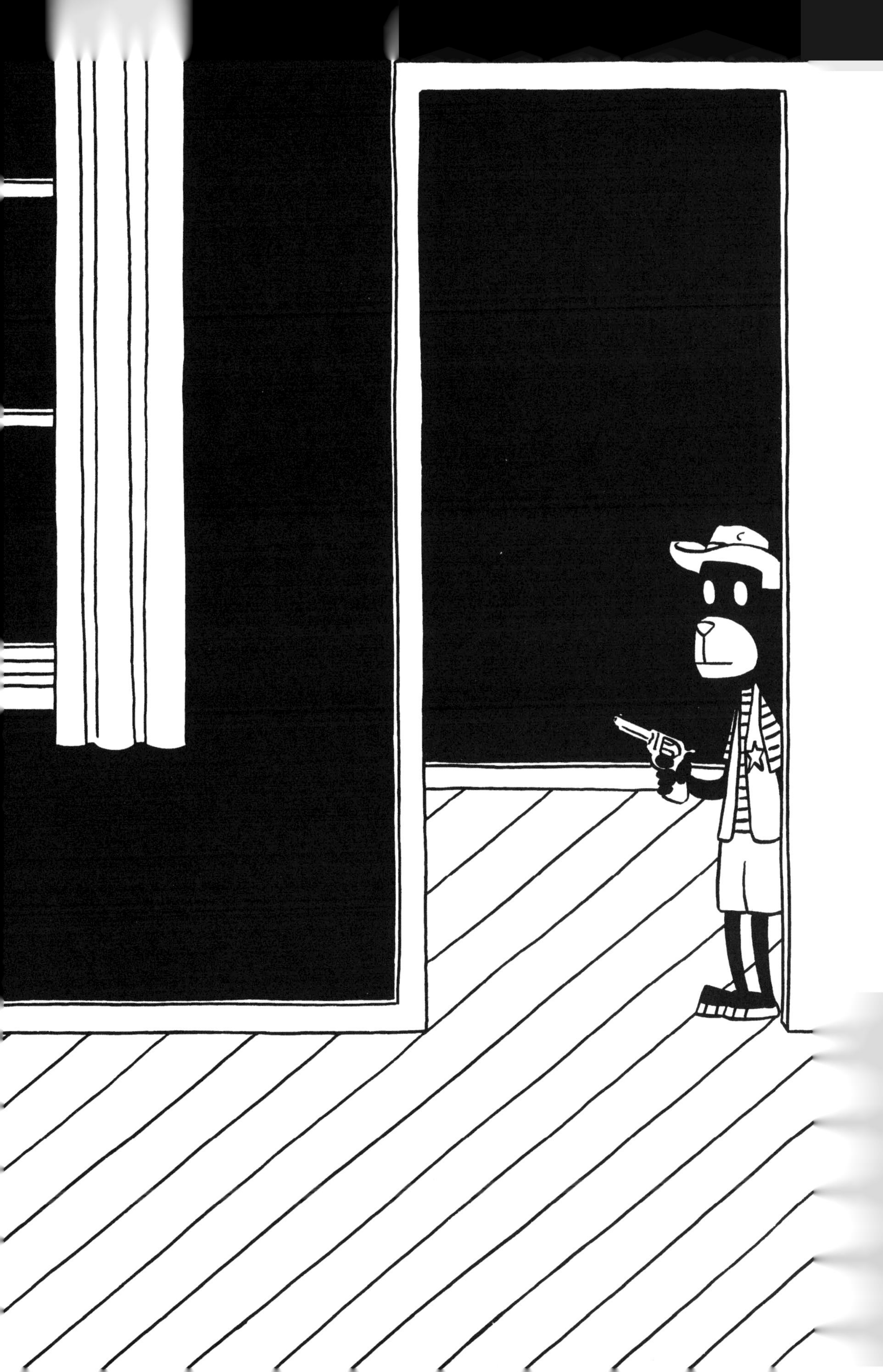

FALLING

BY JASON

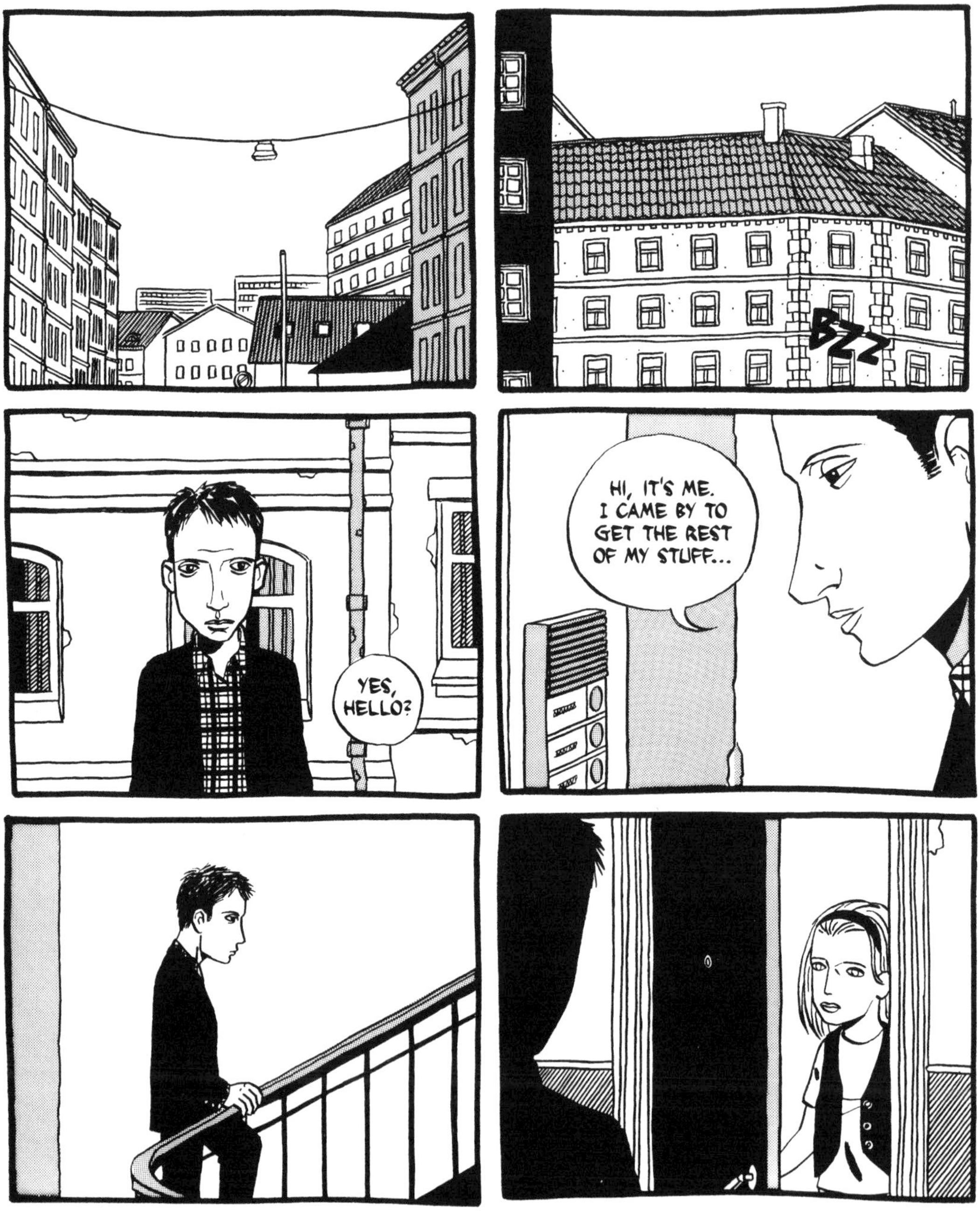
BZZ
YES, HELLO?
HI, IT'S ME. I CAME BY TO GET THE REST OF MY STUFF...

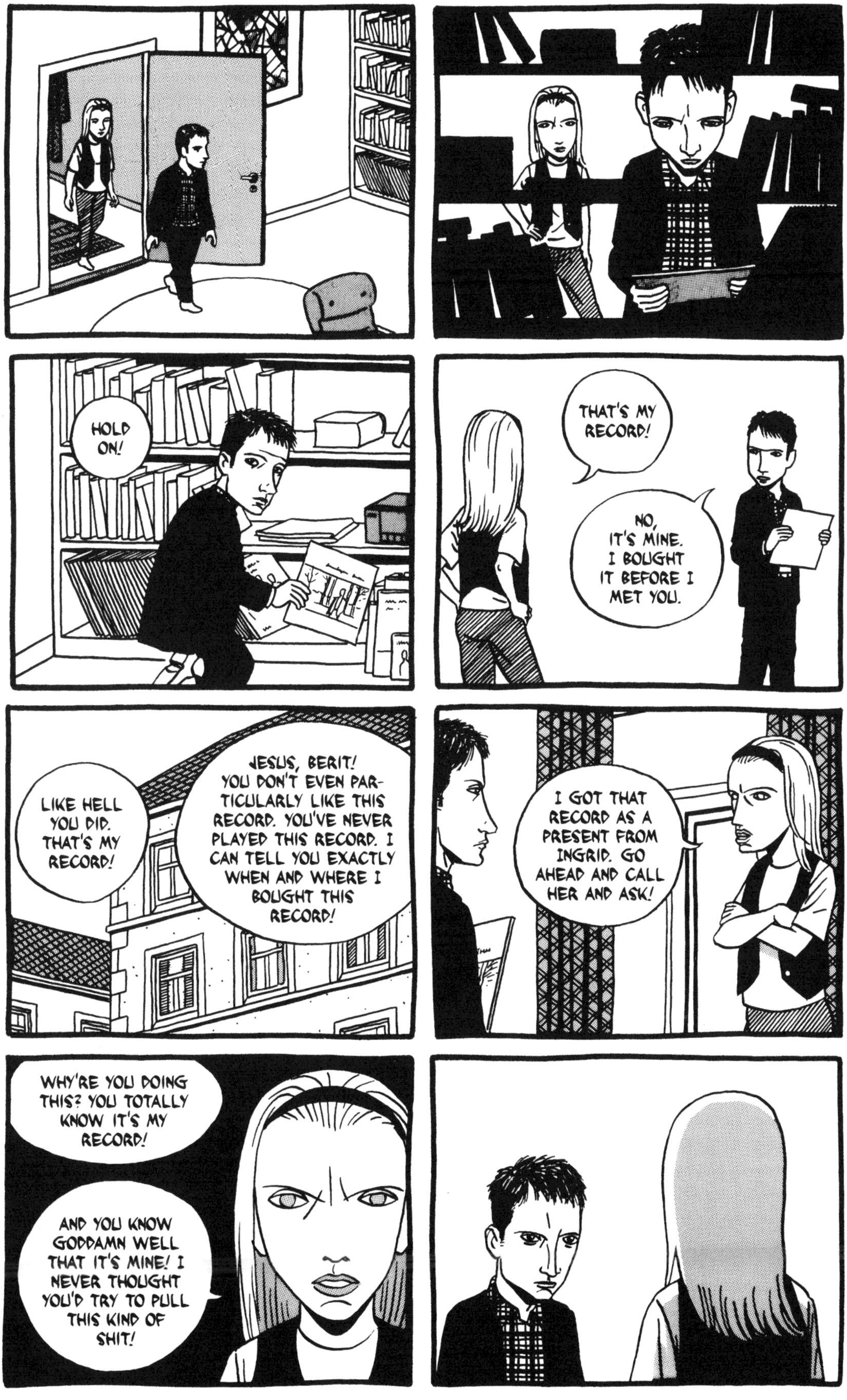
HOLD ON!
THAT'S MY RECORD!
NO, IT'S MINE. I BOUGHT IT BEFORE I MET YOU.
LIKE HELL YOU DID. THAT'S MY RECORD!
JESUS, BERIT! YOU DON'T EVEN PARTICULARLY LIKE THIS RECORD. YOU'VE NEVER PLAYED THIS RECORD. I CAN TELL YOU EXACTLY WHEN AND WHERE I BOUGHT THIS RECORD!
I GOT THAT RECORD AS A PRESENT FROM INGRID. GO AHEAD AND CALL HER AND ASK!
WHY'RE YOU DOING THIS? YOU TOTALLY KNOW IT'S MY RECORD!
AND YOU KNOW GODDAMN WELL THAT IT'S MINE! I NEVER THOUGHT YOU'D TRY TO PULL THIS KIND OF SHIT!

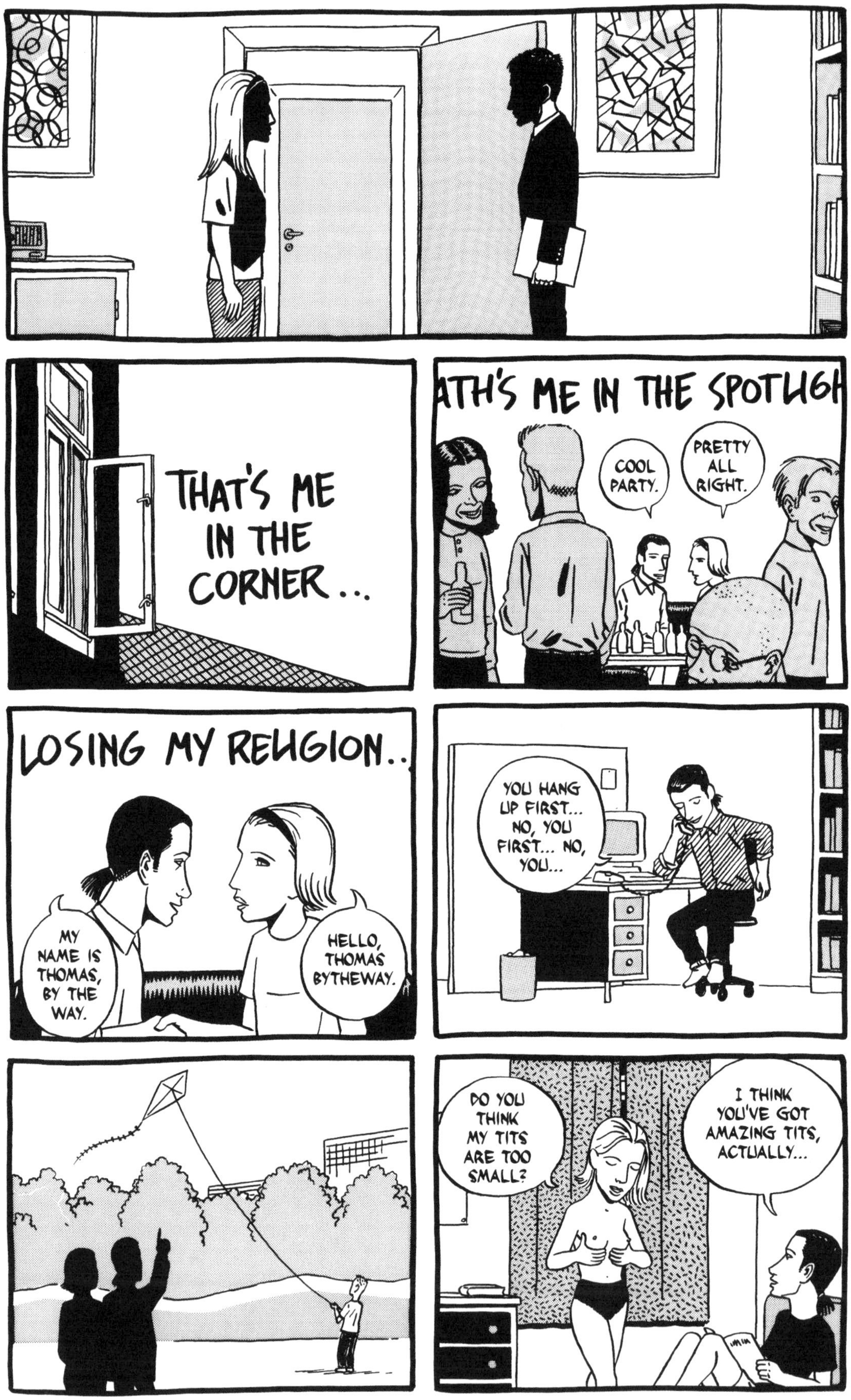
THAT'S ME IN THE CORNER...
ATH'S ME IN THE SPOTLIGH
COOL PARTY.
PRETTY ALL RIGHT.
LOSING MY RELIGION..
MY NAME IS THOMAS, BY THE WAY.
HELLO, THOMAS BYTHEWAY.
YOU HANG UP FIRST... NO, YOU FIRST... NO, YOU...
DO YOU THINK MY TITS ARE TOO SMALL?
I THINK YOU'VE GOT AMAZING TITS, ACTUALLY...

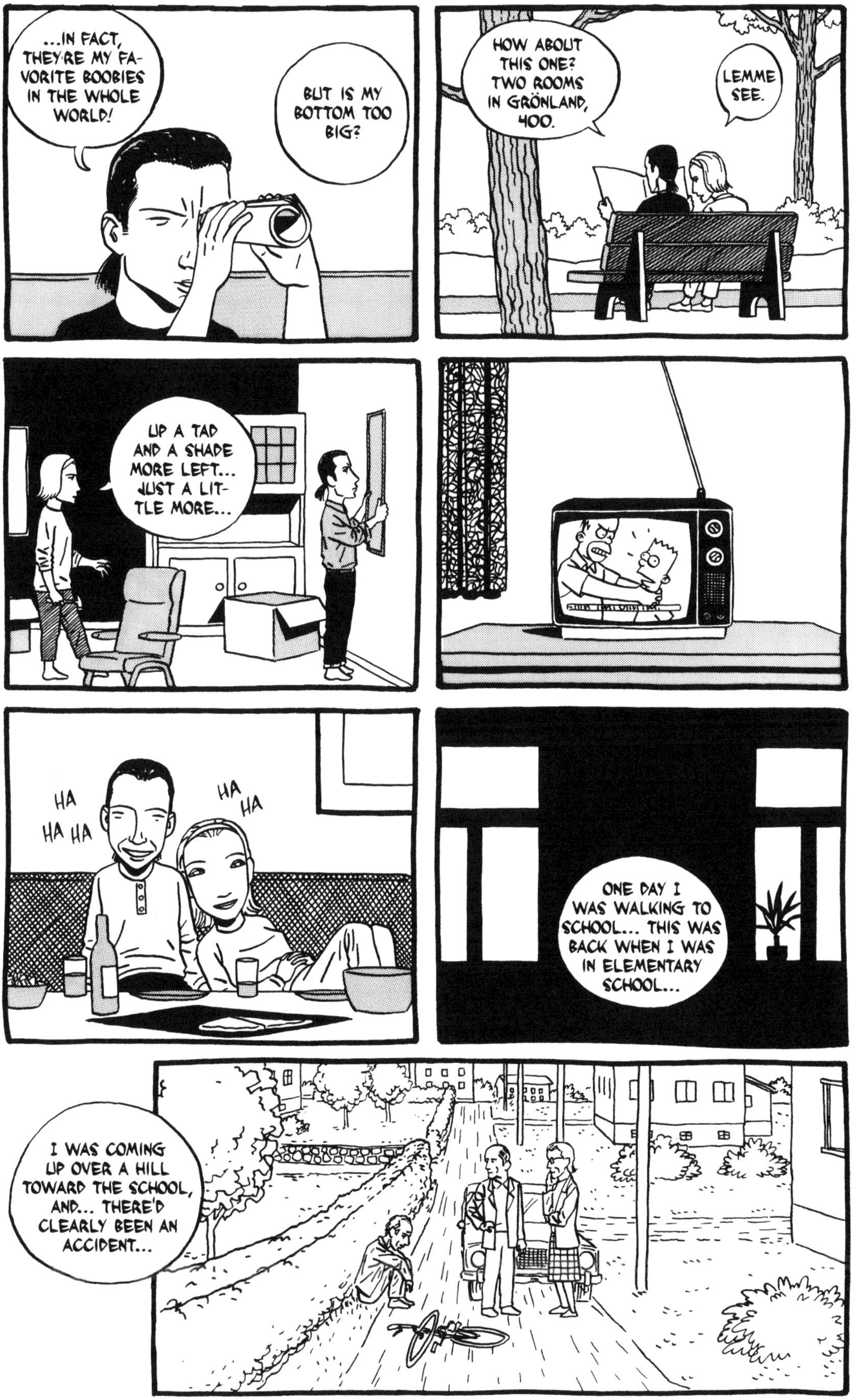
...IN FACT, THEY'RE MY FAVORITE BOOBIES IN THE WHOLE WORLD!
BUT IS MY BOTTOM TOO BIG?
HOW ABOUT THIS ONE? TWO ROOMS IN GRÖNLAND, 400.
LEMME SEE.
UP A TAD AND A SHADE MORE LEFT... JUST A LITTLE MORE...
HA HA HA
HA HA
ONE DAY I WAS WALKING TO SCHOOL... THIS WAS BACK WHEN I WAS IN ELEMENTARY SCHOOL...
I WAS COMING UP OVER A HILL TOWARD THE SCHOOL, AND... THERE'D CLEARLY BEEN AN ACCIDENT...

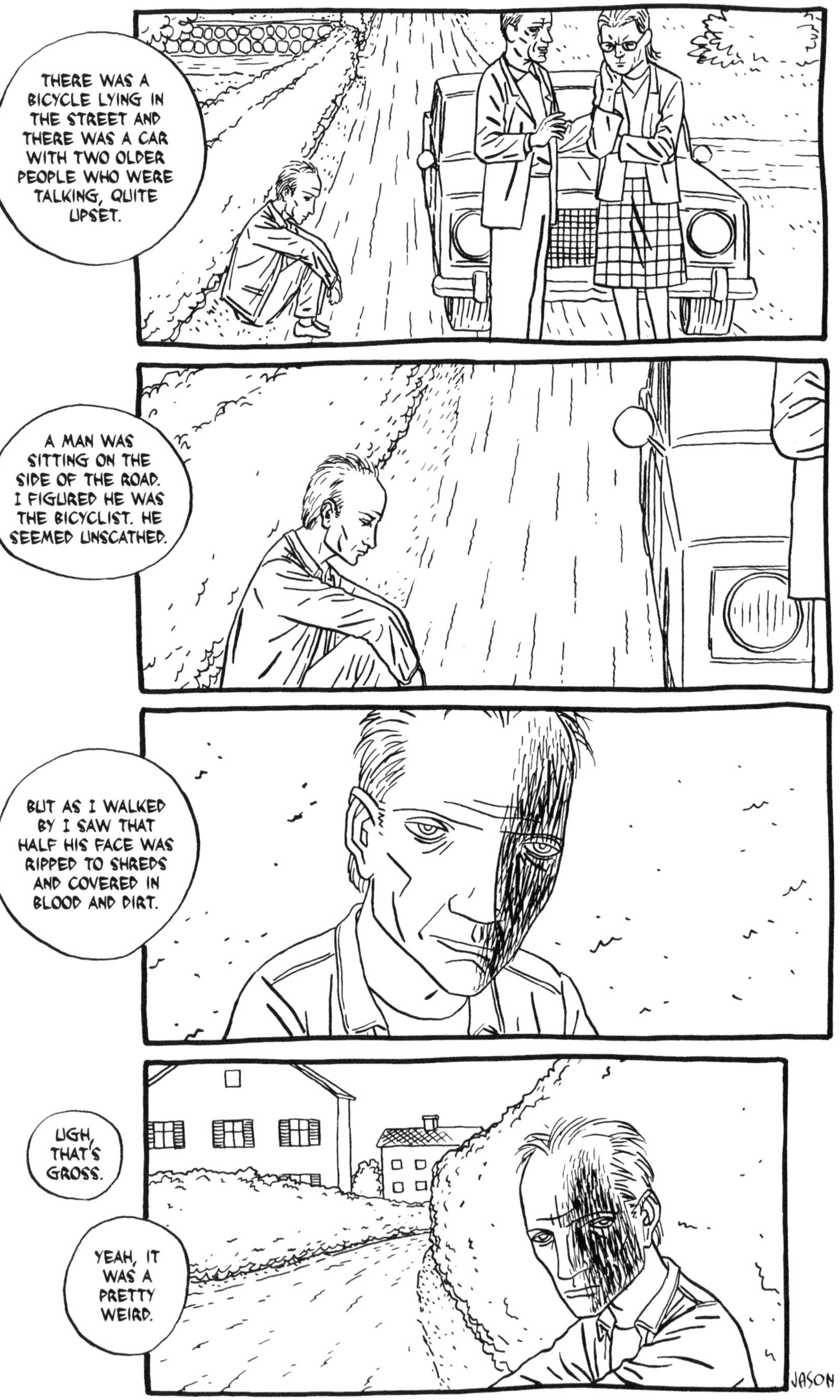
THERE WAS A BICYCLE LYING IN THE STREET AND THERE WAS A CAR WITH TWO OLDER PEOPLE WHO WERE TALKING, QUITE UPSET.
A MAN WAS SITTING ON THE SIDE OF THE ROAD. I FIGURED HE WAS THE BICYCLIST. HE SEEMED UNSCATHED.
BUT AS I WALKED BY I SAW THAT HALF HIS FACE WAS RIPPED TO SHREDS AND COVERED IN BLOOD AND DIRT.
UGH, THAT'S GROSS.
YEAH, IT WAS A PRETTY WEIRD.
JASON

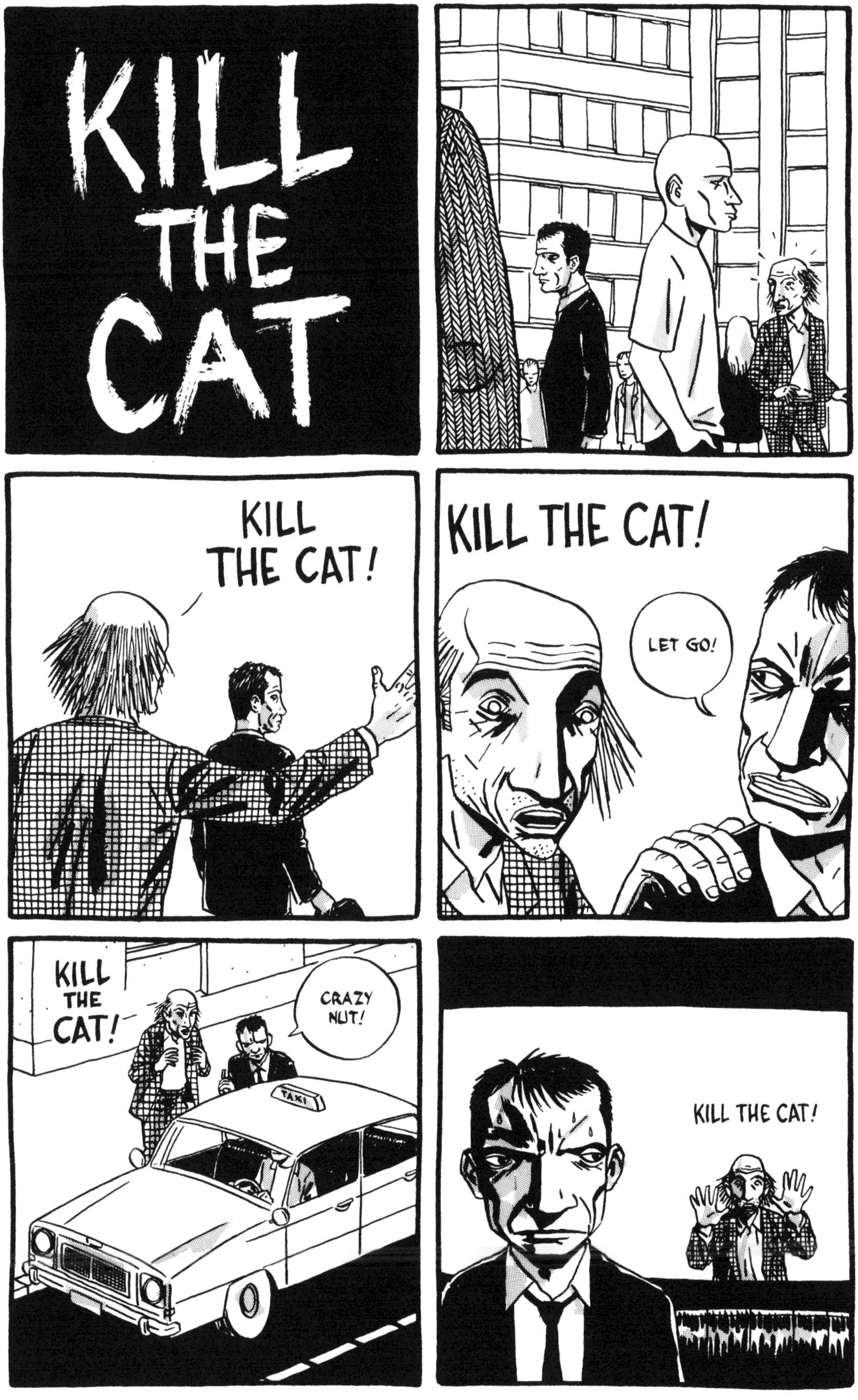
KILL THE CAT
KILL THE CAT!
KILL THE CAT!
LET GO!
KILL THE CAT!
CRAZY NUT!
TAXI
KILL THE CAT!

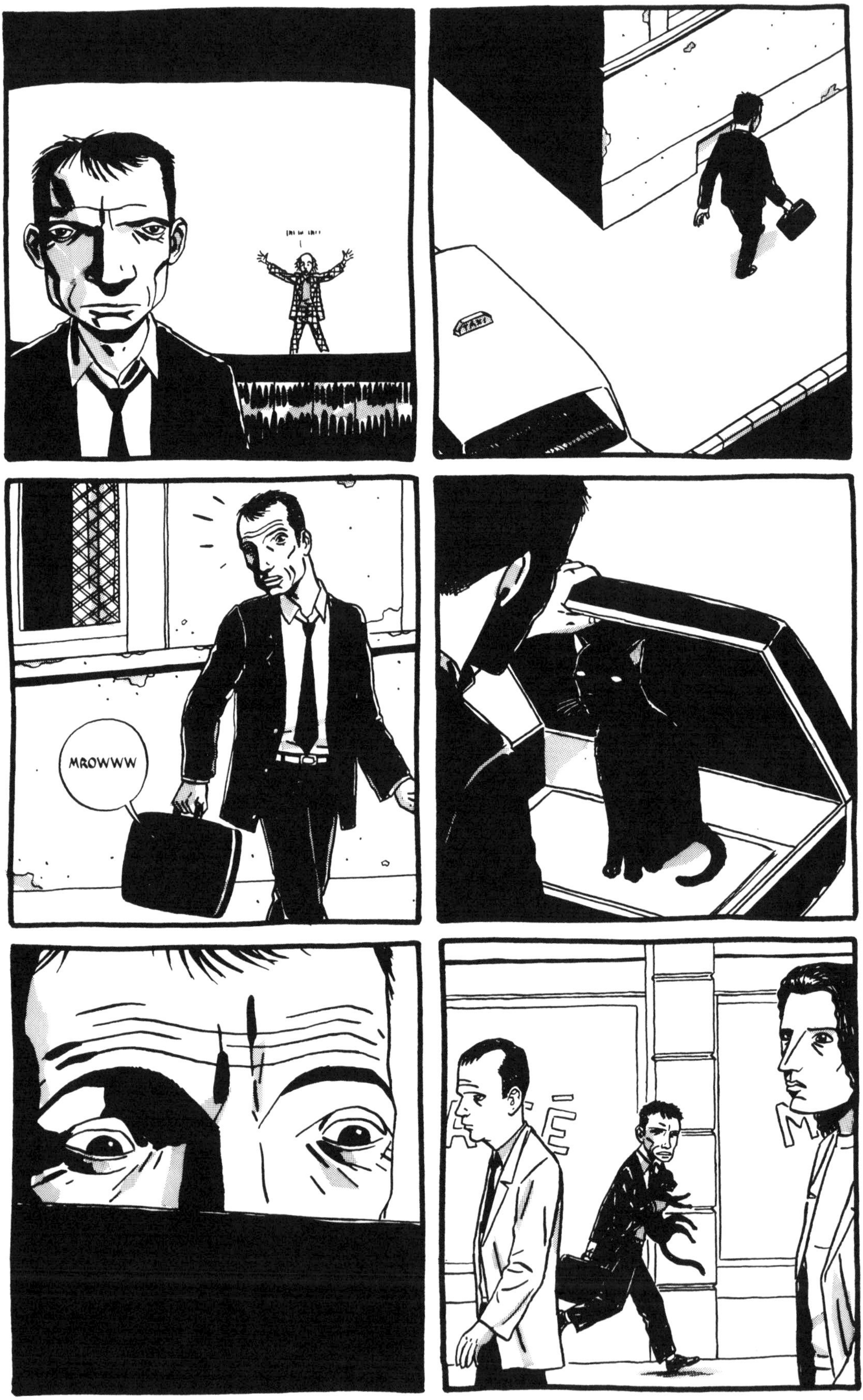
MROWWW

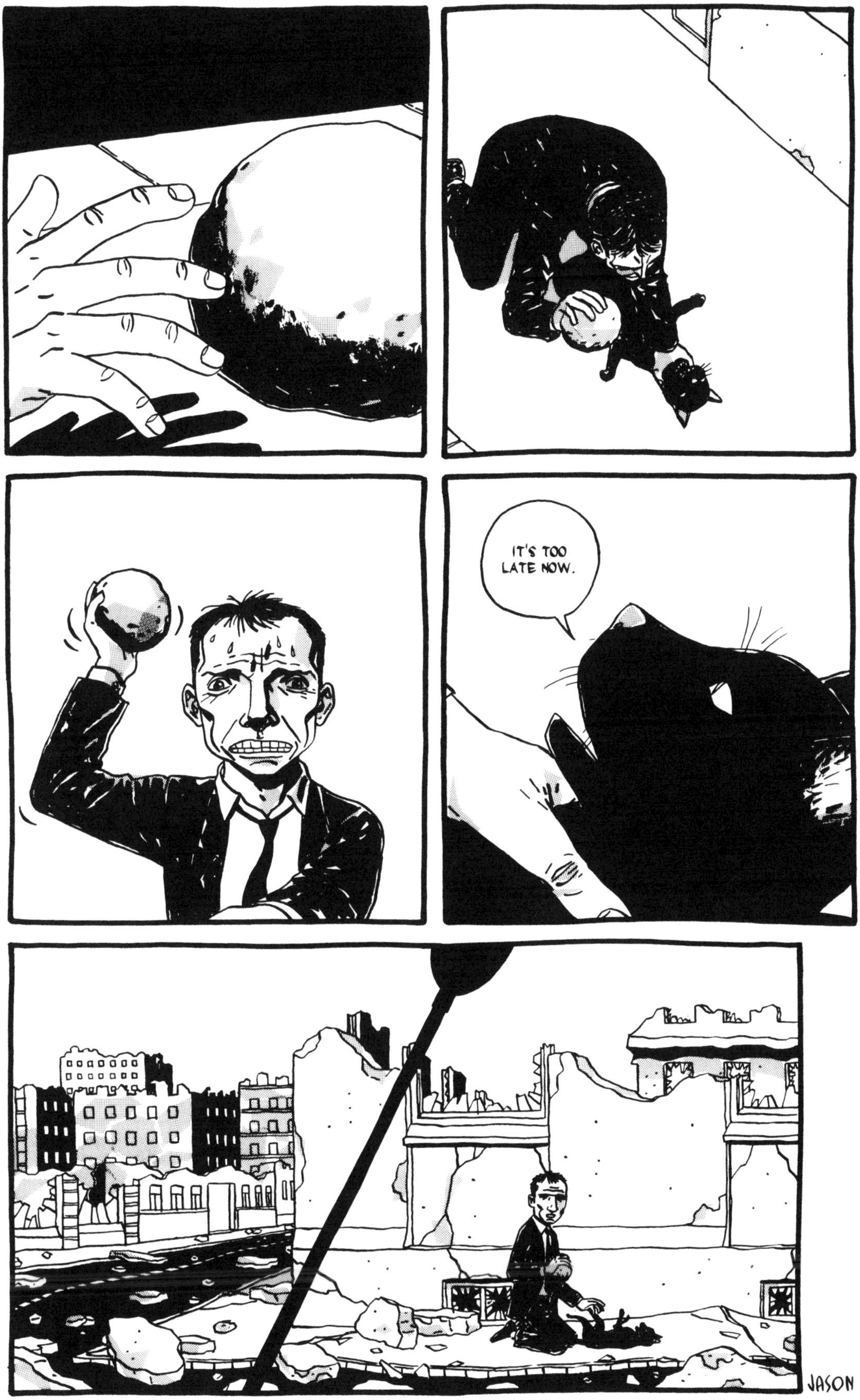
IT'S TOO
LATE NOW.
JASON

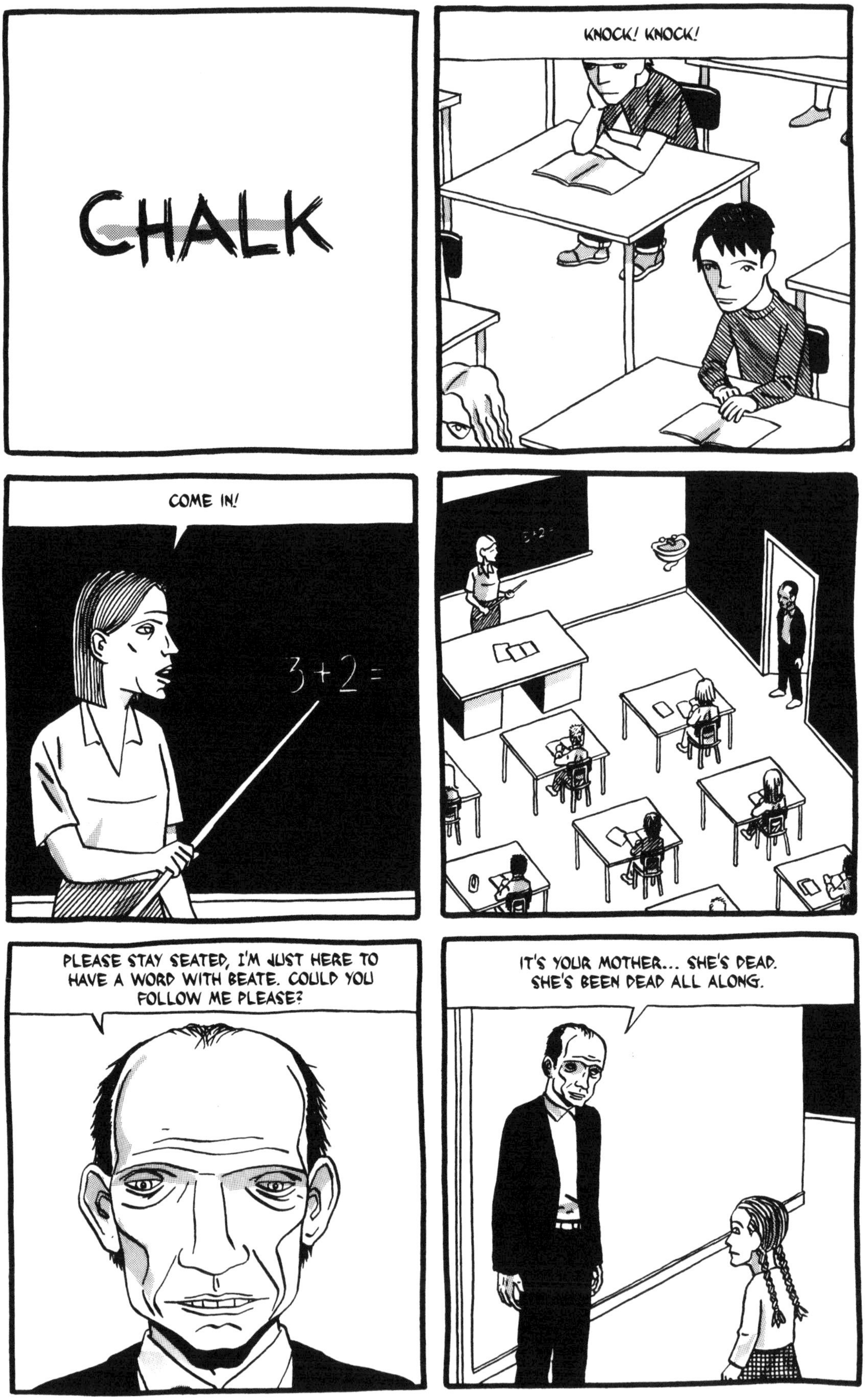
CHALK
KNOCK! KNOCK!
COME IN!
3+2=
PLEASE STAY SEATED, I'M JUST HERE TO HAVE A WORD WITH BEATE. COULD YOU FOLLOW ME PLEASE?
IT'S YOUR MOTHER... SHE'S DEAD. SHE'S BEEN DEAD ALL ALONG.

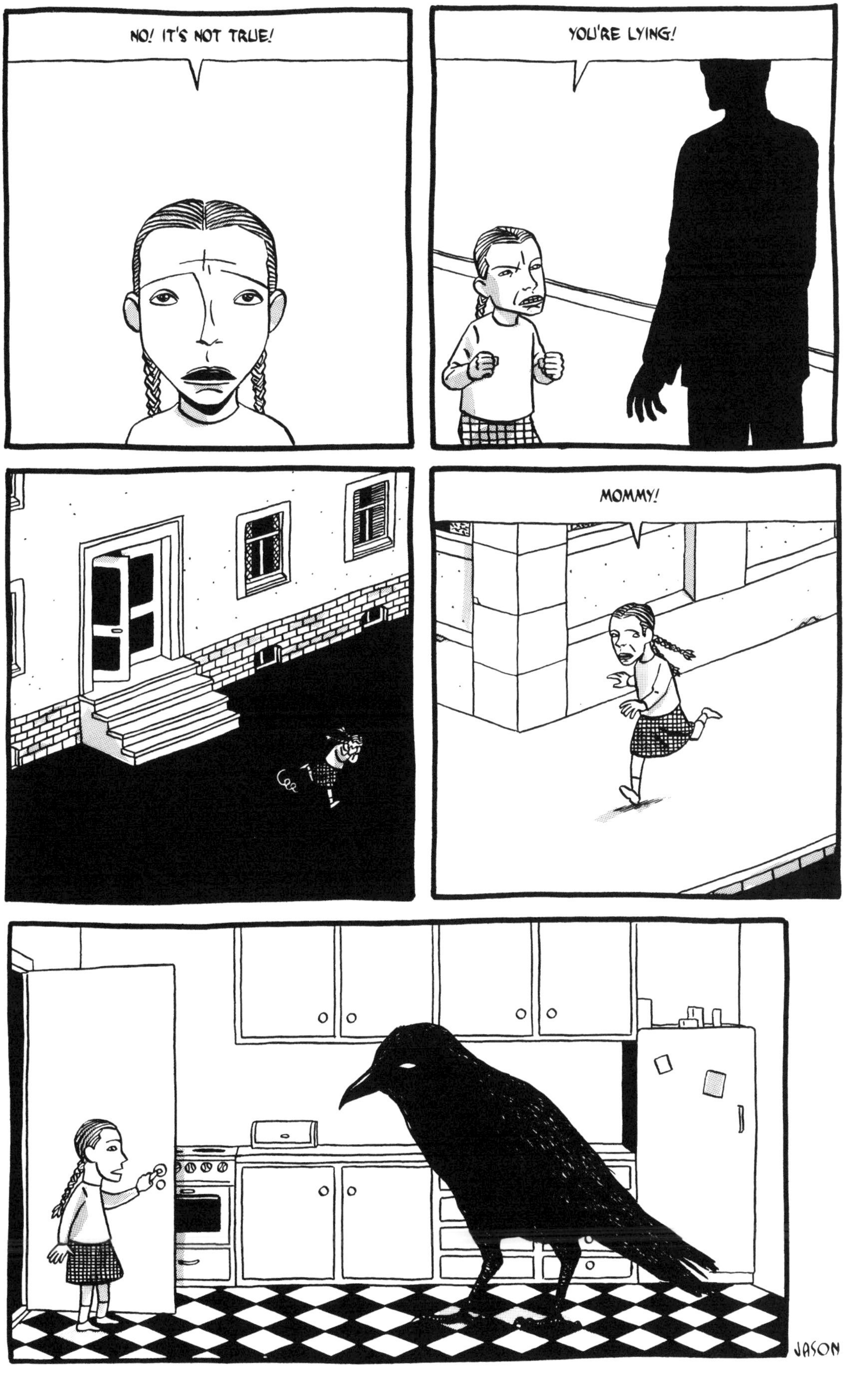

NO! IT'S NOT TRUE!
YOU'RE LYING!
MOMMY!
JASON

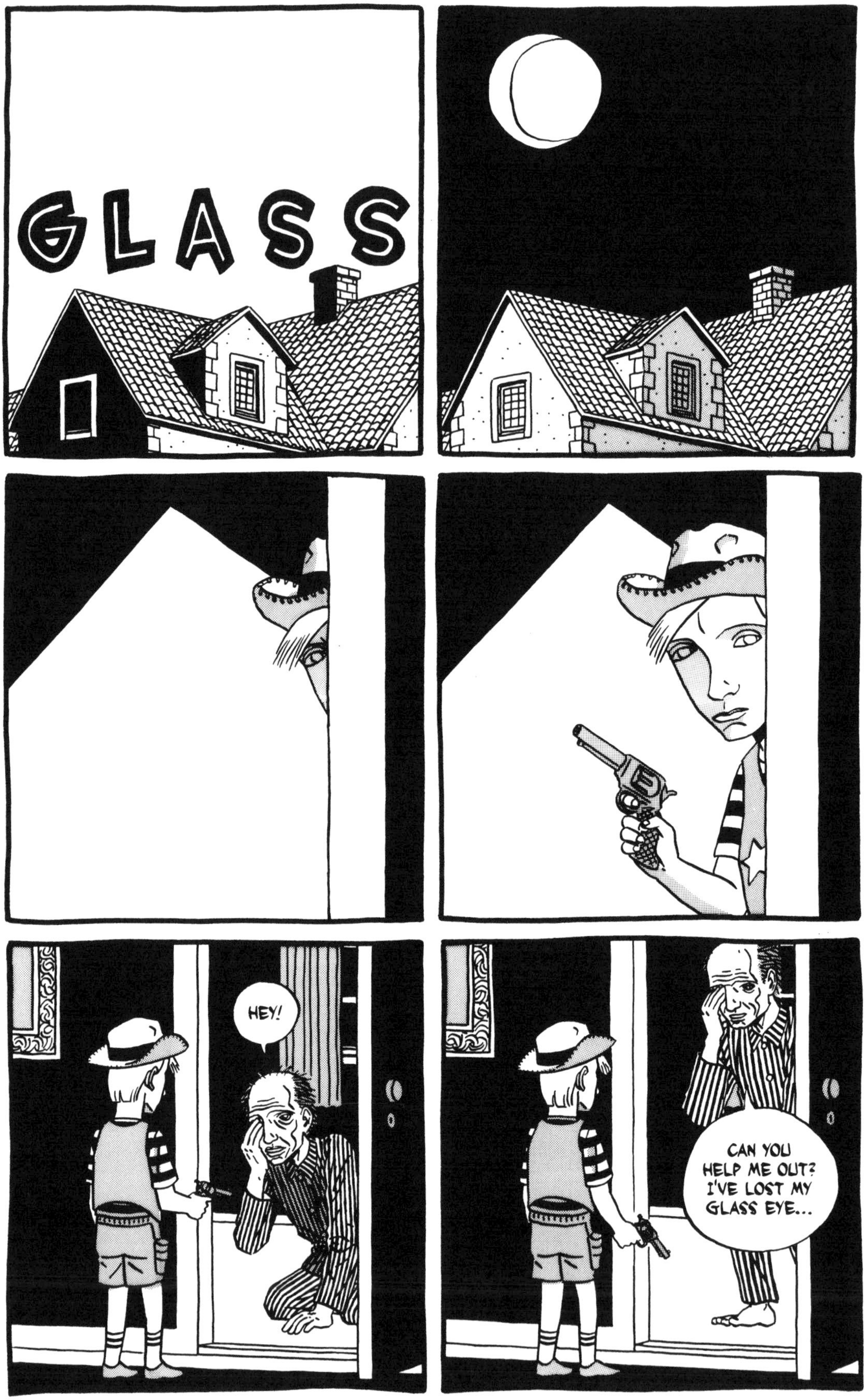
GLASS
HEY!
CAN YOU HELP ME OUT? I'VE LOST MY GLASS EYE...

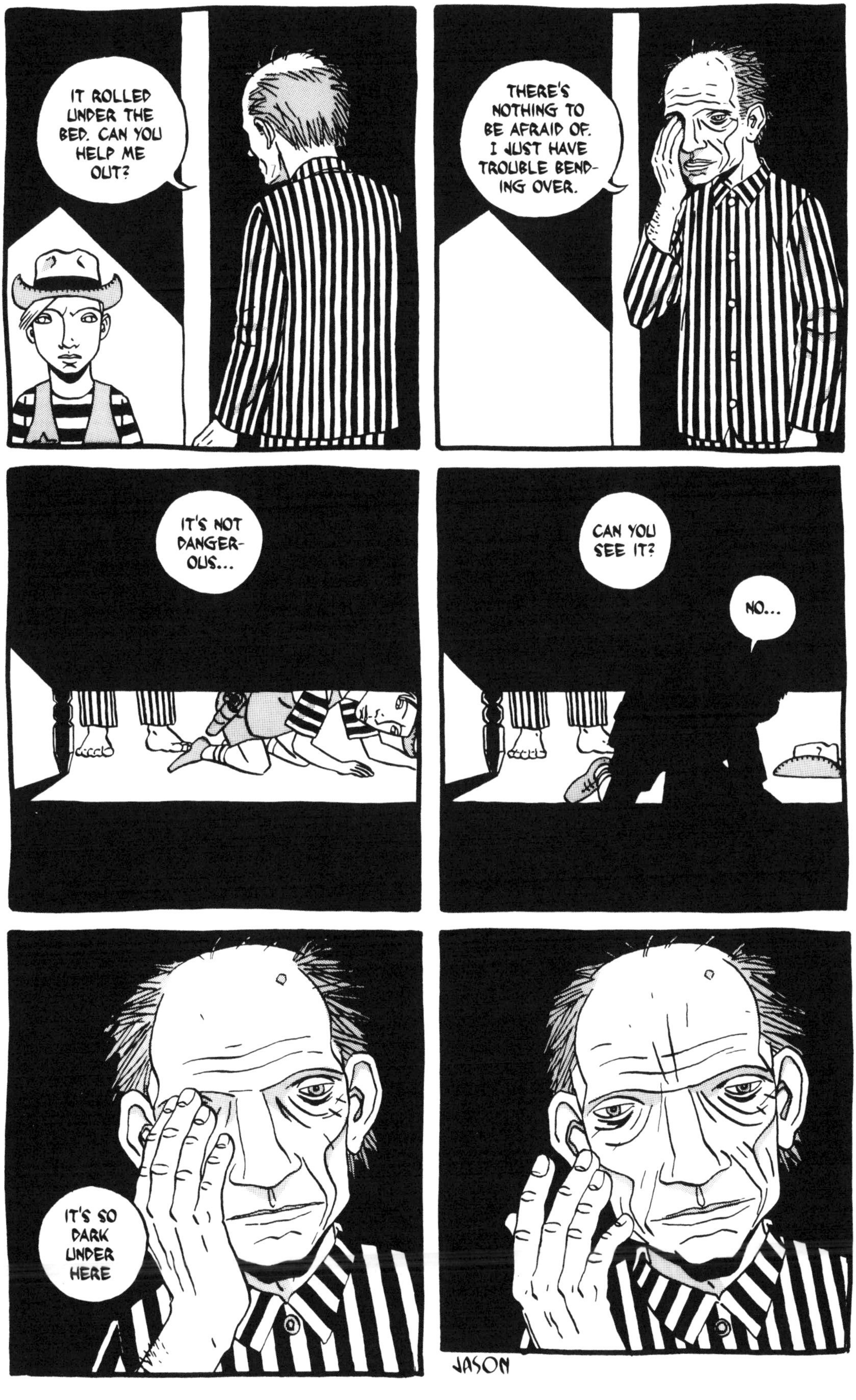
IT ROLLED UNDER THE BED. CAN YOU HELP ME OUT?
THERE'S NOTHING TO BE AFRAID OF. I JUST HAVE TROUBLE BENDING OVER.
IT'S NOT DANGEROUS...
CAN YOU SEE IT?
NO...
IT'S SO DARK UNDER HERE
JASON

the thief

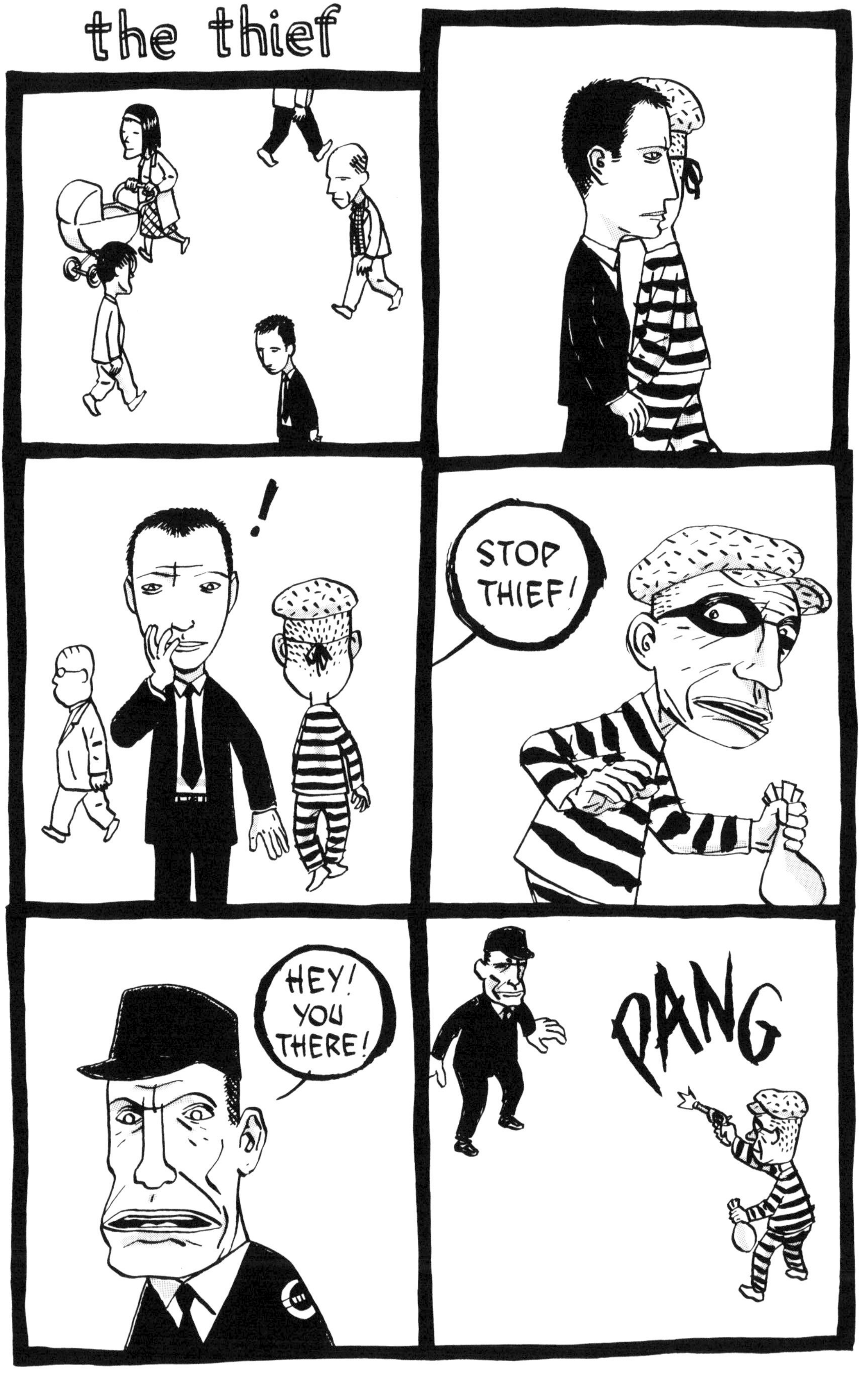
!
STOP THIEF!
HEY! YOU THERE!
PANG

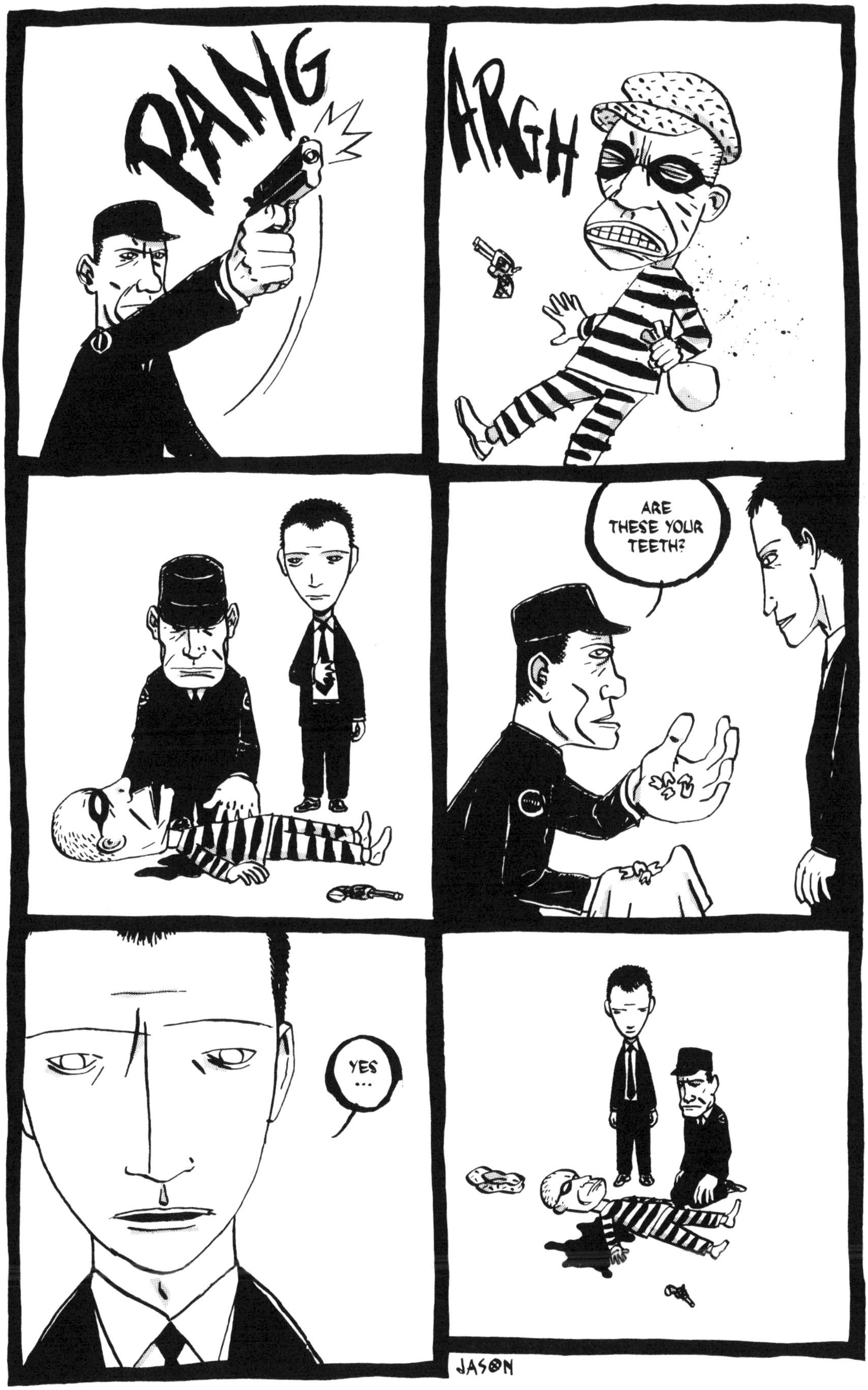
PANG
ARGH
ARE THESE YOUR TEETH?
YES ...
JASON

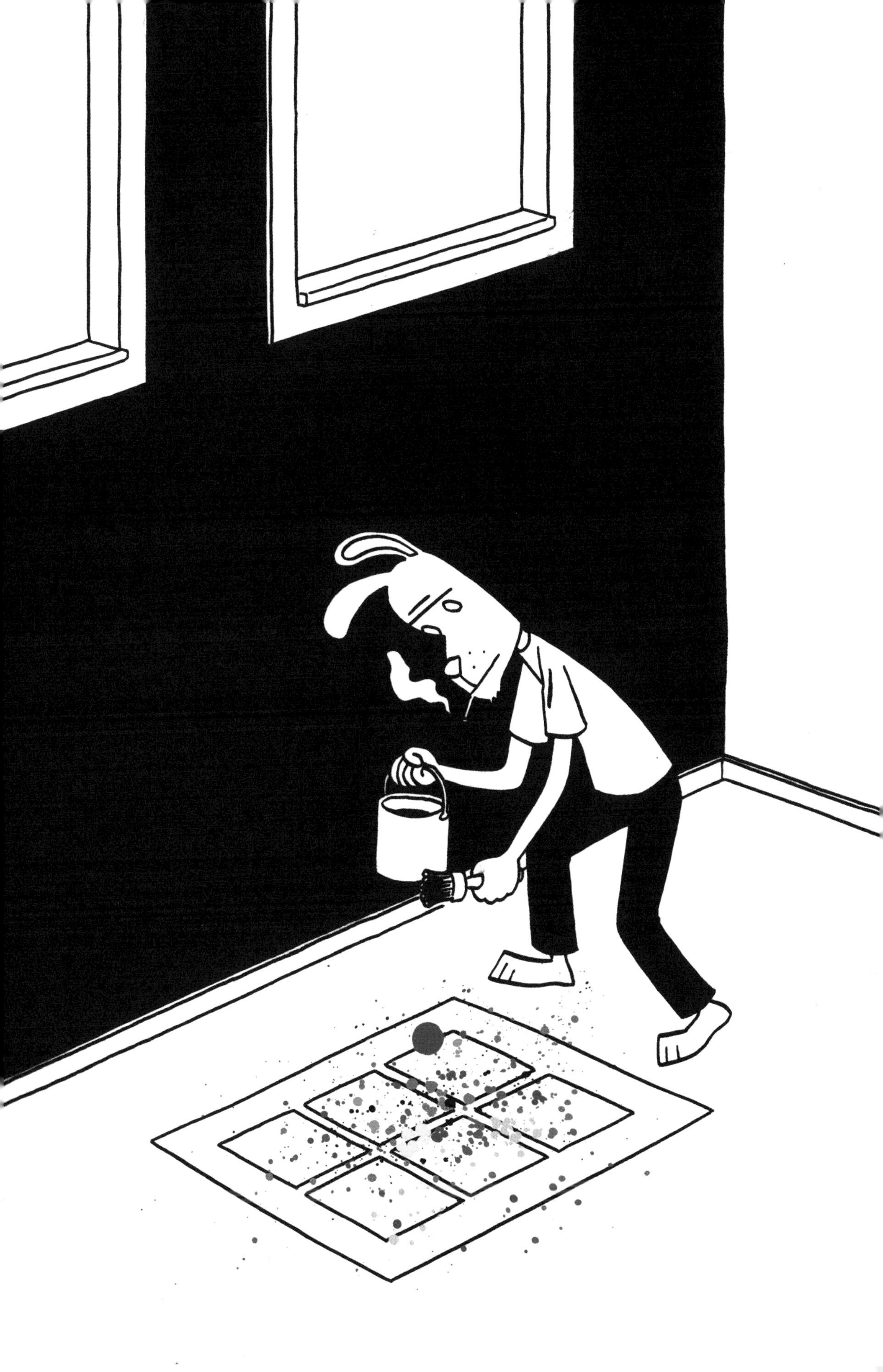

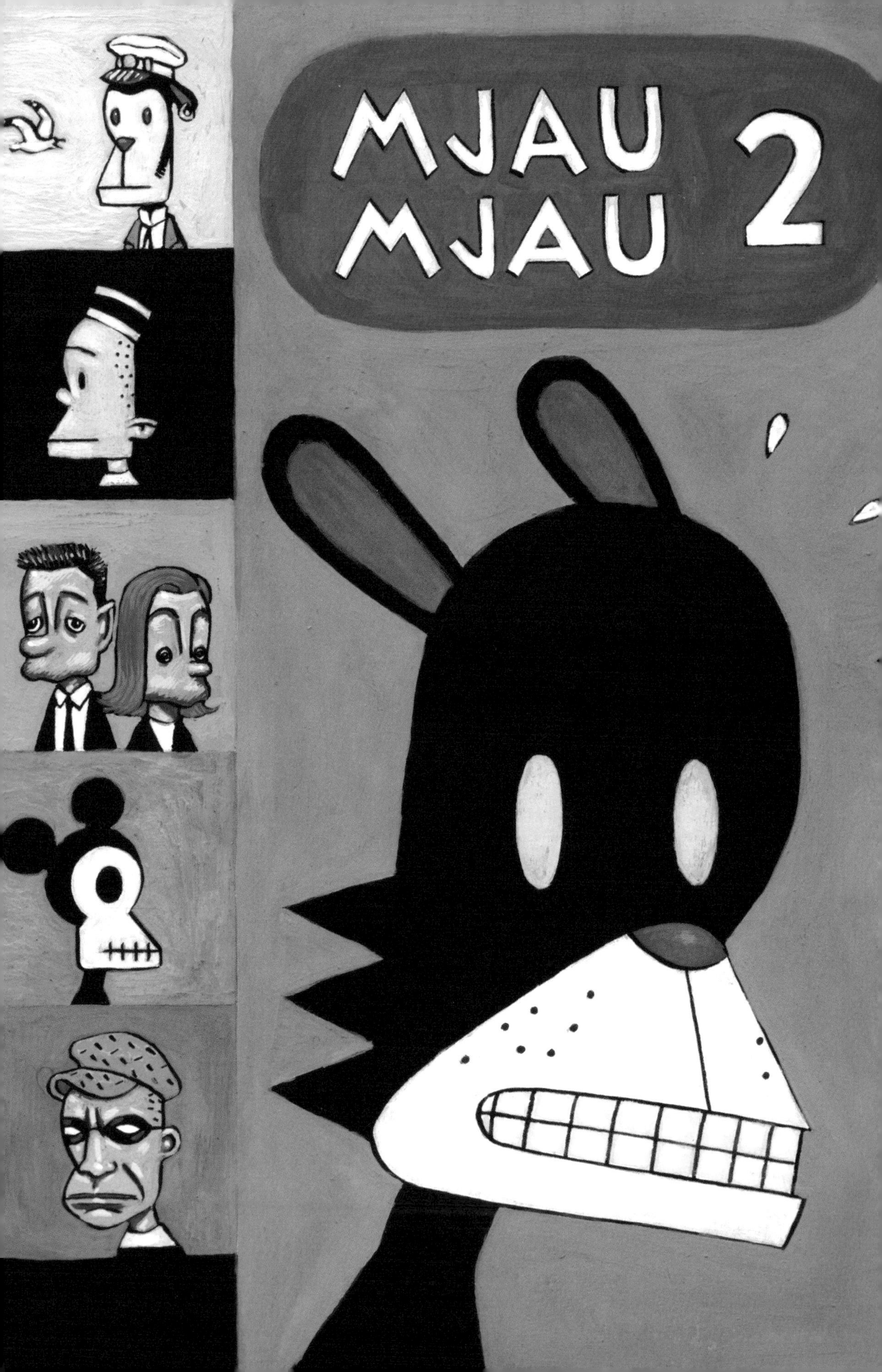
MJAU MJAU 2

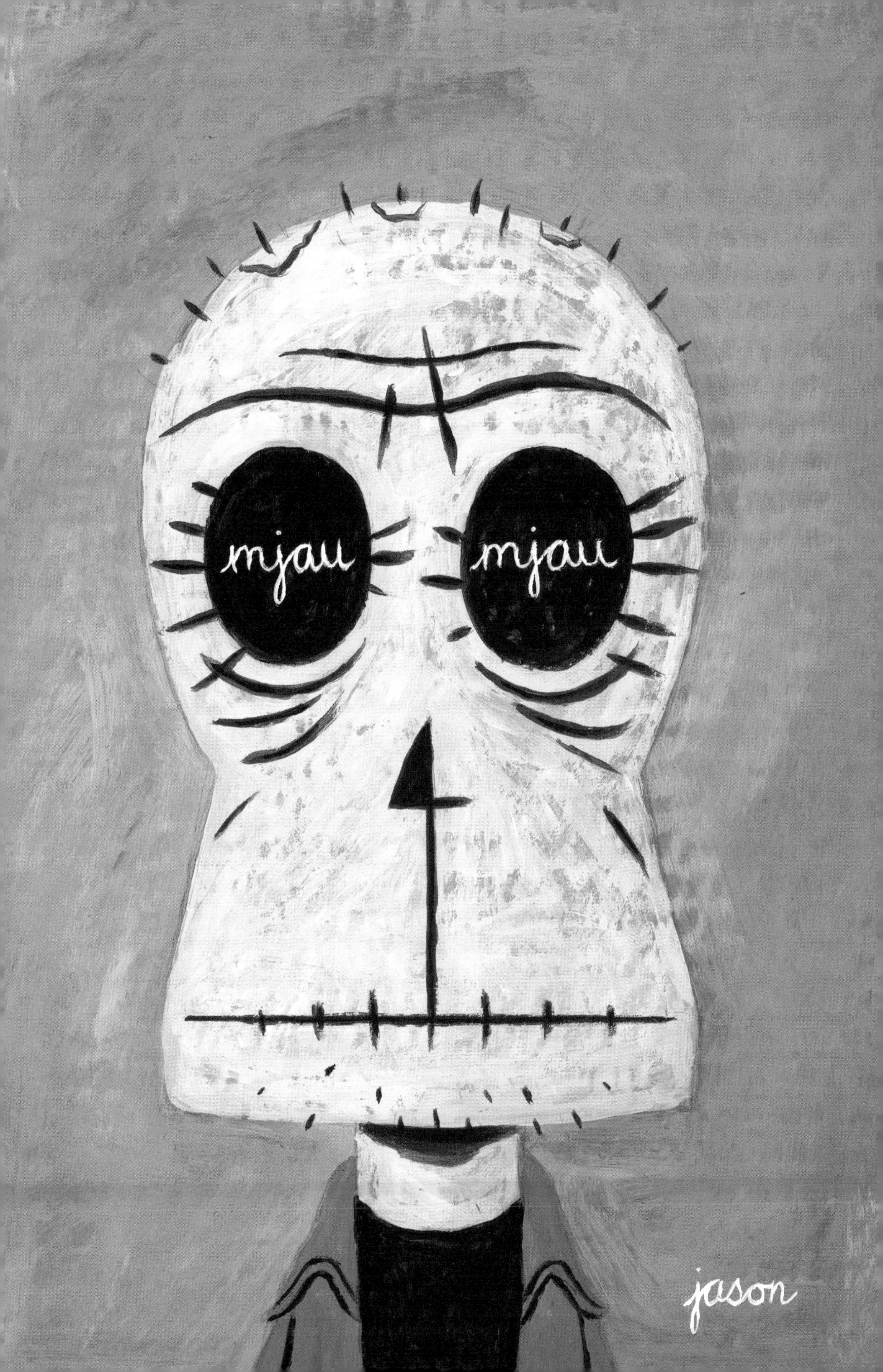
mjau
mjau
jason

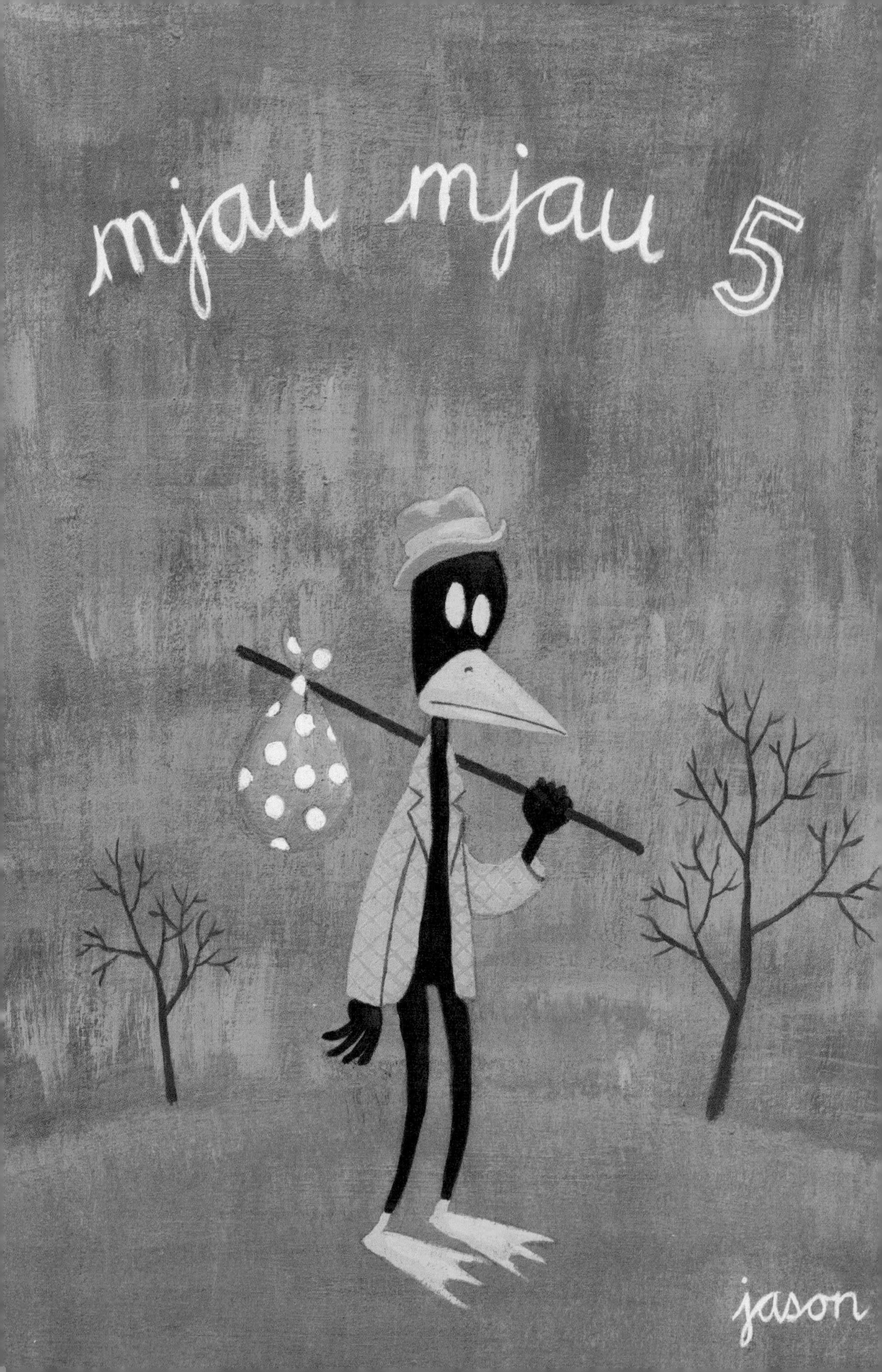
mjau mjau 5
jason

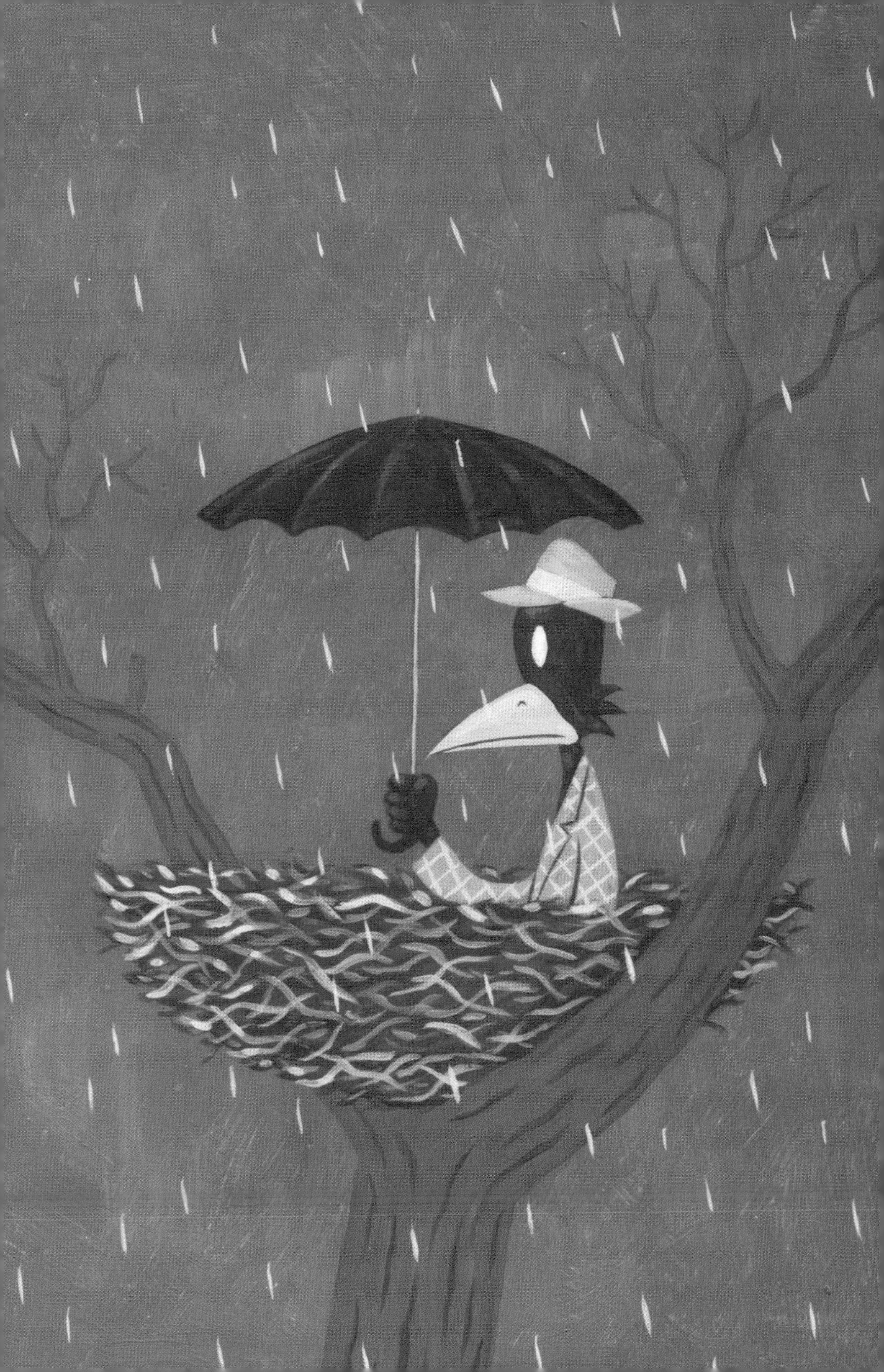

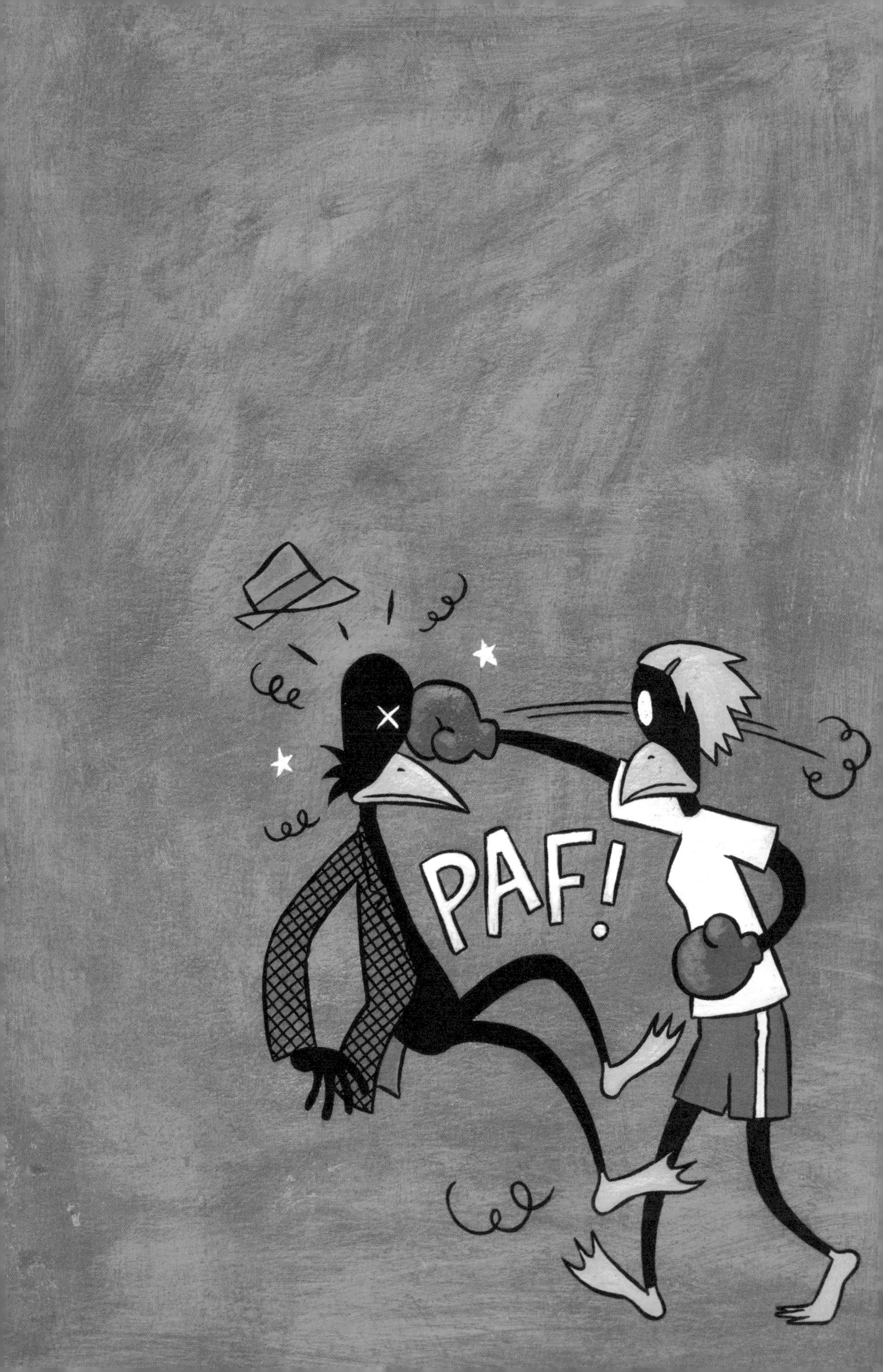
PAF!

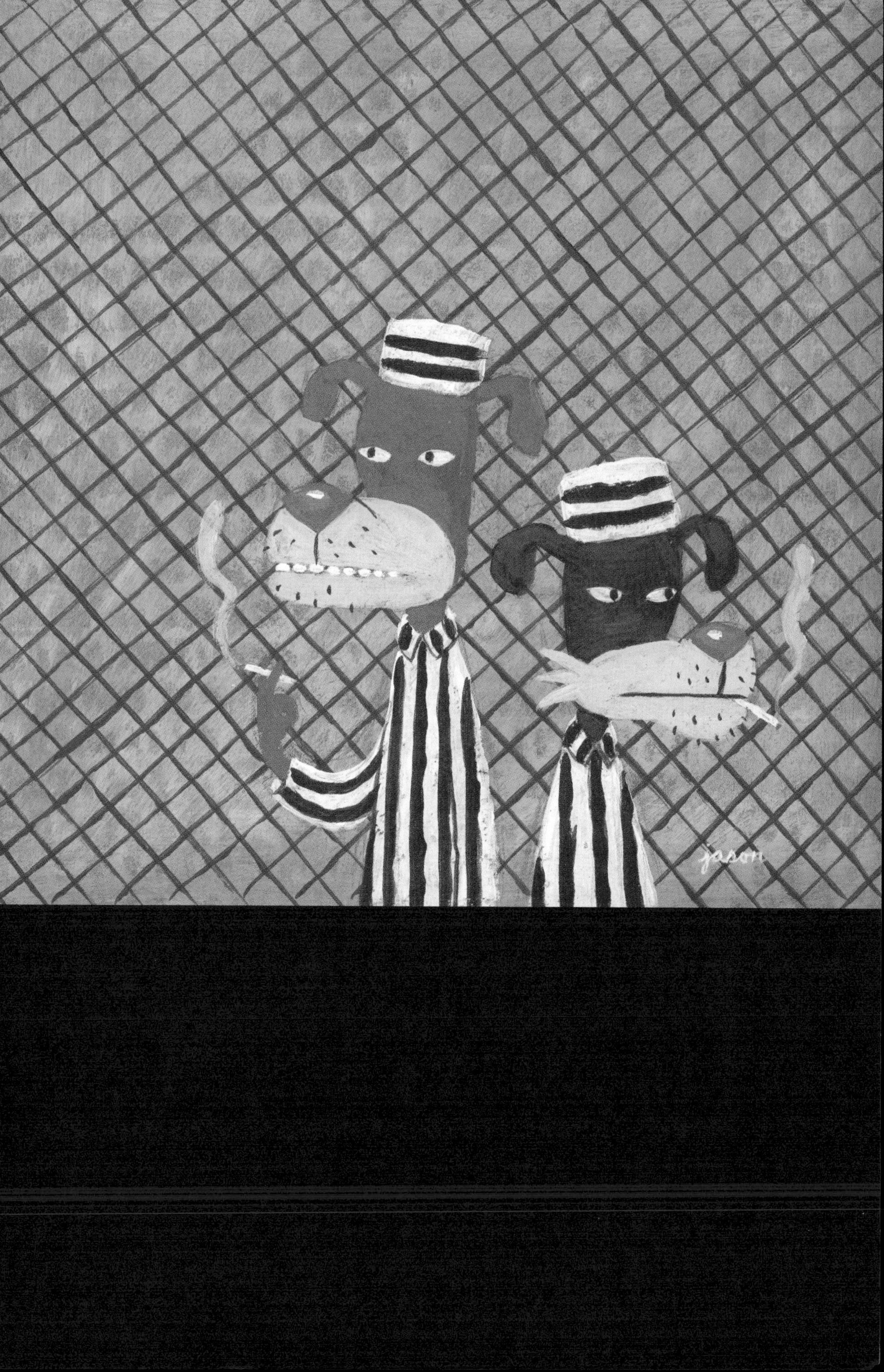
jason

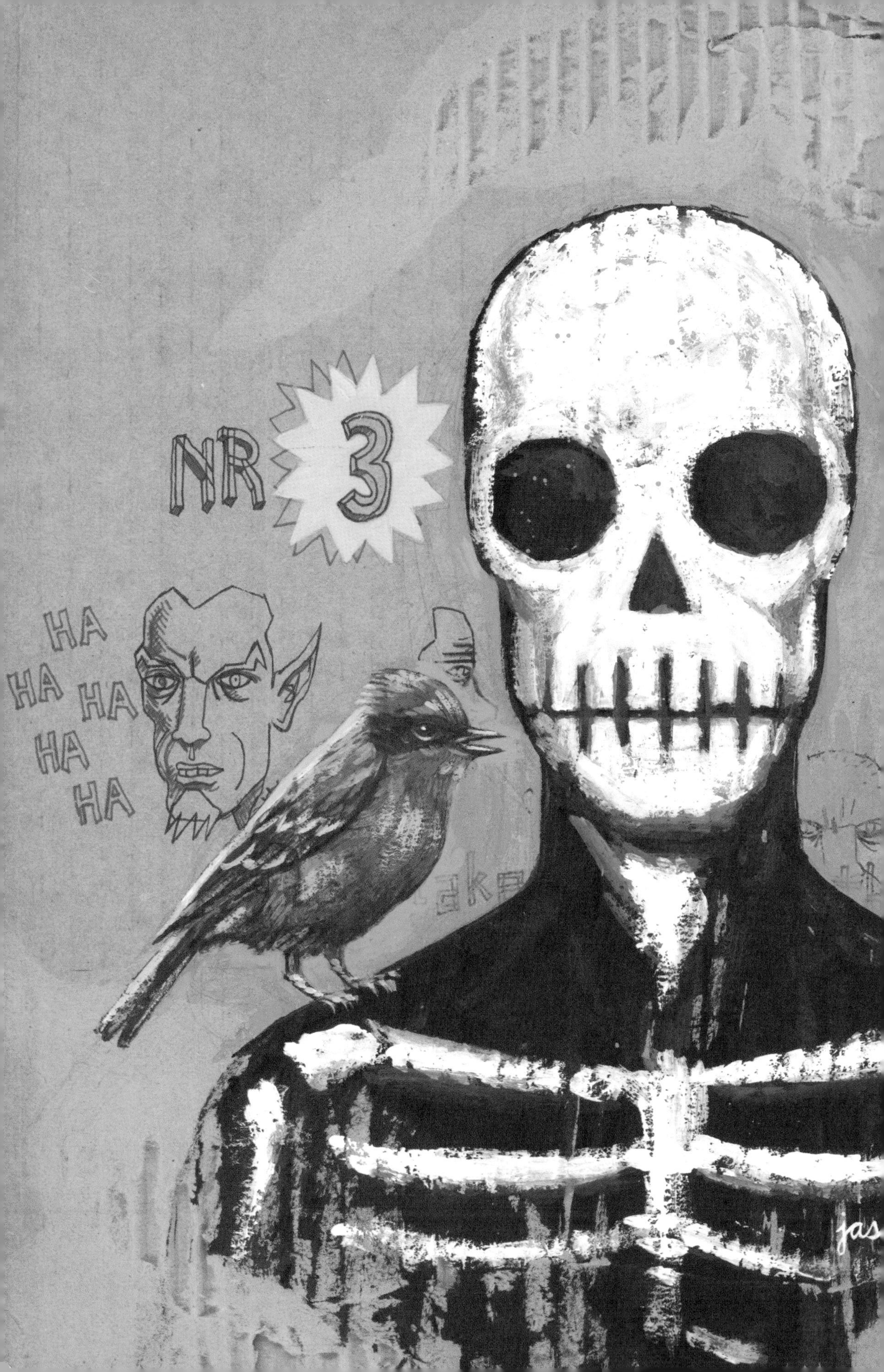
NR 3
HA
HA HA
HA
HA
jas

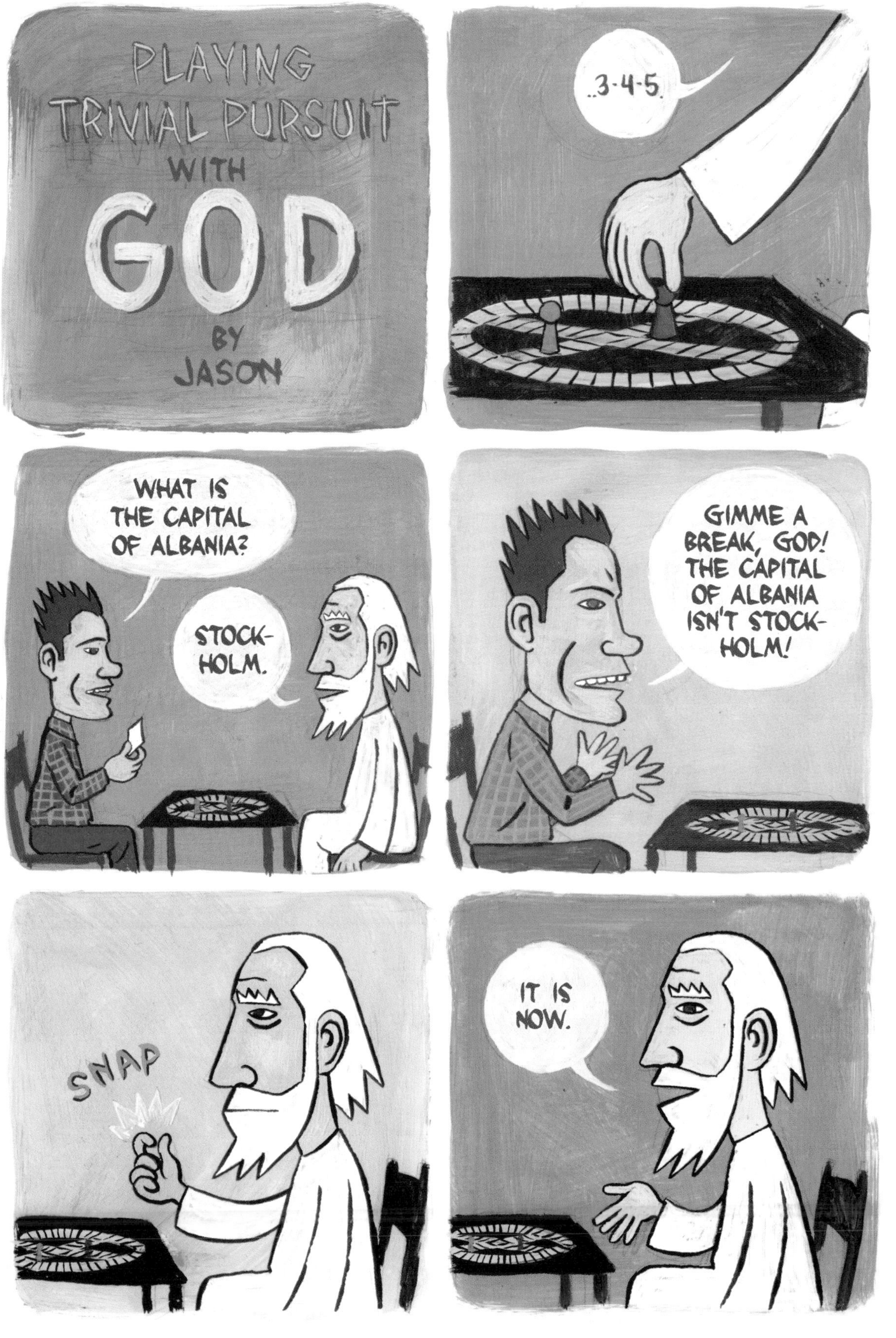
PLAYING TRIVIAL PURSUIT WITH GOD
BY JASON
..3-4-5.
WHAT IS THE CAPITAL OF ALBANIA?
STOCK-HOLM.
GIMME A BREAK, GOD! THE CAPITAL OF ALBANIA ISN'T STOCK-HOLM!
SNAP
IT IS NOW.

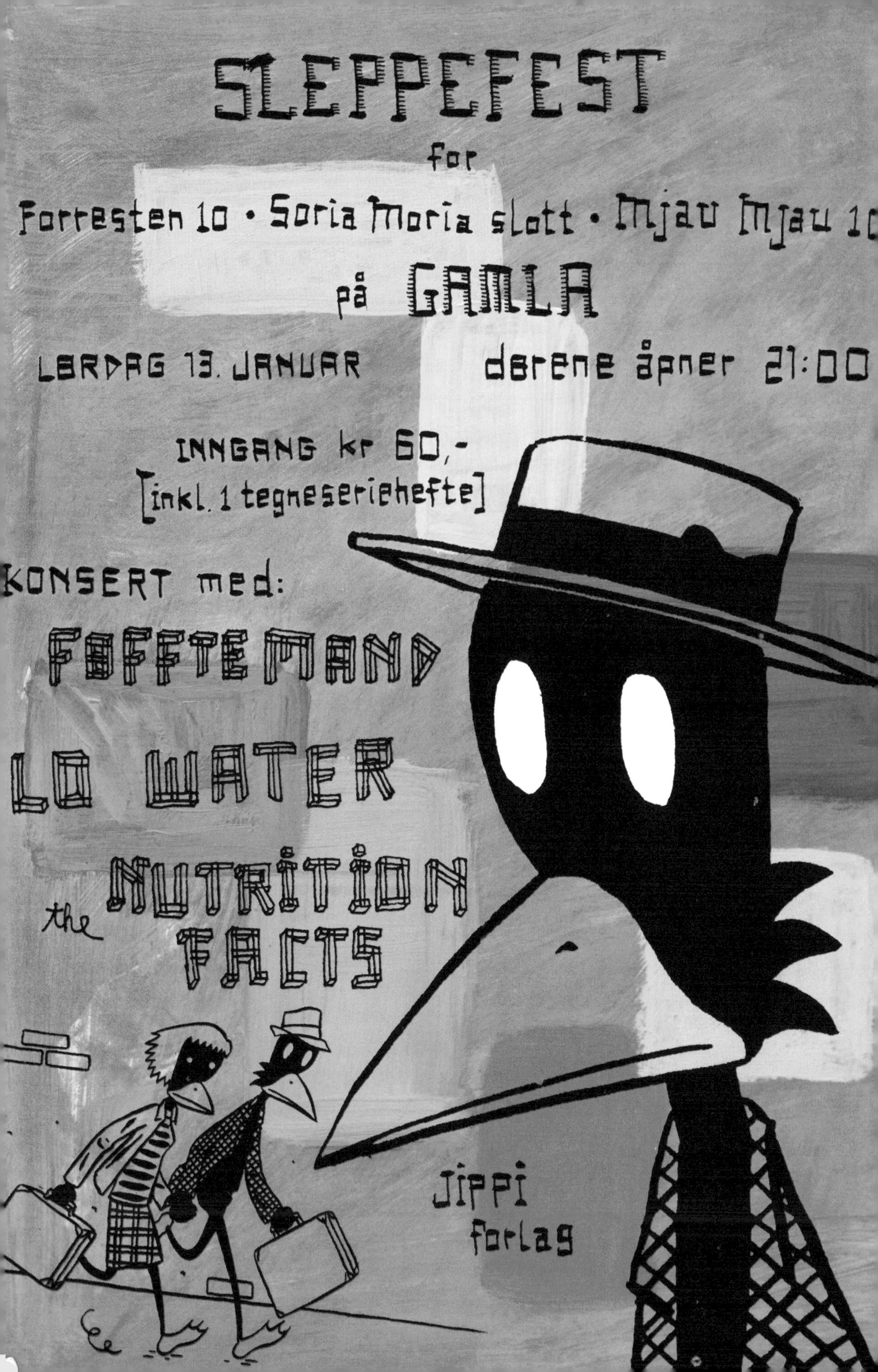
SLEPPEFEST
for
Forresten 10 • Soria Moria slott • Mjau Mjau 10
på GAMLA
LØRDAG 13. JANUAR
dørene åpner 21:00
INNGANG kr 60,-
[inkl. 1 tegneseriehefte]
KONSERT med:
FOFFTEMAND
LO WATER
the NUTRITION FACTS
JIPPI forlag

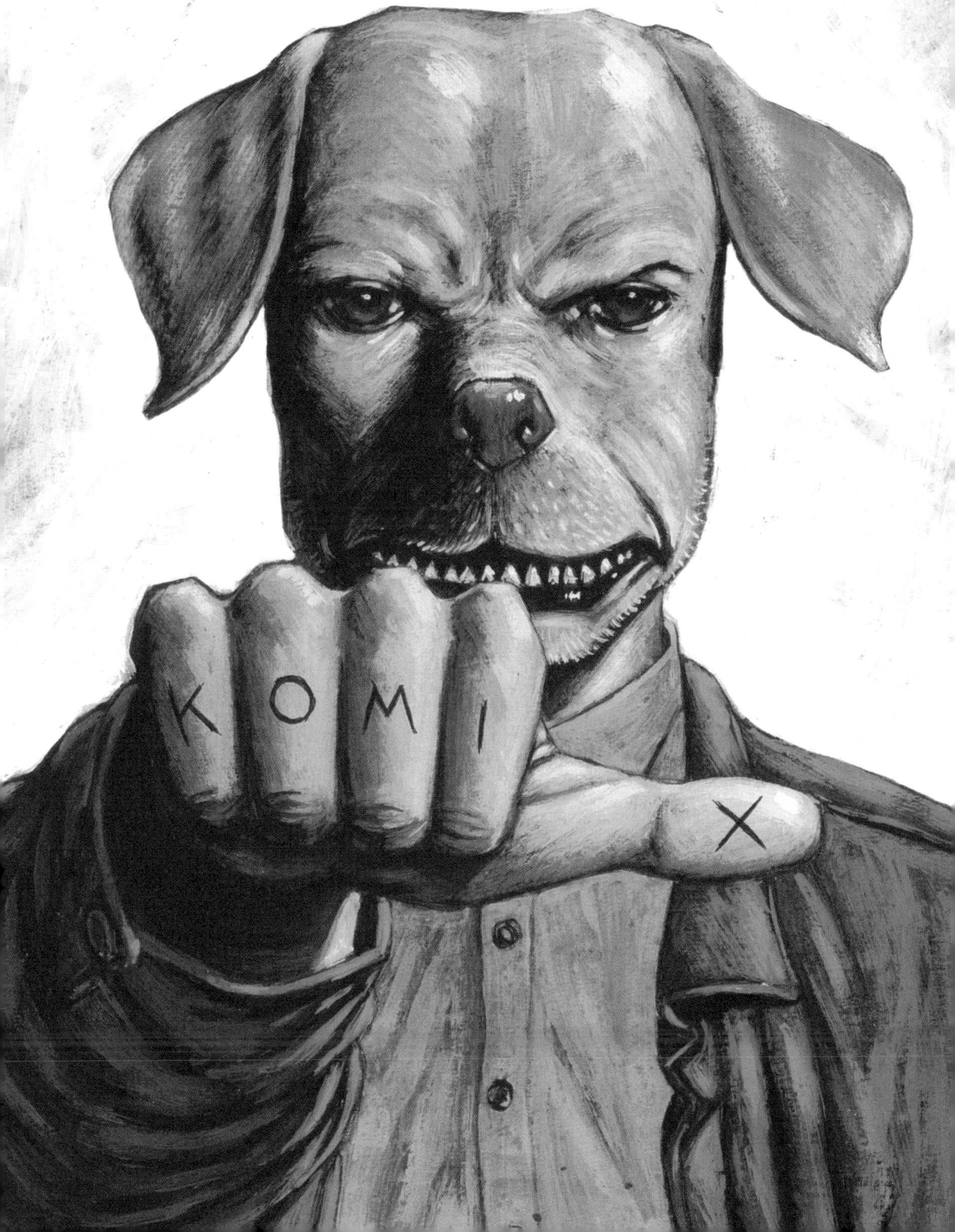
K O M I
X

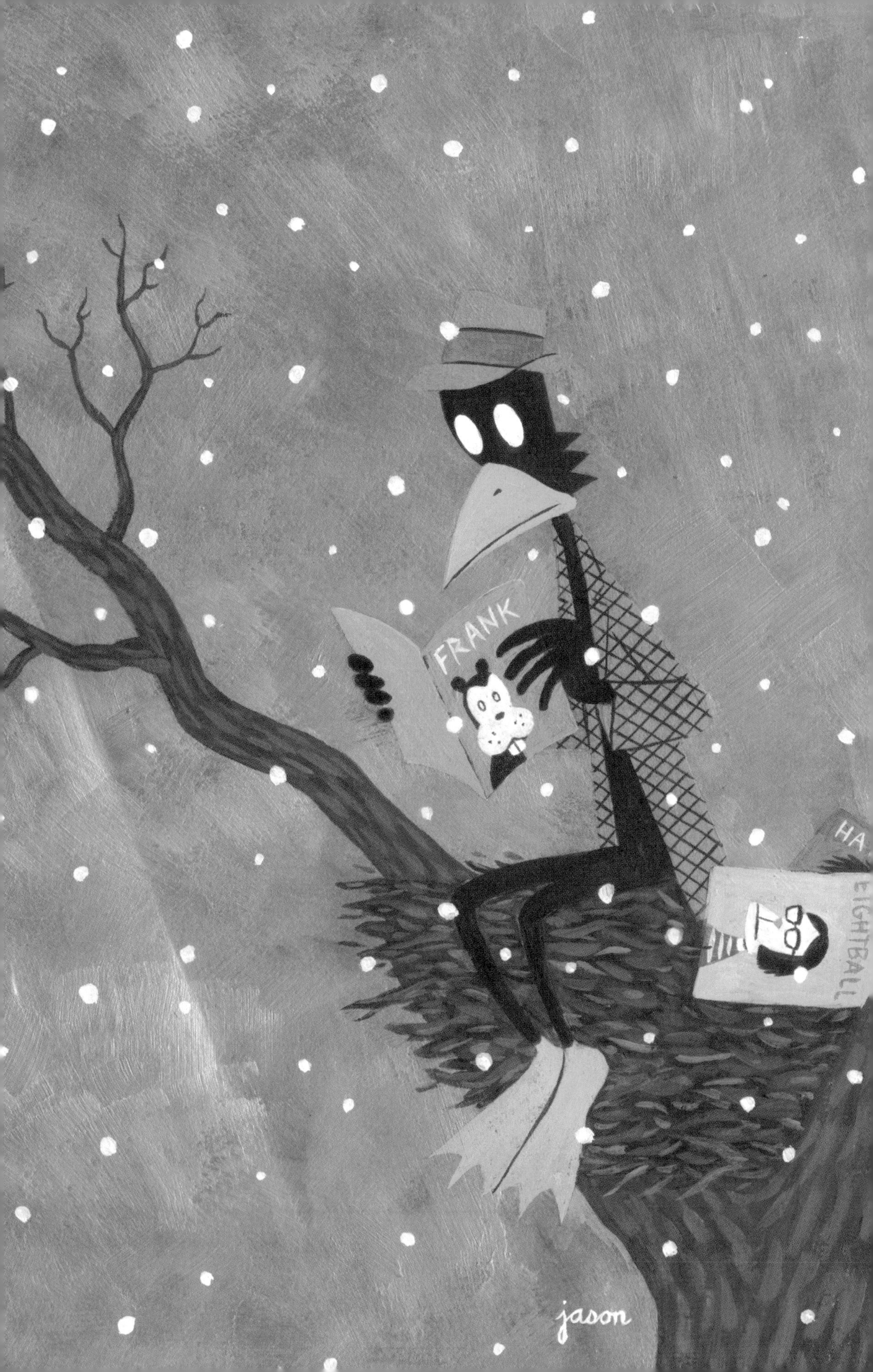
FRANK
EIGHTBALL
jason

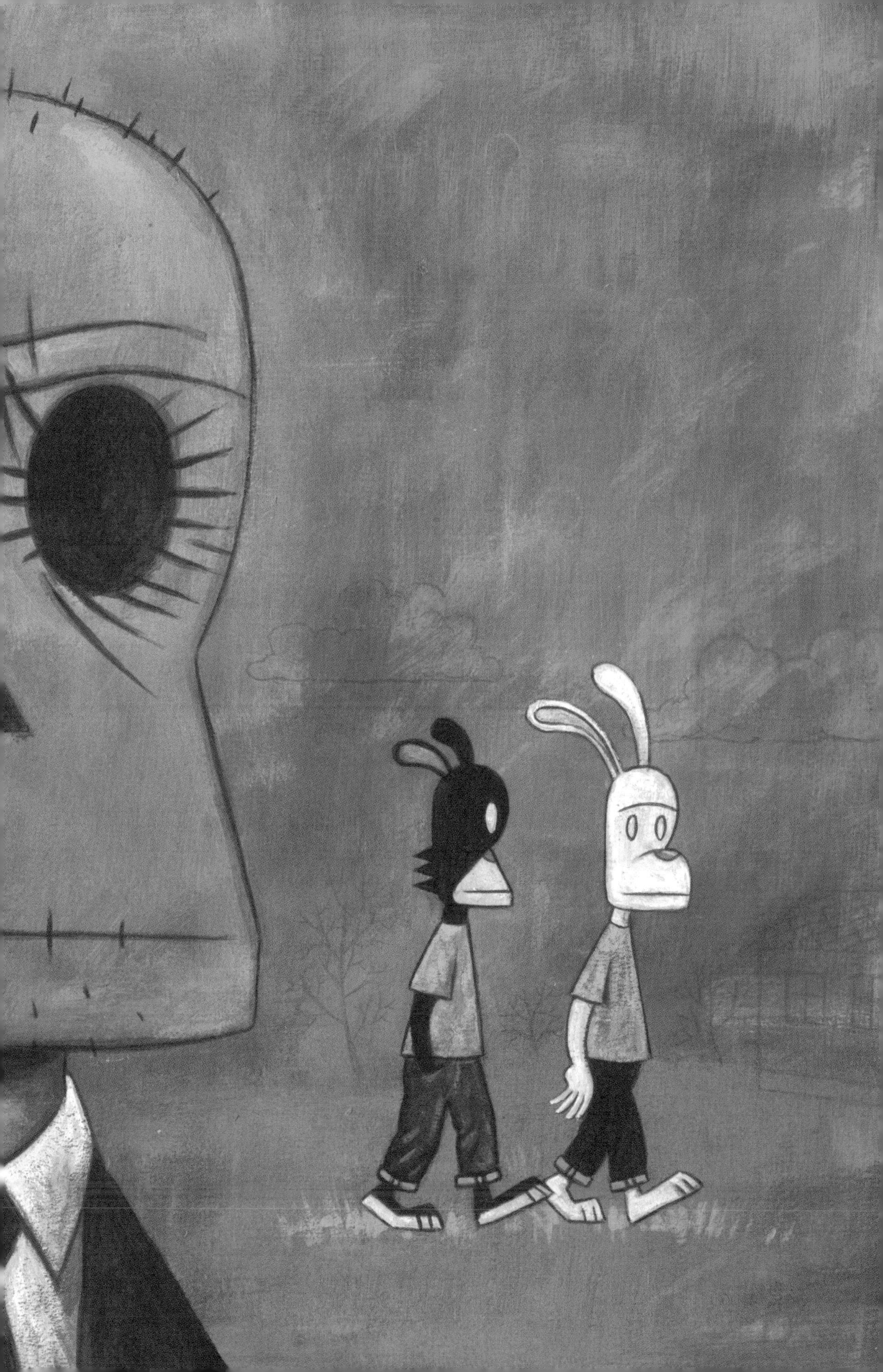

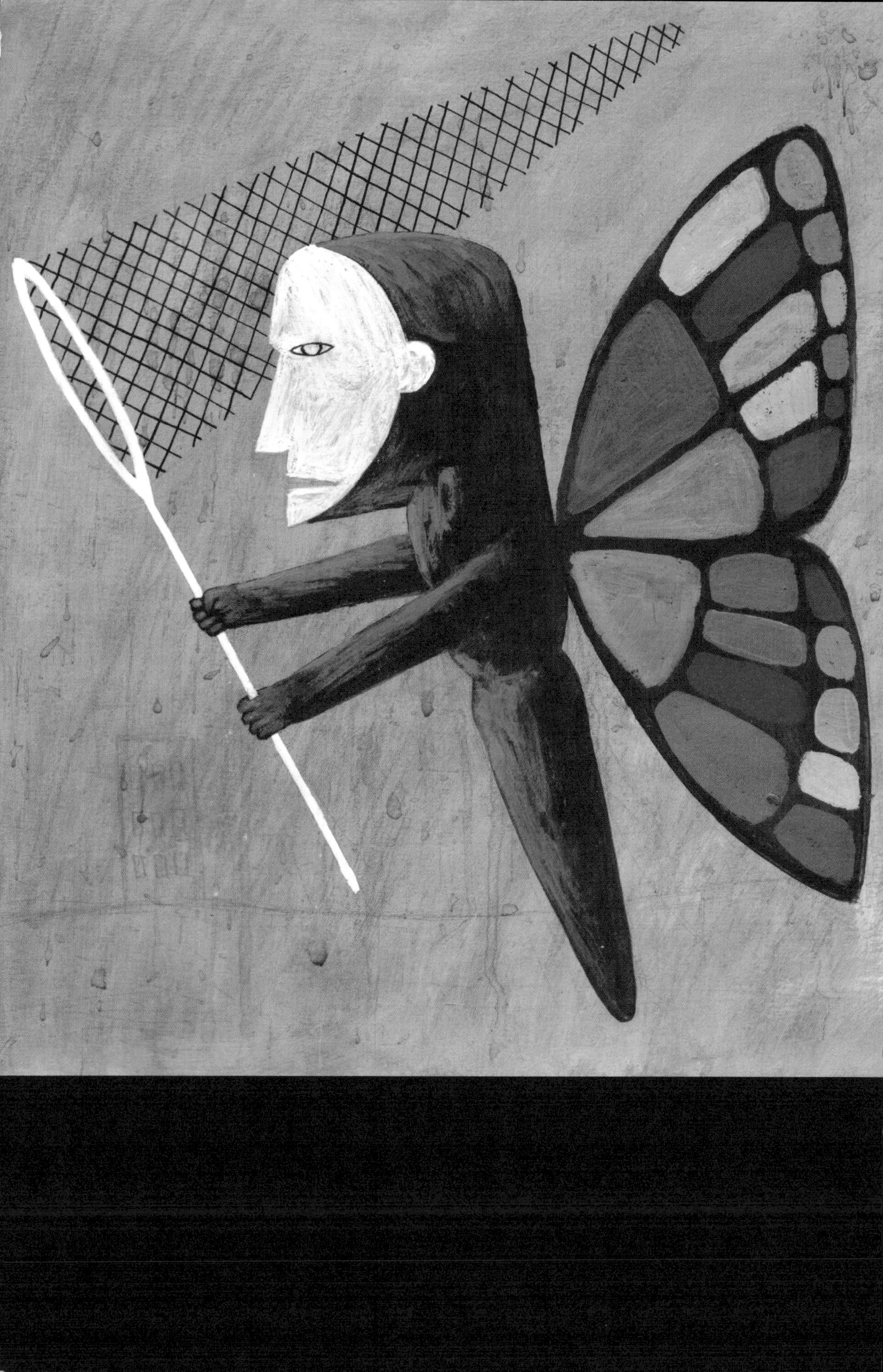

[redacted]

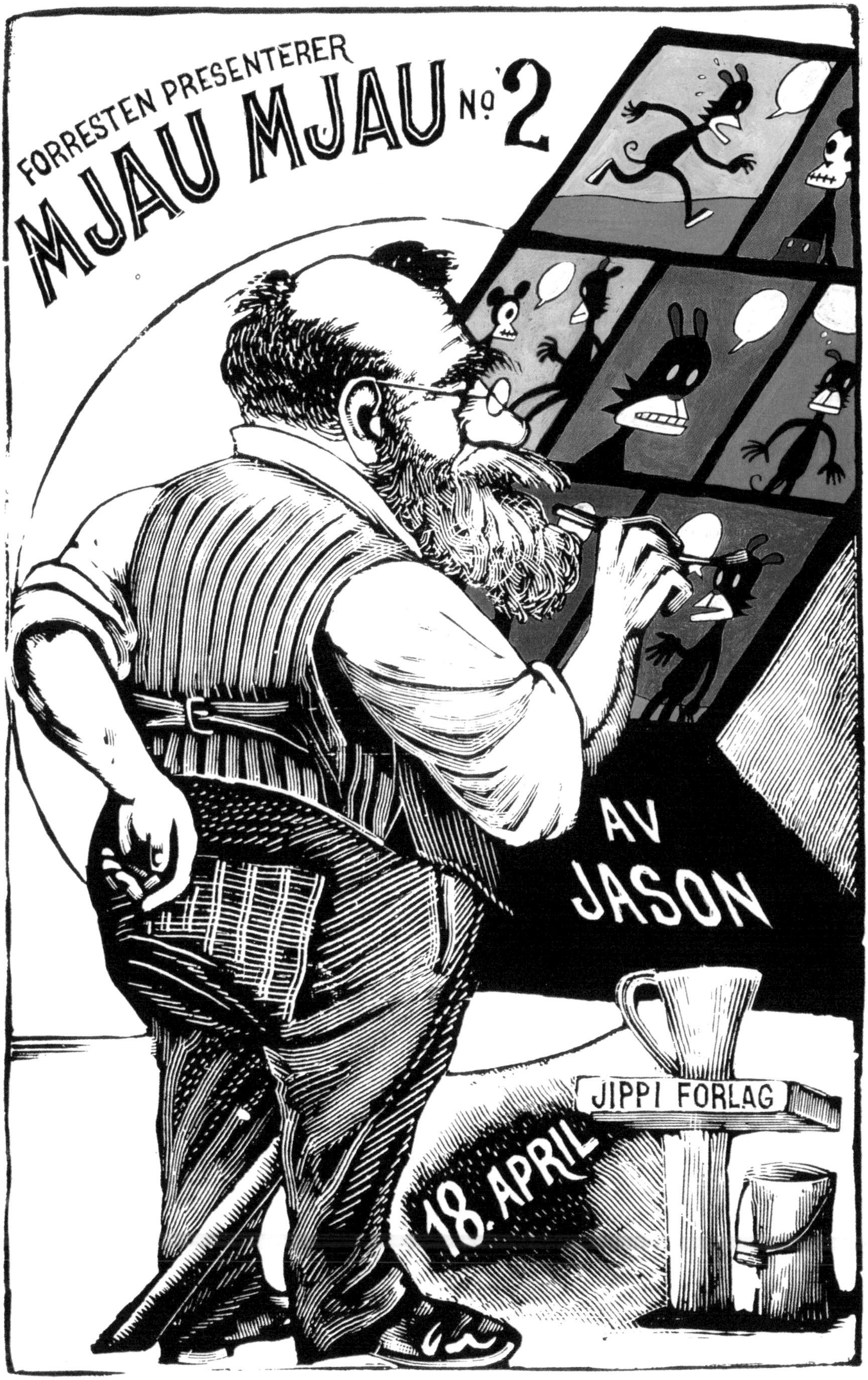
FORRESTEN PRESENTERER
MJAU MJAU No. 2
AV JASON
JIPPI FORLAG
18. APRIL

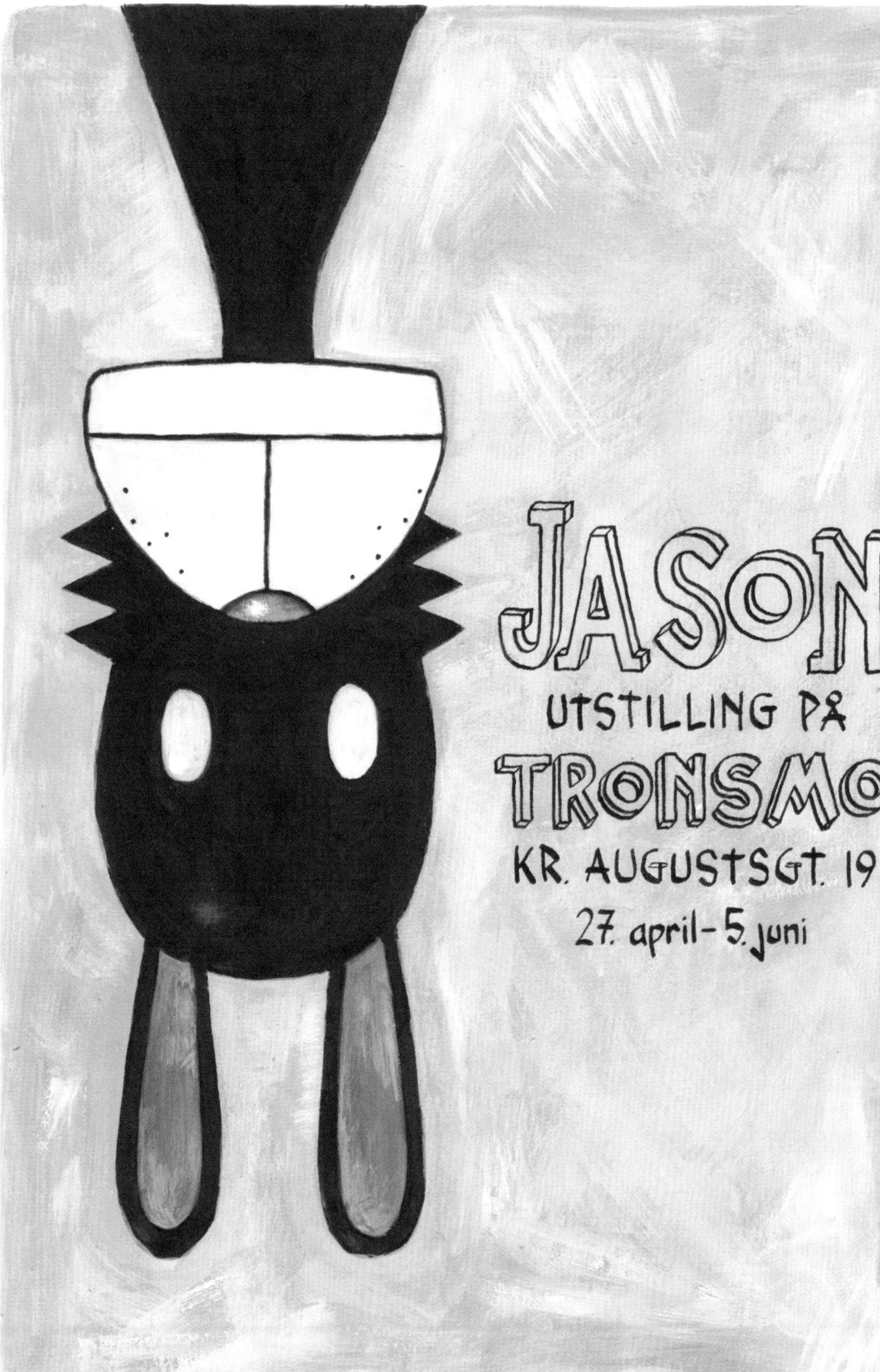
JASON
UTSTILLING PÅ
TRONSMO
KR. AUGUSTSGT. 19
27. april – 5. juni

TABLE *of* CONTENTS

This story was supposed to be just one page long, but I kept coming up with people I found to be annoying and it ended up twice the length. Some of the targets in the original version were Norwegian annoyances which Kim Thompson changed to more internationally known annoyances, but I can't say I disagree with any of them. Anyway, I get what I deserve in the final panel.

Olof Palme was the Swedish prime minister in the early and mid eighties. He was assassinated, and the killer was never found, making Palme a sort of Scandinavian JFK.

I took a lot of photographs from the part of Oslo I was living at the time, and wanted to use them in a story. I came up with this. It was drawn with a beaten up brush, with half the hairs missing. I like the ratty line it gave. The dialogue exchange I stole from Aki Kaurismäki's film *La vie de bohème*.

This story was inspired by me and a friend going out to celebrate after receiving letters that we had been accepted at the National College of Art and Design, in Oslo. For the story, it worked better that the two characters had not been accepted. The cemetery at the end is Vaar Frelsers Gravlund, which also turns up in *Pocket Full of Rain*. The original title was "Preben," which I described to Kim Thompson as a "sissy upperclass name in Norway" and he proposed "Edwin" as an American equivalent. Outraged readers named Edwin should complain to him.

When I first moved to Oslo I rented a small bedsit in the suburbs. The conversation at the first page and a half is pretty much word for word taken from one I had with my alcoholic landlord. He also turns up in "Night." I originally drew this in a realistic style, but was not too happy with the result and redrew it in a funny-animal style several years later.

This is one of three stories I did with the character Sam Space, the only one where I'm still fairly happy with the drawings. I was trying to learn how to draw with a brush at this period. David Mazzucchelli / *Batman Year One* was sort of what I was going for, I guess.

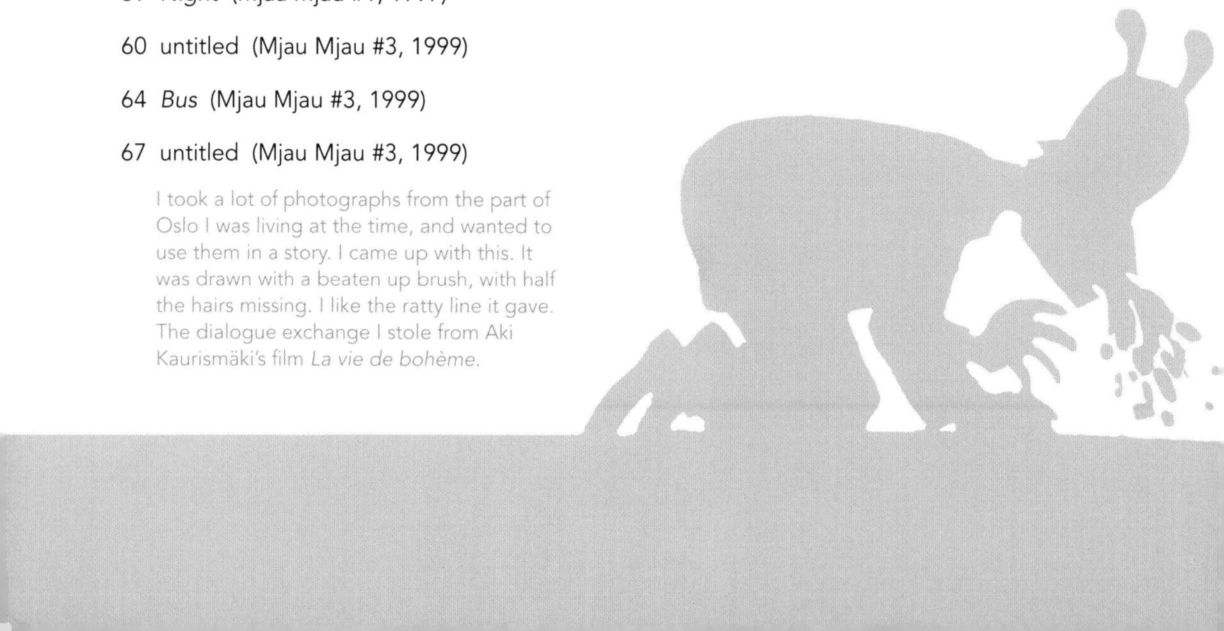

84 *X-pilt* (Mjau Mjau #2, 1998)

Half of the inspiration for this story is obvious. But the other half is a black-and-white children's puppet show, called "Pompel and Pilt," that ran on Norwegian TV in the '70s. This was a really twisted and surreal show that scared the hell out of us kids at the time. Everybody in my generation in Norway vividly remembers it. You can find clips on YouTube; however, avoid those for "Pompel & The Pilts," a Norwegian band that bears the same relationship to the TV show as the band Love and Rockets does to the comic, which is to say, none. Sharp-eyed readers might notice that the two main characters also turn up in a panel in "Pocket Full of Rain."

87 *Corto Meowtese* (Mjau Mjau #2, 1998)

A little homage to Hugo Pratt and Moebius.

88 *Spacecat* (Mjau Mjau #2, 1998)

A pastiche of Basil Wolverton's Spacehawk.

92 *Papa* (Mjau Mjau #1, 1997)

I don't know where my fascination with Hemingway comes from. He's name-dropped in *Pocket Full of Rain*, again in the untitled strip on page 55, and finally appears as a character here. And of course a decade later I made him the star of an entire book, *The Left Bank Gang*. He seems to be one of those writers you're supposed to outgrow, but I still like his books, especially the early ones.

94 *My Life as a Zombie* (Forresten #5, 1998)

102 strips (Mjau Mjau #2, 1998)

I was reading the "Steven" strips by Doug Allen at this time and wanted to create a character a bit like that. Having drawn about 20 of these strips I tried to sell them to a Norwegian newspaper, but they declined. Later the same newspaper had a competition for best new strip. I sent in the same old strips and won, but eventually ran out of ideas.

116 *Falling* (Mjau Mjau #1, 1997)

The flashback at the end is autobiographical. I witnessed a scene like that; it was a very strange and unreal experience. I sometimes wonder what it would be like for the cyclist, if he should happen to run across this story.

121 *Kill the Cat* (Mjau Mjau #1, 1997)

124 *Chalk* (Mjau Mjau #1, 1997)

126 *Glass* (Mjau Mjau #1, 1997)

128 *Thief* (Mjau Mjau #2, 1998)

132 cover, Mjau Mjau #2, 1998

133 cover, Mjau Mjau #4, 1999

134 cover, Mjau Mjau #5, 1999

135 cover, Mjau Mjau #6, 1999

136 cover, Mjau Mjau #8, 2000

137 cover, Doggie Pound CD, 1999

138 cover, Forresten #13, 2002

139 *Playing Trivial Pursuit With God*
       (Forresten #6, 1998)

140 poster, release party for
       Forresten #10, 2000

141 cover, Forresten #4 1997

142 Christmas card for Fantagraphics, 2003

143 cover, *Hey, Wait…*, Optimal Press, 2000

144 advertisement for Jetfly.com, 2000

145 poster for Mjau Mjau #2, 1998

146 poster for art show, 1998

Hey, Wait...
BLACK AND WHITE
68 PAGES / $12.95

Meow, Baby!
BLACK AND WHITE
144 PAGES / $16.95

Sshhhh!
BLACK AND WHITE
128 PAGES / $14.95

You Can't Get There From Here
TWO-COLOR
64 PAGES / $12.95

Why Are You Doing This?
FULL-COLOR
48 PAGES / $12.95

The Left Bank Gang
FULL-COLOR
48 PAGES / $12.95

I Killed Adolf Hitler
FULL-COLOR
48 PAGES / $12.95

The Living and the Dead
BLACK AND WHITE
48 PAGES / $9.95

The Last Musketeer
FULL-COLOR
48 PAGES / $12.95